HENRY VIII
AND HIS SIX WIVES

A GUIDE TO HISTORIC TUDOR SITES

PETER BRAMLEY

The
History
Press

For my mother, Dorothy

.

Cover illustrations. Front, top: Henry VIII by Hans Holbein the Younger; *bottom*: Hampton Court Palace. (James Park-Watt) *Back*: Coughton Court. (Author)

First published 2014

The History Press
The Mill, Brimscombe Port
Stroud, Gloucestershire, GL5 2QG
www.thehistorypress.co.uk

British Library Cataloguing in Publication Data.
A catalogue record for this book is available from the British Library.

ISBN 978 0 7524 8755 7

Typesetting and origination by The History Press
Printed in Great Britain

CONTENTS

PREFACE

The concept of this guide derives from the belief that the understanding and enjoyment of history can be enhanced by visiting the actual sites of key historical events, as well as the monuments or memorials to the people involved. Television documentaries on historical topics now routinely follow this approach, using on-location shots of appropriate sites. This guidebook is different because it focuses on one particular episode in English history – Henry VIII and his six wives.

I could not have completed the task of researching and writing this book without the help of my family. My daughter, Lucy, has produced the maps and family trees and helped me with the digital photography, and my wife Sheila has provided a challenging ear throughout. Many thanks are due to Rachel Howkins, with whom, as always, it has been a pleasure to work.

PICTURE CREDITS

All images are from my own collection unless otherwise credited. I am grateful to the
following organisations for permission to reproduce images from their collections:

British Museum
British Library
Getty Images
National Portrait Gallery
Royal Collection Trust

All maps and family trees have been drawn by Lucy Bramley.

ONE

INTRODUCTION TO THE GUIDE

The saga of Henry VIII and his six wives is amongst the best known in English history. No other king comes close to this number of wives – Edward III is next, with three. In his desperate twenty-eight-year search for a male heir, Henry turned England upside down, and heralded the English Reformation.

Even after 500 years, a considerable number of historic sites survive from these dark, turbulent times and can help to reconstruct the events and personalities of the period. Such sites occur in the form of houses, castles, churches and cathedrals, monasteries, plaques, obelisks and church monuments. The objective of this guide is to introduce the reader to the best of these, by providing for each site:

- A short description of what there is to see.
- A brief account of any events in the Tudor period that occurred there, and/or a biography of the person(s) commemorated, covering their role in the dramas.
- Summary directions on how to find the site and other entry details. These directions are designed to complement modern road atlases.
- A broad-brush 'star' rating.

The guide covers those historic sites in England and Wales which I consider to be the most interesting and important. I have visited more than 200 sites over the last four years, selecting those to visit by consulting recent historical literature (see Bibliography), including the Pevsner and Arthur Mee county guides. My criteria for including sites in the guide are:

- There must be something memorable to see to act as a focus of interest. So, churches where someone is known to have been buried but where no memorial has survived have been excluded.

- The Tudor monarchs and their subjects were great builders and imposed themselves on both the urban and rural landscapes through houses of different designs in brick, stone and timber round the country. Examples of such properties are included, usually with a connection to our story.
- Last but not least, each site must be accessible or at least visible to the public.

I have visited all the sites included in this guide at least once. In order to provide the reader with background for their visit to the site, the guide includes a summary of the key dates of the period, together with profiles of the main historical characters involved. The latter have been drawn from a number of sources, including the *Oxford Dictionary of National Biography*.

Please note that the scope of this book is limited to Henry VIII and his six wives; it does not cover all aspects of Henry's reign. Henry only visited the north of England once, when he travelled to York with Katherine Howard – the Tudor power base was in the south – so there are but nine sites to visit north of Sheffield. One final point: dates of birth were rarely recorded in Tudor times outside royalty; where possible I have included best-guess estimates.

TWO

HISTORICAL BACKGROUND

THE WARS OF THE ROSES

The Tudor dynasty was very much a product of the Wars of the Roses – the series of battles between the rival Plantagenet houses of Lancaster and York, stretching over thirty years from 1455 to 1487, in three clear phases. The wars arose because the four sons of Henry IV (who had usurped the throne in 1399) produced between them only one male heir – the son of Henry V, who became Henry VI in 1422 on the premature death of his illustrious father.

Unfortunately, the young king had inherited his mother's mental instability so that, once his last uncle had died in 1447, the country descended into chaos as a vacuum developed at the centre of power. This ensured the loss of Normandy and Gascony and the end of the Hundred Years War, and allowed Richard, Duke of York to promote a rival claim to the throne, based on his descent from not only the fourth son of Edward III (the House of Lancaster was descended from the third son, John of Gaunt) but also through his mother, Anne Mortimer, from the second son Lionel, Duke of Clarence.

It was unclear in England at that time whether the throne could be inherited through a female. It had happened in the twelfth century, when Henry I's daughter Matilda had inherited, but that had led to a long civil war. Ever since then the Plantagenets had produced sons.

The first phase of the wars ended in 1461, when Edward, son of Richard, Duke of York, triumphed at the large scale and hard fought Battle of Towton, near York. Henry VI was not present at the battle, and was driven into hiding, leaving the throne to Edward IV who was supported by Warwick the Kingmaker. The second phase, from 1469–71, involved Warwick changing sides, driving Edward into exile and restoring Henry VI who was, by now, a complete puppet. However, in 1471 Edward returned from exile and decisively beat and killed Warwick at the Battle of Barnet, and then defeated the Lancastrian forces at Tewkesbury. Henry VI was murdered in the Tower, and that should have been it.

England enjoyed twelve years of relative peace, until Edward IV died after a fishing trip, just before his fortieth birthday. This instigated the third and final phase of the wars. Edward IV was succeeded by his son, Edward V, who was still only 12 years old, with his uncle Richard, Duke of Gloucester acting as Lord Protector. Richard could not resist the temptation, and in the summer of 1483 split the Yorkist party, usurped the throne as Richard III, and imprisoned his two nephews in the Tower. They disappeared from view and were never seen again.

After Henry VI's murder in 1471, because of the small size of the Lancastrian royal family, there were no mainstream candidates for their claim to the throne (Henry VI's son, Edward, had been killed at Tewkesbury). However, an alternative did exist through the Beauforts. In the 1360s, John of Gaunt produced four illegitimate children with his established mistress, Katherine Swynford. As adults, the children were legitimated by Richard II and the Pope in 1396. From John, the eldest son, was descended John Beaufort, Duke of Somerset (1408–44), whose only child was Lady Margaret Beaufort – born in 1443.

Lady Margaret was, thus, a great heiress and was married, at 12 years of age, to Edmund Tudor, the eldest son of Owen Tudor and Katherine of Valois (mother to Henry VI). Katherine was somewhat fun-loving and had become involved with Owen, her Groom of the Wardrobe. Edmund had a younger brother, Jasper. Henry VI much favoured his half-brothers as his only living relatives. Edmund, keen to secure his wife's income, quickly ensured that Margaret was pregnant. In 1457 she gave birth to Henry at Pembroke Castle.

Henry was brought up by the Herberts in Raglan Castle, but by 1483 was safely in exile in Brittany with a small band of Lancastrian stalwarts. Through his paternal line, Henry had no claim to the throne at all and the Beaufort line was fraught because of the illegitimacy, and because Henry IV had specifically ruled out any Beaufort claim (although this was never ratified by Parliament). If there was a claim, then actually that rested with Lady Margaret, his mother. The accession of the Yorkist kings had established that succession through the female line *could* occur, but England was not yet ready for a female ruler. Lady Margaret was more than happy to pass on her controversial claim to her son.

Now 26 years old, Henry was not, on the face of it, a strong candidate for the throne. He had lived in exile in France for over ten years, and was not well known in England. Few people of importance had even met him. He was tall, but somewhat reserved and had no military experience. However, there were still Lancastrian diehards in the country and Richard III's treatment of the princes in the Tower had alienated many Yorkist followers. What changed Henry Tudor's fortunes dramatically was the combination of Buckingham's revolt, in the autumn of 1483, and his promise at Christmas of that year to marry Edward IV's daughter, Elizabeth.

Much plotting between Lady Margaret Beaufort, Dowager Queen Elizabeth Woodville and the Duke of Buckingham had resulted in armed demonstrations by the gentry and some peers across the south of England, in support of the Tudor and Woodville factions. Buckingham's execution by Richard III in November 1483, left Henry Tudor as the de facto leader of this faction, with the promise of marriage to unite Tudor and Woodville. Although Richard's executions after the uprising were limited, many rebels fled to Tudor in France, and the Yorkist party was split again.

The Tudor drive for the throne was underway. Its eventual triumph at Bosworth owed much to the southern gentry backbone inherited originally from Edward IV, and to further clever intrigue and plotting by Lady Margaret, to the extent that, by Bosworth, Richard III could not count on the battlefield loyalty of much of his army.

THE TUDOR CLAIM TO THE THRONE

It has been calculated that, at the time of the Battle of Bosworth, there were twenty-nine other people with a better claim to the throne of England than Henry Tudor! His claim was obscure and flawed, but there were no other Lancastrian claimants. This was why it was essential for him to marry Elizabeth of York, who, with the disappearance of the princes in the Tower, was Prince Edward IV's heir.

However, in Parliament, he relied solely on a claim based on his victory at Bosworth, and from day one he played down any dependence on his wife's claim. Furthermore, he had only two blood relations – his uncle Jasper Tudor, whom he made Duke of Bedford but who had no children, and his mother, Lady Margaret Beaufort, who continued to play such an important role behind the scenes for the next twenty years and more.

The Tudors, dynastically, were on a knife-edge from the beginning. Elizabeth, however, produced a boy, named Arthur, within eight months, and the couple had seven further children, of whom three survived, two girls and Prince Henry. The elder daughter, Margaret, became Queen of Scotland, so that once Prince Arthur had died in 1502, the dynasty was back to square one, with Henry as the only male Tudor from 1509 until Edward's birth in 1537. This is why Henry VIII was so obsessed with a male heir – there was absolutely no back-up.

Who could threaten them? The main Yorkist alternatives came from Princess Elizabeth Plantagenet, Edward IV's younger sister, who had married John de la Pole, Duke of Suffolk; Princess Katherine Plantagenet, Queen Elizabeth's younger sister who married William Courtenay, Earl of Devon; and from Edward Plantagenet, son of George, Duke of Clarence who was Edward IV's middle brother, and his sister, Margaret. Henry VII married her to a Tudor stalwart, Sir Richard Pole. They all, in various ways, demanded the attention of the two Henrys, and not many died in their beds.

RISE OF THE GENTRY

Edward IV developed a powerbase in southern England by directly retaining upwardly mobile gentry, who were benefitting from the loosening of the traditional feudal ties between themselves and the nobility. He was supported throughout by some members of the peerage, but not in the same numbers as those who leaned towards the Lancastrians.

The Lancastrians were really the party of the 'clubbable' nobles, who fought together in the Hundred Years War and for whom the House of Lords was the focus of government. Edward IV appealed direct to the gentry and the burgesses in the City, who saw the House of Commons as the natural focus of government.

By the 1470s, the nobles had fought themselves to a standstill and the power of magnates, like the Nevilles, had been broken. The clever realignment of the Tudor political position between 1483 and 1485 ensured that Henry Tudor swept to power in 1485, having inherited Edward IV's southern gentry supporters as well. They found that they were not to be disappointed – if any one factor ensured the survival of the knife-edge Tudor dynasty, it was the continued overlooking of the established peerage, and the promotion of men of talent from the ranks of the gentry and below, by both Henrys.

THE MEDIEVAL CHURCH

Christianity had been around in England since St Augustin established his church at Canterbury in AD 675. It had been a force for stability and restraint in a violent society. The Norman Conquest brought the Church more fully back into the fold of Rome. It survived the challenges of Thomas Becket's dispute with Henry II, and the rise of Lollardy at the end of the fourteenth century.

Otherwise, the English Catholic Church in the early sixteenth century was considered amongst the most conservative in Europe. Luther's pronouncements in 1517 ignited the flame of church reform throughout Europe, and intellectuals and radicals began working on a programme of evangelical change.

Initially, progress in conservative England was slow because Henry VIII himself was a very traditional Catholic, and had written a tract opposing Luther. Henry died a Catholic, and was still burning Protestant heretics until the end. The whole of Henry's campaign to break with Rome was pursued for political reasons against the papacy, rather than for doctrinal reasons.

A small number of reforms undertaken by the Church of England in the 1530s did result in changes to the fabric of the religion. Otherwise, the change of the Church of England to Protestantism took place in the reigns of Edward VI and Elizabeth I.

St George's Chapel, Windsor, founded by Edward IV. The Wars of the Roses were not all bad news.

In a similar vein, monasticism had been established by the Anglo-Saxons but was much enhanced by the Normans. By the thirteenth century, up to 40 per cent of the land area of England was owned by monasteries – a huge area. Many were big sheep farmers. However, by the fifteenth century they were becoming less well used and some of the smaller ones closed in the early 1500s. This massive accumulation of scarce resources under the Church's control must have been highly coveted by landowners.

THE REIGN OF HENRY VII

In January 1486, after a delay to obtain a papal dispensation, Henry Tudor was married to Elizabeth of York in Westminster Abbey and the rival factions of Lancaster and York were finally united. Tudor withstood the expected Yorkist backlash at the Battle of Stoke (near Newark) in 1487, where John de la Pole, Earl of Lincoln, was killed. He dealt with the later Perkin Warbeck conspiracy, and a number of other plots, even including Sir William Stanley, the hero of Bosworth.

By the late 1490s, the dynasty was safely established. Henry proved a cautious but shrewd king – perhaps the greatest 'accountant' king since Henry I. He built on the policies of his father-in-law, Edward IV, and left the public finances in a very sound state. However, when state ceremony was needed, Henry was very willing to make the money available.

Charming tomb brass at Coughton.

Tudor chimneys at Rotherfield Greys.

Henry's success financially meant that he was able to reward his followers in the House of Commons by not calling Parliaments very often, and not imposing too many taxes – such a contrast to the bad old days of Henry VI and the disastrous Normandy project in the 1430s and 1440s.

In the area of foreign policy, Henry was surprisingly bold. In 1489, only three years after his triumph at Bosworth (which had been bankrolled and supported on the ground by France), Henry allied himself with the newly emergent Spain, through a marriage alliance between his son, Arthur, and Catherine of Aragon, the youngest daughter of Ferdinand of Aragon and Isabella of Castile. It was this unusual move which set the framework for much of our story. Ahead of the wedding, the Spanish monarchs became concerned about the number of rival claimants to the English throne. In 1499, one of the most prominent, Edward, Earl of Warwick (who was the son of Clarence, Edward IV's brother) was executed on a trumped-up charge, despite being mentally feeble.

Arthur and Catherine were married in St Paul's Cathedral in November 1501, aged 15 and 16 years respectively. In midwinter, they travelled up to Ludlow where the prince was based but, in April 1502, Arthur died of sweating sickness. Further tragedy hit the royal family in 1503, when Elizabeth of York died after giving birth in an attempt to 'replace' Arthur with a new baby. Quite soon afterwards, the king's thoughts turned back to his Spanish alliance and he arranged for a papal dispensation to be obtained so that Catherine could marry Prince Henry, Arthur's younger brother. Such a marriage was against canon law and the teachings of Leviticus. The dispensation was obtained, but the new marriage negotiations stalled.

Twenty-five years later, the King's Great Matter – Henry VIII's need to annul his own marriage to Catherine – revolved around whether Arthur and Catherine had actually consummated their short marriage.

Yorkist emblem in Worcester Cathedral.

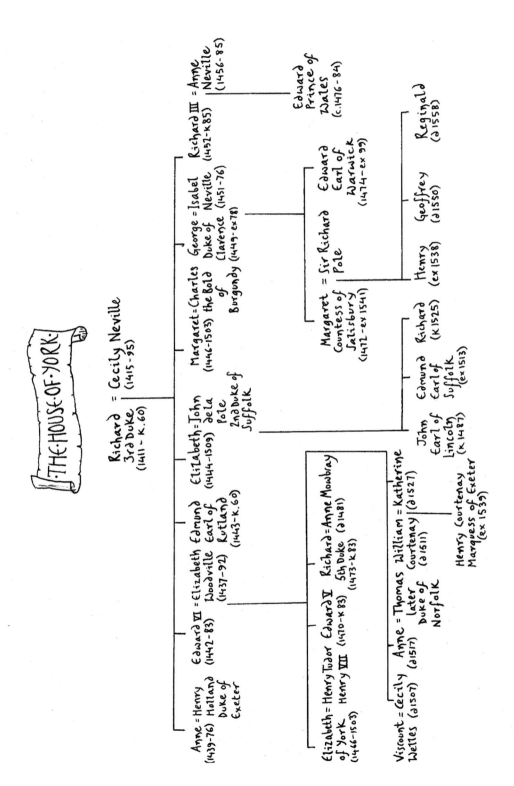

KEY DATES

1485	**August**	Battle of Bosworth, where Henry Tudor gains the throne of England.
	December	Birth of Catherine of Aragon, to King Ferdinand and Queen Isabella of Spain.
1486	**January**	Marriage of Henry Tudor and Elizabeth of York.
	September	Birth of Prince Arthur, to Elizabeth of York.
1489	**March**	Treaty of Medina Campo, in which Arthur and Catherine of Aragon are betrothed.
1491	**June**	Birth of Prince Henry, to Elizabeth of York.
1501		Birth of Anne Boleyn, to Sir Thomas and Elizabeth Boleyn.
	November	Prince Arthur and Catherine of Aragon married at St Paul's.
1502	**April**	Death of Prince Arthur at Ludlow.
1503	**June**	Catherine of Aragon betrothed to Prince Henry.
1505	**June**	Prince Henry repudiates betrothal.
1508		Jane Seymour is born to Sir John and Margery Seymour.
1509	**April**	Death of Henry VII; accession of Henry VIII.
	June	Marriage of Henry VIII and Catherine of Aragon; coronation of Henry VIII and Catherine of Aragon.
		Death of Lady Margaret Beaufort.
1510	**January**	Stillborn daughter delivered to Queen Catherine.
	August	Execution of Dudley and Empson.
1511	**January**	Birth of Prince Henry, to Queen Catherine.
	February	Death of Prince Henry.
1512		Birth of Katherine Parr, to Sir Thomas and Maud.
1513	**June**	Queen Catherine appointed regent while Henry VIII invades France.
	August	Henry wins Battle of the Spurs in northern France.
	September	Earl of Surrey routs Scots at Battle of Flodden.
	October	Stillborn son delivered to Queen Catherine.
1514		'Bessie' Blount first linked to Henry VIII.
	November	Birth of son to Queen Catherine; dies the same day.
1515	**September**	Birth of Anne of Cleves, daughter of the Duke of Cleves in Düsseldorf.
		Wolsey takes over from Archbishop Warham as Lord Chancellor.
1516	**January**	Death of King Ferdinand of Spain, Catherine of Aragon's father.
	February	Birth of Princess Mary, to Queen Catherine.
1517		Outbreak of sweating sickness.
1518	**November**	Birth of a daughter, to Queen Catherine – she dies soon after.

1519	**February**	Election of Charles V of Spain, Catherine of Aragon's nephew (Holy Roman Emperor).
	June	Birth of Henry Fitzroy, to 'Bessie' Blount (Henry's only acknowledged bastard).
1520	**June**	The Field of the Cloth of Gold meeting between Henry VIII and Francis I of France.
1521	**May**	Execution of the Duke of Buckingham.
1524		Queen Catherine has passed the age for having children; birth of Katherine Howard to Lord Edmund and Joyce Howard.
1526	**February**	Henry begins to court Anne Boleyn.
1527	**May**	Sack of Rome by army of Charles V; ecclesiastical court set up at Westminster to annul Henry and Catherine's marriage.
1528	**September**	Cardinal Campeggio arrives in England to judge the annulment with Wolsey.
1529	**July**	Campeggio adjourns the case indefinitely to Rome.
	October	Wolsey falls from power.
1530	**November**	Death of Wolsey.
1531	**February**	Henry recognised as Supreme Head of the Church of England by Reformation Parliament.
	July	Queen Catherine banished from court.
1532	**September**	Anne Boleyn made Lady Marquess of Pembroke.
1533	**January**	Henry and Anne marry secretly.
	May	Cranmer declares marriage between Henry and Queen Catherine to be unlawful; a few days later Cranmer declares marriage of Henry and Anne Boleyn to be lawful and valid.
	June	Coronation of Anne Boleyn.
	September	Birth of Princess Elizabeth, to Queen Anne Boleyn.
1534	**March**	Act of Succession passed by Parliament giving succession to children of Anne Boleyn.
	Summer	Stillborn baby to Queen Anne Boleyn.
1535	**January**	Thomas Cromwell appointed king's vice regent.
	June	Stillborn baby to Queen Anne.
	Summer	Royal progress to West Country, including Wulfhall.
1536	**January**	Death of Catherine of Aragon. Birth of stillborn son to Queen Anne Boleyn.
	February	Dissolution of smaller monasteries.
	May	Anne Boleyn arrested and escorted to the Tower; trial and execution of Anne; marriage of Henry and Jane Seymour.
	June	Parliament passes another Act of Succession, handing the succession to the children of Jane Seymour and the king; Princess Mary submits to the king.

	October	Pilgrimage of Grace breaks out in the north.
1537	**October**	Birth of Prince Edward, to Jane Seymour; death of Jane Seymour.
1539	**January**	Execution of the Marquess of Exeter and other members of the conservative faction.
	December	Anne of Cleves arrives in England.
1540	**January**	Marriage of Henry to Anne of Cleves.
	April	Henry begins to court Katherine Howard.
	July	Marriage of Henry and Anne of Cleves annulled; execution of Thomas Cromwell; marriage of Henry and Katherine Howard.
1541	**November**	Cranmer informs the king of Queen Katherine's indiscretions.
1542	**February**	Parliament passes Act of Attainder against Queen Katherine – she is executed.
1543	**July**	Marriage of Henry and Katherine Parr.
1544	**Summer**	Queen Katherine acts as regent while Henry invades France.
1547	**January**	Execution of Henry Howard, Earl of Surrey; death of Henry VIII; accession of Edward VI; Edward Seymour becomes Lord Protector.
	April	Katherine Parr marries Thomas Seymour.
1548	**September**	Death of Katherine Parr after childbirth.
1549		Protector Somerset deposed and John Dudley seizes power and becomes Duke of Northumberland.
1553	**July**	Death of Edward VI.
		Nine-day reign of Lady Jane Grey.
		Accession of Queen Mary I.
1554	**July**	Marriage of Mary I to Philip II of Spain.
1557	**July**	Death of Dowager Queen Anne of Cleves.
1558	**November**	Death of Queen Mary I.
		Accession of Queen Elizabeth I.
1603	**March**	Death of Queen Elizabeth I.

THREE

THE MAIN CHARACTERS

HENRY VIII AND HIS WIVES

HENRY VIII (1491–1547, king from 1509) was the second son of Henry VII and Elizabeth of York. His elder brother, Prince Arthur, died in 1502. As a boy, Henry was highly intelligent and academic, well-educated and precocious. He spent most of his time in the company of his sisters and his mother at **Eltham Palace**, whilst Arthur was despatched to **Ludlow** in 1492.

Henry adored Queen Elizabeth, and is said to have been inconsolable when she died in 1503. It has been said that she was the only person he truly loved. As he entered his teenage years he grew to be multi-talented – he composed music, danced and sang extremely well and loved to discourse on religion. He also became very tall for Tudor times, at 6ft 2in, which gave him a natural royal bearing. He retained a high voice.

In the later years of Henry VII's reign, father and son failed to get on, with the result that Henry had little or no experience of government when his father died. Incredibly, he still managed to hit the ground running as king – he announced himself by quickly marrying Catherine of Aragon and famously arresting, and finally executing, Dudley and Empson for financial extortion crimes during his father's reign.

However, for the next few years of his reign his personal achievements were limited. He was naive in his dealings with his father-in-law, Ferdinand of Spain, which resulted in disappointing military expeditions overseas. In fact, if you look at two of the key roles of a medieval monarch, internal law and order and the defence of the realm, his record is patchy.

There was certainly no reoccurrence of the Wars of the Roses (the big Tudor selling point), but on the other hand, the Pilgrimage of Grace, organised in the north in 1536, was one of the most serious threats to the Crown during the Middle Ages. It was, nevertheless, ruthlessly suppressed by the Dukes of Norfolk and Suffolk.

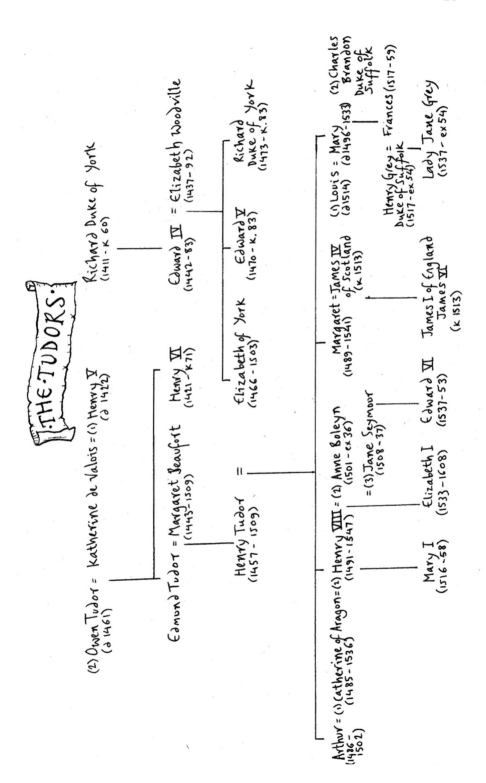

Henry's record on the defence of the realm and on overseas military expeditions is little better. The French fleet briefly landed on the Isle of Wight in 1546, but were driven away after the Battle of the Solent. Henry spent extravagantly on military expeditions, but gained little of any significance. In truth, he was no war leader like his illustrious predecessors, Edward III and Henry V, or even his grandfather, Edward IV. He led from the rear, not from the front as they had.

Henry was an obsessive – he was obsessed with hunting, as were so many of the ruling classes; as a young man he was obsessed with jousting, and spent hours jousting with his favourites like Charles Brandon in this dangerous sport. He was good at it, although he was sometimes allowed to win since he liked to win at everything he did.

Another obsession was the building of palaces. Henry owned more of these than any other monarch before or since, even though they were mainly confined to the Home Counties. This obsession proved very expensive, but led to architectural delights such as **Nonsuch Palace**. Another, **Hampton Court**, was originally built by Cardinal Wolsey but much modified by Henry.

However, this obsessive nature came to England's rescue. The third key accountability for a medieval monarch was to provide a male heir who would be likely to reach adulthood before inheriting the throne. There had not been a female monarch in England since Queen Matilda in the twelfth century, whose reign had led to twenty years of civil war. The demise of the Tudor royal family from 1502, and the marriage of Henry's sister, Margaret, to the King of Scotland, meant that on Henry VIII's accession there were only three surviving members of the family in England – Henry's 13-year-old sister, Mary, plus Henry and his new queen Catherine of Aragon. Henry's nearest male relative was Henry Courtenay, Earl of Devon, a somewhat lacklustre performer whose mother, Katherine, was Elizabeth of York's younger sister.

England needed a male heir quickly, because the new king's premature death would be likely to reopen the Wars of the Roses. Queen Catherine produced one for Henry as early as 1511 and he was named Henry, but died after fifty-two days. It would take another twenty-six years, and two more wives, to finally achieve the goal when Jane Seymour gave birth to Prince Edward in 1537.

In order to succeed, Henry had had to turn England upside down and overcome every possible obstacle. He was able to draw on not only his obsessiveness but also his utter ruthlessness and cruelty, his love of conspiracy (inherited no doubt from his grandmother, Lady Margaret Beaufort) and his incredible love of detail – he was a micro-manager. Yes, he had the right skill set for this task.

When, around 1520, Henry's conscience began to tell him that he should not have married his brother's wife, there were two main obstacles to obtaining an annulment of their marriage from the Pope. Firstly, a papal dispensation had been issued in 1504 which specifically allowed Henry to marry Catherine of Aragon, his brother's widow. Secondly, in 1519, Charles V of Spain (Catherine's nephew), was elected, through her sister, to Holy Roman Emperor.

From 1527, Charles put his considerable diplomatic and military resources behind Catherine's cause. In that year, to make matters worse, Charles' military successes over the French in Italy meant that, in effect, he had Pope Clement as a prisoner. This combination of circumstances proved insurmountable for Henry, and led directly to the break with Rome in 1531, the establishment of the Church of England, early 'Protestant' reforms and the Dissolution of the Monasteries – the biggest change in land ownership in England since the Norman Conquest.

The massive legislative programme that constituted Henry's major legacy as sovereign stemmed from his need to secure a male heir – the 'King's Great Matter' as it became known. Henry unscrupulously used Wolsey and then Cromwell to implement these actions, but kept well abreast of the detail. Perhaps surprisingly, Henry remained very much a traditional Catholic on a personal level. In the late 1530s, he actually slowed the pace of religious reform by issuing the 'Six Articles'. The English Reformation proper had to wait until the reign of his son, Edward VI, a decade or so later.

The Dissolution provided Henry with a one-off opportunity to enhance the loyalty of his aristocratic subjects (who also served as members in one or other of the Houses of Parliament) to the new religious order and to the Tudor dynasty. He was able to sell off or grant the lands confiscated from the monasteries to the gentry and the nobility. A large number of these sub-jects became tied in to the new order because to go back would entail much personal loss. At least from 1536, Henry is revealed as a 'man with a consistent plan'. Although personally conservative in his religion, he steadily built up the number of religious reformers on his council; in particular, Edward Seymour, Queen Jane's brother (and therefore Edward VI's uncle), whom Henry nominated to lead the council during Edward's minority.

Also favoured was John Dudley, son of Edmund, who had been executed by Henry at the beginning of his reign. Henry also chose as his sixth wife Katherine Parr, who favoured religious reform. With her help, the king also ensured that Prince Edward's

Henry went on pilgrimage to Little Walsingham in 1511.

tutors were of a reforming bent, so that the prince grew into a reformer himself, if a rather serious-minded one. It was no coincidence that the religious environment in Edward VI's reign was proto-Protestant. From 1538, Henry also took steps to ensure that the conservative faction at court was kept in check. The Poles and the Courtenays were destroyed in the late 1530s and, right at the end of his reign, Henry moved against his one-time supporters, the Howards. By 1547, therefore, the reformers dominated the council and his young son's reign looked secure.

However, even Henry VIII could not control events after his own death! Disastrously, Seymour and Dudley fell out in 1549, with the outsider Dudley proving the more accomplished political operator. Seymour was executed. In 1553 Henry's dream was shattered when Edward VI died, aged only 15 years, unmarried and without issue. Dudley vacillated, which let in the Catholic Mary I, whom Henry had consistently rejected as heir.

A return to Rome looked on the cards and, even worse, the marriage of Mary I to King Philip of Spain, which might result in the founding of an Anglo-Spanish dynasty. All Henry's efforts would have been in vain, but Mary was not able to have children. This left the way open for her sister, Elizabeth, to be made queen and to finish the job begun in her father's reign and create a Protestant state. This is surely one of the most moving episodes in English history; the daughter of Anne Boleyn, executed for adultery in 1536, bides her time, accedes to the throne and then is able to ensure just the long-term religious settlement with which her mother would have been delighted. The double irony being that Henry himself did not favour female rulers.

Another controversial element of the King's Great Matter revolves around Henry's sexual potency, or rather lack of it. Modern historians frequently question it, but of course evidence is scarce. Why did it take him twenty-eight years to produce a male heir who survived infancy? In these matters he was certainly an intensely private man and conducted his affairs under a veil of secrecy. However, Catherine of Aragon was pregnant six times before they stopped sleeping together, whilst Anne Boleyn may have been pregnant four times in less than four years. So, maybe there was no problem there?

However, there was a period of fourteen years, from the birth of the illegitimate Henry Fitzroy in 1519 to that of Princess Elizabeth in 1533, during which time he appears to have made no one pregnant, unless he was the father of Mary Boleyn's children in the mid-1520s (Henry never acknowledged them). This long hiatus was driven by Catherine's opposition to annulment, and was to have the disastrous consequence that Edward VI was only 9 years old when Henry died. Furthermore, after Jane Seymour's death in 1537 there is no further evidence of pregnancy with any of his final three wives, certainly not Anne of Cleves! And yet Henry really needed a back-up for Prince Edward, the lack of which was to lead to the collapse of his dream. So, we seem to have sporadic impotency perhaps?

The only telling evidence that there was a problem for Henry comes from the revelation made by George Boleyn, at his trial for adultery with his sister in 1536.

George was asked to confirm, or otherwise, to the court that a written statement on the subject of Henry's lack of virility was true. Instead, he chose to read it out, virtually guaranteeing his own execution. The statement claimed that Anne had told George's wife, Jane Rochford, that Henry 'was no good in bed with women and that he had neither potency nor force'.

This portrait captures the later personality of Henry better than any other. (British Museum)

Henry was utterly ruthless and brutal in his pursuit of the Great Matter, but was he a tyrant? He was too clever for there to be a simple answer to this question. It is important to recognise that, throughout his reign, Henry received strong backing from Parliament for most of the controversial measures he instigated, especially in the 1520s and 1530s. At least in the south of the country, he was very popular with the gentry and the middle classes. So much so that in July 1536, just after Anne Boleyn's execution, Parliament passed a statute which enabled him to issue proclamations which would have the same force of law as an Act of Parliament – a power which has never been granted to any other king or prime minister in England before or since. Parliament was, in effect, giving him tyrannical powers!

CATHERINE OF ARAGON (1485–1536) was the first wife of Henry VIII, and queen for twenty-four years until her marriage was annulled in 1533. She had previously been married to Prince Arthur, Henry's elder brother, in 1501, but was widowed only five months later. Catherine was the youngest of the five surviving children of King Ferdinand of Aragon and Queen Isabella of Castile. Isabella was monarch in her own right so their marriage, in 1469, brought together the key parts of Spain for the first time.

They were both extremely vigorous rulers – Isabella even campaigned during pregnancy. They expelled the Moors from Granada, the last Muslim stronghold in Spain; they sponsored Columbus' expedition; they instigated the Spanish Inquisition; and in between, they found the time to produce a male heir and four daughters, who were to be used to advance the cause of the New Spain in Europe. (Their splendid tomb survives in the Alhambra Palace in Granada.)

Soon after Catherine's birth, Ferdinand proposed a marriage alliance with anti-French overtones, between her and Prince Arthur, Henry VII's first born. Surprisingly perhaps, Henry signed the Treaty of Medina del Campo in 1489, ratifying the match.

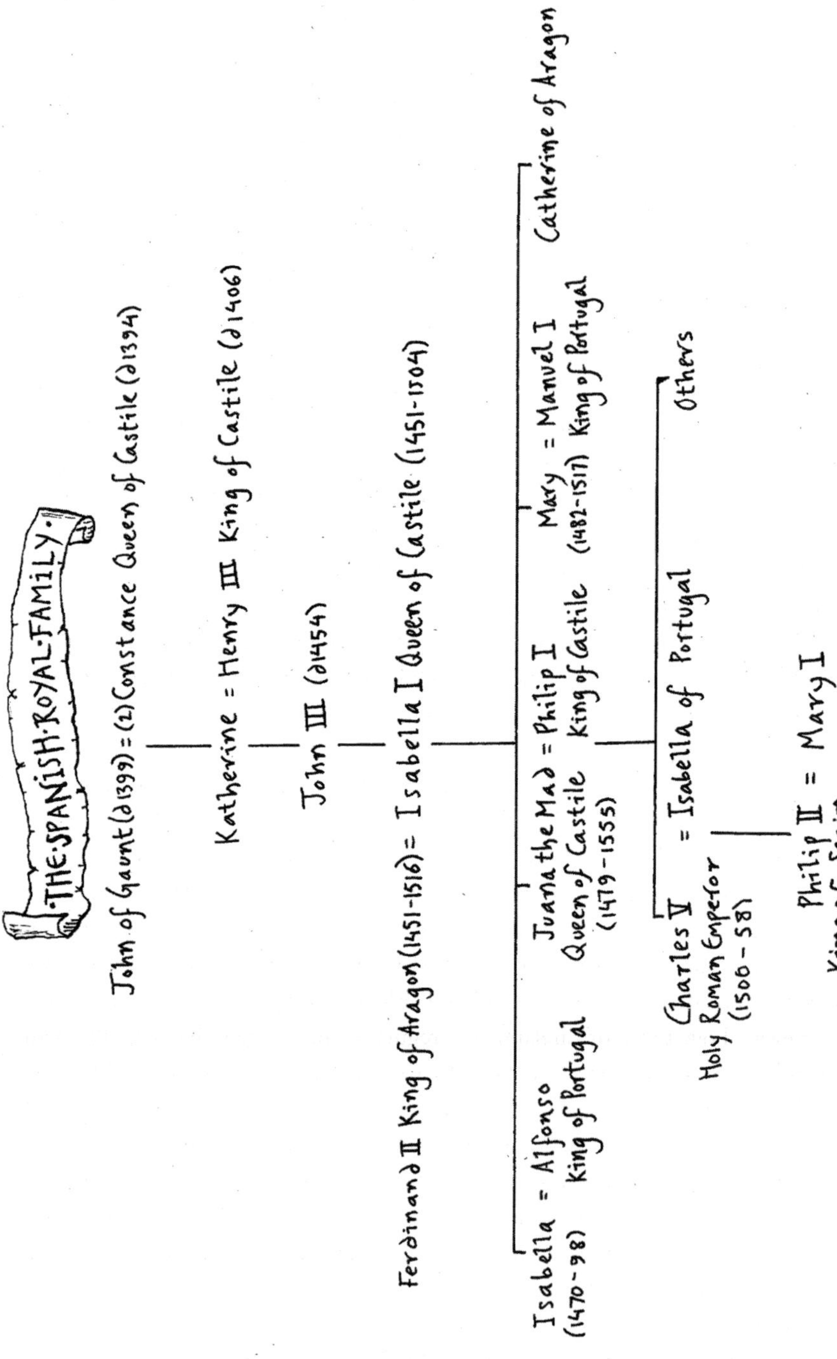

·THE·SPANISH·ROYAL·FAMILY·

John of Gaunt (d1399) = (2) Constance Queen of Castile (d1394)

Katherine = Henry III King of Castile (d1406)

John III (d1454)

Ferdinand II King of Aragon (1451-1516) = Isabella I Queen of Castile (1451-1504)

Isabella = Alfonso
(1470-98) King of Portugal

Juana the Mad = Philip I
Queen of Castile King of Castile
(1479-1555)

Mary = Manuel I   Catherine of Aragon
(1482-1517) King of Portugal

Charles V = Isabella of Portugal   Others
Holy Roman Emperor
(1506-58)

Philip II = Mary I
King of Spain
(1527-98)

This despite the fact that France had supported him in exile before Bosworth, and provided troops and military support on the day. From a military point of view, the alliance was to achieve very little and was to lead indirectly, forty years later, to seismic changes in England and to the Armada invasion, 100 years after.

Isabella oversaw her daughter's education and gave her a good grounding in Latin. She was intelligent and well-read, but no linguist – she struggled early on in England to learn the language. She grew into a pretty and plump young woman with red-gold hair and perhaps the colouring of her maternal great-grandmother, Katherine, daughter of John of Gaunt (after whom she was named). Although possessing a degree of reserve, Catherine was tenacious and single-minded and very proud. She had strong principles, and was conventually pious to a degree which deepened as her travails with Henry VIII increased. On the other hand, she had a natural kindness which she used to good effect to make friends amongst her English household and the nobility.

After Prince Arthur's untimely death early in 1502, Henry VII moved quickly to obtain the papal dispensation necessary to allow the young Prince Henry to marry Arthur's widow, Catherine. The dispensation did recognise that Arthur and Catherine had consummated their marriage. However, negotiations with Ferdinand and Isabella dragged on and stalled. Nonetheless Catherine stayed put in England – she was obviously determined to get her prize.

On Henry VII's death in 1509, however, the new king moved rapidly and Henry VIII and Catherine were married in June by Archbishop Warham at Greenwich – she was almost six years older than Henry. Their joint coronation followed later the same month. Catherine quickly became a very effective queen consort, her intelligence, beauty and love of pageantry ensuring her popularity with the crowds, especially with women.

In the early years there was also demonstrable mutual affection between the royal couple. Queen Catherine was a successful regent in 1513, during Henry's expedition to France; she seems to have had real substance. However, as far as Henry was concerned, she made mistakes during the reign in three crucial areas. Firstly, she still managed to put the interests of her father, Ferdinand of Spain, on an equal footing with or even above those of England. She regularly encouraged Henry to ally with Ferdinand and to model himself on her father. Oddly, early on in the reign she wrote to her father referring to England and Wales as 'these kingdoms of your Highness' – slip of the pen, or revelation of a cunning Spanish plan, which nearly worked when Mary I came to the throne? However, in 1513 Ferdinand double-crossed Henry by doing a secret deal with the French. On top of that, the Holy Roman Emperor rejected Henry's sister, Mary, as a match for Archduke Charles. Henry took this insult badly and blamed Ferdinand and Catherine. He upbraided her 'icily' and announced that, henceforth, he would rule England without her.

Secondly, after the stupendous victory at Flodden in 1513, Catherine had written to Henry in France, '… the great victory that our Lord hath sent to your subjects in your absence. To my thinking, this battle hath been more than you should win all the crown of France.' Not the tone that a man like Henry wanted to hear – tactless or what?

But the most important mistake Catherine made, of course, was to fail to produce a male heir for Henry. When Lady Margaret Beaufort died, six days after Henry's coronation, there were only two other members of the Tudor Royal House alive – Henry's elder sister, Margaret, who was Queen of Scotland, and his unmarried younger sister, Mary. However, there were still a number of rival male claimants (actually with a technically better claim) from the House of York. If the Tudor dynasty was to continue, it was vital that a male heir was produced.

Actually Catherine and Henry did try – Catherine had six full-term pregnancies between 1510 and 1518, three of each sex. One daughter was stillborn; one daughter and one son died the same day; two sons lived a short while, particularly little Henry born on New Year's Day 1511 who lived for fifty-two days. Had this boy lived this book would be very short! In 1516 Princess Mary was born, their only surviving child (see **Westminster Abbey**).

From the second pregnancy onwards Henry took mistresses, despite Catherine's attempts to dissuade him. This was not unusual for kings at the time. There is a long list of his suspected mistresses, but actually Henry was very discreet with his affairs. There are only three which are proven – Lady Anne Hastings, sister of the Duke of Buckingham, whom we know about because the duke was very put out and had rows with Sir William Compton (Henry's manservant), and with the king himself, although there is some ambiguity over who actually slept with Lady Anne (see **Stoke Poges**); Bessie Blount, with whom Henry started an affair in 1514 and who gave birth to a boy in 1519, which Henry acknowledged as his own and named Henry Fitzroy (see **South Kyme** and **Framlingham**); and finally in 1536, Henry admitted to an affair with Mary Boleyn, Anne's elder sister (see Henry Carey in **Westminster Abbey**).

Curiously, as early as 1514, rumours began to circulate in Rome that Henry intended to put aside his wife because she could not produce children, and then marry a daughter of the French Duke of Bourbon. Sometime after 1521, Henry first confided to his almoner (or confessor), Bishop John Langland of Lincoln, his doubts about the validity of his marriage. He was 'troubled in his conscience' every time he read the passage in the Bible from Leviticus which stated that 'if a man shall take his brother's wife, it is an unclean thing: he hath uncovered his brother's nakedness; they shall be childless'. His lack of a male heir was God's way of punishing him for his incestuous marriage to his brother's widow. The whole affair became known as the 'King's Great Matter'.

From 1524, he ceased to sleep with Catherine who, soon after, reached the menopause. However, he did not raise the topic of annulment with her until June 1527, a month after Wolsey, as papal legate, had convened a special ecclesiastical court to consider the king's request for an annulment of his marriage to her. She was overcome with grief at the news. However, she soon recovered and embarked on a campaign of unflagging opposition to Henry's proposals.

Catherine was greatly aided by the news of the sack of Rome, in May 1527, by the forces of Charles V, the Imperial Emperor, and of the virtual imprisonment of Pope Clement. Charles was the son of Catherine's sister, Juana 'the Mad', and was also King of Spain. He was able to ensure that the Pope fully looked after her interests, whilst she identified with her nephew Charles' interests in the same way she had done with her father, Ferdinand. The whole process dragged on until a papal legate, Campeggio, arrived in London in the autumn of 1528. He came from the Pope with a suggestion that Catherine should retire to a nunnery, allowing Henry to remarry and produce male heirs. Henry was keen on this idea, but Catherine rejected it out of hand.

Her determination to oppose Henry extended to lodging an appeal with the Pope against the case being tried in England, on the basis that every subject's loyalty to his sovereign prevented objectivity in the proceedings. The case was heard in May 1529 in the Black Friars, by Campeggio and Wolsey, but postponed indefinitely in July. Eventually Henry was summoned to appear before a papal court in Rome at the end of 1530. This was a step too far for the king and triggered the break with Rome. In February 1531 he stood in Parliament and demanded that the Church of England recognise him as its 'sole protector and supreme head'.

Throughout all these events, Catherine and Henry had occasionally spent time together but, not surprisingly, had often argued. In mid-July 1531, they had been at Windsor together when Henry rode away without telling Catherine. They were not to meet again. Henry sent her to 'The More' near St Albans, a house which had been Wolsey's, and banned her from court. In May 1532, she was moved again to the **Bishop's Palace** at **Hatfield**, and then to Enfield. By now, Catherine's communication with the outside world was heavily restricted and Cromwell's spies were watching her. In February 1533, she was moved again to Ampthill in Bedfordshire, even further from London.

Since the king had married Anne Boleyn in January, Catherine was instructed that, henceforth, she must be addressed only as Dowager Princess of Wales, her title after Prince Arthur had died, not as Queen. She absolutely refused to accept this change. When Lord Mountjoy arrived in July 1533, to inform her of the annulment of her marriage by the new Archbishop of Canterbury, Thomas Cranmer, she again refused to co-operate and was removed to **Buckden Palace** in Huntingdonshire, further from London, very remote and next to a fen. Her household was much reduced and there was little to do except pray and embroider.

Catherine bore her trials with fortitude. Finally, a year later, Catherine was moved to nearby **Kimbolton Castle**, which at least was further from the dreaded fen. Her gaolers were Sir Edmund Bedingfield and Sir Edward Chamberlayne. Catherine became ill in December 1535, and died a few weeks later in early January 1536. The condition of her heart would today suggest cancer of the heart as the cause of death – at the time poisoning was suspected, so the autopsy report was suppressed. Catherine was buried in nearby **Peterborough Cathedral** (then an abbey).

Catherine's ordeal had demanded courage and strength of character. She had conducted her 'campaign' with intelligence and, in the early stages particularly, she managed to stay one step ahead of the king. But what were her motivations for such stoical behaviour? Clearly from her point of view, she knew for definite that she had come to Henry VIII's bed in 1509 as a virgin. Any other interpretation was incorrect to her, and Cranmer's judgement on her second marriage was, therefore, just wrong. Her marriage was valid, and she would die a queen.

Catherine needed her marriage to be valid to preserve the legitimacy of her daughter, Princess Mary. Was there also an element of pride? Catherine was, after all, the daughter of the highly successful 'Catholic Kings' of Spain, who did so much to promote the cause of their country in Europe. Presumably she was expecting the Pope to rule that her marriage was valid; after all she held all the aces in Rome through her nephew. She will not have anticipated that her husband would go so far as to break with the papacy.

The problem with Catherine's approach comes when we consider the strategic issue underlying the King's Great Matter – the succession to the throne of England. In 1525, Henry found himself with only one surviving daughter and a wife who had probably reached the menopause. He himself was still young. Only twice in the last 500 years had the country been in such a position – in 1066, because Edward the Confessor had no children, and in the 1120–30s, after Henry I's son was drowned in the White Ship disaster, leaving only his daughter Matilda (or Maud) as heir. The effect in 1066 was truly catastrophic for England (well, at least for the ruling classes!), while Matilda's attempts at ruling the country led to prolonged civil war (the Anarchy from 1135–54).

So, this vast weight of historical precedent surely pointed out the need for Henry VIII to have a male heir. This had only recently been demonstrated when Lady Margaret Beaufort had passed on her claim to the throne to her son, Henry Tudor. Henry VIII was only reflecting what would have been the majority view amongst the aristocracy: a clear male succession when Henry died would ensure that the country was not at risk (England had just been mired in the Wars of the Roses in the middle of the last century).

In Catherine's single-minded defence of her marriage there does not appear to be any thought for the future welfare of England, her adopted country of thirty years. Offered the chance to retire to a nunnery by the Pope in 1528, she rejected the idea out of hand. Presumably she was very interested in her daughter remaining Henry's only heir – after all, Catherine herself was the daughter of the formidable and successful Isabella, queen regnant of Castile. Did she think that the time had come to establish queens regnant in England as well? Or would the succession position provide the ideal opportunity for her daughter Mary, as queen regnant of England, to marry a nice Spanish prince – which is exactly what happened eighteen years after Catherine's death. Had Catherine been alive, she would surely have loved the day, in

July 1554, when Mary I married Philip of Spain in **Winchester Cathedral**. But, had Mary borne children, whither England?

ANNE BOLEYN or BULLEN (1501–ex. 1536) was the second wife of Henry VIII. She was only queen from her coronation, in June 1533, until her execution for adultery less than three years later. It was in order to marry Anne that a passionately in love Henry broke with Rome and instigated the English Reformation, yet within eighteen months the marriage was in trouble.

Anne was only the second commoner in England to become queen (the first was Elizabeth Woodville, Edward IV's queen). Anne was the second daughter of Sir Thomas Boleyn and Elizabeth Howard, sister of the 3rd Duke of Norfolk. The Boleyns were upwardly mobile members of the Norfolk gentry, who owned land at **Salle**. Anne's great-grandfather, Geoffrey, had been Mayor of London and bought more land at nearby **Blickling**, and at **Hever**, in Kent, where Sir Thomas is buried. By dint of good marriages into the nobility over two generations, Sir Thomas was put in a position to marry into the Howard family, the premier family in Norfolk and one of the most powerful in England. Sir Thomas and Elizabeth produced a child a year for ten years, but only three survived to adulthood – Anne, an elder sister, Mary, and the youngest, George.

Anne was most probably born at **Blickling**, but spent much of her childhood at **Hever** which was convenient for the court, where her father was making a name for himself as a linguist. In 1513, Sir Thomas went on an embassy to the Low Countries and managed to secure a position for his younger daughter in the household of the regent, Margaret of Austria. The following year, Anne joined her sister as maid of

Catherine of Aragon's emblem: the pomegranate.

A lovely oriel window at Thornbury Castle, the home of the Duke of Buckingham.

Buckden Palace. Catherine of Aragon hated the cold fen here.

honour to Mary Tudor, Henry's younger sister who was to marry the aged Louis X, King of France. Louis died soon after the wedding and Mary probably returned home with the dowager queen, who was by now secretly married to Charles Brandon, Duke of Suffolk! Anne, however, joined the household of Queen Claude, long-suffering wife to the new King of France, Francis I. Here she remained, absorbing all things French, until in 1521 she was ordered home as relations between England and France deteriorated towards war.

Anne had grown into an intelligent, vivacious and witty woman who exuded sex appeal – not so much from her figure as from her personality and her eyes. She enjoyed gambling, cards, dice and a good joke. On her return to court she became maid of honour to Queen Catherine, and was selected for the celebrated 'Chateau Vert' court revel on Shrove Tuesday, 1522, in which the king partnered Mary Boleyn (with whom he was having, or had just had, an affair). Other ladies involved were Anne herself; Gertrude Blount, the new Countess of Devon; and Jane Parker, soon to become Anne's sister-in-law as Lady Rochford (remember those names!).

From 1522, Anne's father began receiving preferments from the king (perhaps because of Mary's favours). He was made Treasurer of the Royal Household that year and, in 1525, Viscount Rochford. Perhaps from 1523, and certainly from 1525, King Henry developed an interest in the younger sister, but her attractions were such that so did other courtiers; Henry Percy, the heir of the powerful earldom of

Northumberland, contracted to marry Anne in front of witnesses and had to be leant on hard by Cardinal Wolsey, who thus made himself an enemy of both Percy and Anne; and the poet Thomas Wyatt developed a passion, but it was not requited.

Henry made his first public indication of his feelings in early 1526, by embroidering his jousting outfit with the words 'Declare I dare not'. However, Anne did not take the normal route of becoming Henry's mistress, as her sister had. She is said to have refused to sleep with the king unless they were married, which was currently impossible. This unleashed a stream of letters from Henry to press his suit, although there are some suggestions that it was actually Henry who held back from intimacy. Finally, in late spring 1527 Anne accepted his proposal of marriage once he was free to so do. Shortly afterwards, Henry instigated the proceedings for annulment of his marriage by asking Wolsey, as papal legate, to convene the secret meeting at Westminster.

From then on, Anne largely withdrew from court and returned to **Hever**. However, from July 1528, Anne was given an apartment at Greenwich, and courtiers began to pay court to her there. At the fall of Wolsey in October 1529, Anne also received Wolsey's York Place, which was renamed Whitehall and renovated as a palace. She was queen in all but name. Soon after, her father was made Earl of Wiltshire, releasing his title of Lord Rochford for his son, George, and Anne became Lady Boleyn.

However, the King's Great Matter dragged on, and Henry still attended state occasions with Catherine of Aragon. It is clear that the stresses and strains began to affect the relationship between Anne and Henry. Anne became very edgy, and quarrels occurred, Henry sometimes being reduced to tears. Anne was also falling out with her uncle, the powerful Duke of Norfolk. She was not popular in England in the way that Catherine had always been. Probably in France she had developed an interest in the reform of the Church, as had her father and brother. Consequently, her reputation in Europe was even worse – she was called a whore, adulterous and even a heretic (which she wasn't).

This difficult situation came to an end, first with the Act of Supremacy in 1531, and second with the death of the elderly Archbishop Warham in August 1532. Now Henry could see the way to appointing a new archbishop who was amenable to annulment of the king's first marriage. At this good news, Anne and Henry are thought to have consummated their relationship – more than five years after her agreement to marriage. On 1 September, she was made Marquess of Pembroke in her own right.

In these first few months their love life seems to have been very satisfactory so, by Christmas, Anne knew she was pregnant. In late January 1533, the couple were married at Whitehall Palace in a private ceremony. The service was most probably conducted by Dr Rowland Lee, while Henry Norris and Thomas Heneage were amongst the witnesses. The only trouble was that Henry now had two wives! His first marriage was finally annulled by Cranmer in May 1533. Anne was crowned on 1 June the same year. The details of the ceremony suggest that, very unusually, she was crowned not just as a queen consort but as a queen regnant.

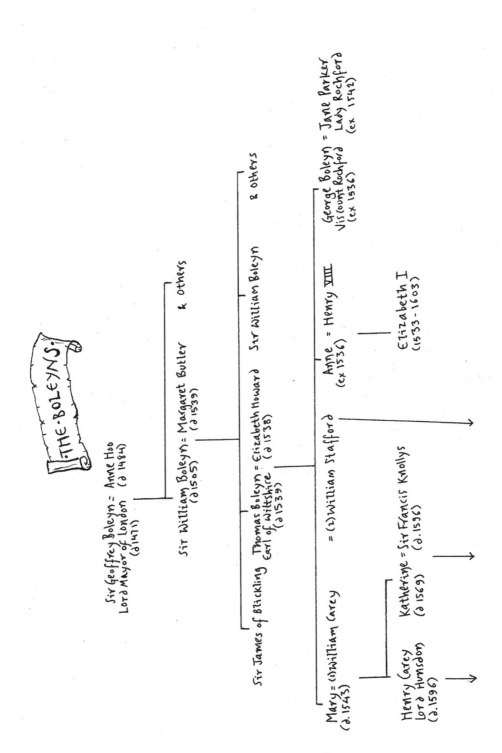

·THE·BOLEYNS·

Sir Geoffrey Boleyn = Anne Hoo
Lord Mayor of London   (d 1484)
(d 1471)

Sir William Boleyn = Margaret Butler   & others
(d 1505)   (d 1539)

Sir James of Blickling   Thomas Boleyn = Elizabeth Howard   Sir William Boleyn   & others
                          Earl of Wiltshire   (d 1538)
                          (d 1539)

Mary = (1) William Carey   = (2) William Stafford   Anne = Henry VIII   George Boleyn = Jane Parker
(d 1543)   (ex 1536)   Vis (ount Rochford   Lady Rochford
                                                                                        (ex 1536)   (ex 1542)

Katherine = Sir Francis Knollys   Elizabeth I
(d 1569)   (d 1596)   (1533-1603)

Henry Carey
Lord Hunsdon
(d 1596)

Anne's unique contribution, before and after being queen, revolves around her interest in religious reform. Doctrinally she was not a Lutheran – she died a Catholic. However, she desired to reform the many abuses in the medieval Church, such as those within the monasteries. She was also very interested in reading the new books on religion, even where these were officially suppressed in England. Henry seems to have been quite indulgent towards these interests; Anne owned a copy of the New Testament by William Tyndale. The king was happy for her to advise him on some religious issues. Her identification with the cause of reform, however, did ensure a vitriolic response both from abroad and from her conservative opponents at home.

The years of stress from 1527 seem to have warped Anne's character. Temperamentally, she was incapable of handling Henry's philandering with other women at court; she failed to control her temper when upbraiding him and she was indiscreet and increasingly unstable. What's more, her role as queen led to increasing arrogance, so that she fell out with too many important people, for example, Cromwell, Mary Tudor (Henry's sister) and even her uncle, the Duke of Norfolk.

Anne was never going to get on with Catherine of Aragon, but her handling of Catherine's tricky daughter, Princess Mary, was not a success either. Inevitably, however, it was her performance at child bearing which was of crucial importance. Actually, Anne conceived very easily – four times in less than four years. The birth of Princess Elizabeth in September 1533 provides the high point. The other three pregnancies were lost, one almost at full term, so there was still no son for Henry.

Anne became pregnant for the last time while on the summer progress of 1535, during which the royal couple stayed at **Wulfhall**, the home of the Seymours (see also **Sudeley**, **Iron Acton**, **Painswick**, for that progress). It is often assumed that Henry's affair with Jane Seymour started at **Wulfhall**. In fact, Jane, as lady-in-waiting to Queen Anne, would have already been in the royal party. Regardless, by November, Henry was seen with Jane at court.

An incredible concurrence of events, in 1536, led to disaster for Queen Anne. On 7 January, Catherine of Aragon died; on 24 January, Henry suffered a very bad fall in the tiltyard and was unconscious for two hours; and on the day of Catherine's funeral, 29 January, Anne caught Henry with Jane Seymour on his knee! That evening, Anne suffered a miscarriage of a male foetus aged around 16 weeks. The king was not amused, but Anne could not stop herself from putting the blame on him because of Jane. Henry retorted that 'she should have no more boys by him'. Later that evening, Cromwell reported to the Imperial ambassador that Henry believed 'he had made this marriage seduced by witchcraft and for that reason he considered it null and void'. During February, Henry determined to get rid of Anne, and his relationship with Jane became closer as she moved into Cromwell's apartments at Greenwich, chaperoned by her brother, Edward, and his wife Anne Stanhope.

Unfortunately, Anne chose to fight the king rather than go quietly. On 7 April, Anne instructed her almoner, John Skip, to preach the sermon in the **Chapel Royal** at **Hampton Court**, in front of Henry and Cromwell, on a theme of lightly disguised opposition to the Dissolution of the Monasteries – then a hot political topic, and the cornerstone of Henry's popularity with the aristocracy. Anne, being ahead of her time, had often called for the monasteries to be used for educational purposes. Henry was livid, and Anne had a massive row with Cromwell. During April, Cromwell told Henry that his spies had provided information which raised suspicions that the queen, desperate for a male heir, had resorted to adultery, and plotted to kill the king to save her skin. Adultery by a queen was not, at that time, high treason – hence the second charge. He was told to gather evidence. On 14 April, Parliament was dissolved and the legal process against Anne commenced.

An early indicator of the way the political scene was changing came on St George's Day, with the choice of Sir Nicholas Carew for Knight of the Garter rather than George Boleyn, Lord Rochford. On 24 April, Lord Chancellor Audley appointed a commission to investigate treasons. By 29 April, the Privy Council had been told, and Cromwell had presented the full evidence to Henry. Cromwell claimed that the queen had committed adultery with five men – Sir Henry Norris, Sir Francis Weston, William Brereton, Mark Smeaton and, worst of all, her brother, George (Lord Rochford). Sir Henry Norris was the king's Groom of the Stool and one of his closest friends. The next day, Henry was ensconced with the council. Smeaton, who was not a gentleman but a musician, was arrested, probably racked, and subsequently confessed.

At the May Day tournament at Greenwich, Henry and Anne presided. But, unusually, before the end the king abruptly stood up and departed, never to see Anne again. Norris was arrested after the joust (he was one of the participants); Henry offered him a pardon if he confessed, but he refused. The next day, 2 May, George Boleyn was arrested and taken to the Tower. Anne, who still seemed unaware of her fate because the whole process had been undertaken so discreetly, was summoned to appear before the Privy Council. There, she was confronted by Norfolk, Fitzwilliam and Paulet, all looking very serious. They, straight away, read out the formal charges being made against her. Anne was stunned and did not reply to the charges. She may not yet have realised the full gravity of her situation – after all, queens of England were not executed for adultery.

That afternoon, she was transported by barge to the Tower, where she was met by the constable, Sir William Kingston. Sir William was known to her from her coronation and was, at heart, a kind, if austere, man. Nevertheless, at this point Anne was overwhelmed by her experience and broke down. Once in the Tower, Anne was allocated a number of ladies-in-waiting, some of whom were expected to inform on the queen. They included her aunt, Lady Anne Shelton, *née* Boleyn; Mrs Cosyn, wife of Anne's master of horse and widow of Richard Vernon; and Lady Kingston, wife of the constable. In this stressful environment Anne could not stop talking, no doubt providing much incriminating material.

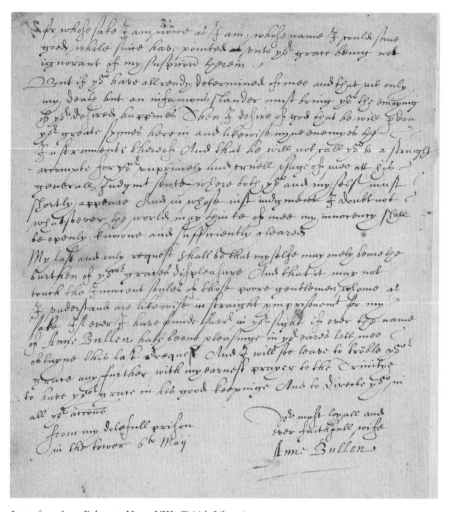

Letter from Anne Boleyn to Henry VIII. (British Library)

On 12 May, Norris, Brereton, Weston and Smeaton were tried in **Westminster Hall**. Norfolk, as High Steward of England, presided. All were found guilty by the jury and sentenced to the full horrors of medieval execution: being hung, drawn and quartered. On 15 May, the queen and her brother were tried by twenty-six of their peers in the great hall of the Tower. They unanimously found them guilty, and the siblings were sentenced to death by their own uncle, the Duke of Norfolk. Many modern historians consider Anne not guilty, because detailed research reveals that much of the evidence does not stand up, since places and dates cannot be reconciled.

So, what was Anne's crime? One clue might be that, during George's trial, he was presented with written evidence and asked to confirm or otherwise whether the evidence was true. The note read that his sister, Anne, had told George's wife, Jane

Rochford, that 'the king had not the ability to copulate with a woman, for he has neither potency nor vigour'. However, instead of indicating his agreement or otherwise, George bravely chose to read out the note in open court thus, in effect, condemning himself to death. Popular sentiment had expected him to be acquitted, so we can perhaps assume that the allegations were true. If so, they do not fit easily with the fact that Anne was pregnant four times in less than four years – actually a strong record for Henry.

Was this, and other shocking breaches of royal confidentiality, the real reason why Anne was found guilty? Were there other revelations from her time in the Tower? Anne could not stop talking while there – giving Cromwell plenty of material. Possibly, the key question in this book is why did Anne have to die? No queen since at least the Norman Conquest had been executed. If there were major issues then, traditionally, the queen could retire to a nunnery, as had been offered to Catherine of Aragon by the Pope. However, given Anne's temperament, she was unlikely to go quietly and, indeed, had chosen to fight Henry on religious matters.

Anne's 'lovers' were executed on 17 May, on **Tower Hill**, their sentences all being commuted to beheading. On 19 May, Anne was executed on **Tower Green,** by an experienced executioner using a specially imported French sword.

JANE SEYMOUR (1508/09–37) was the third wife of Henry VIII. She was queen only from June 1536 to October 1537. She died at **Hampton Court**, probably of puerperal fever, two weeks after the birth of Prince Edward. Given Henry's twenty-eight year struggle to produce a legitimate male heir who survived infancy,

By tradition, Anne Boleyn resided in the Tower before her execution. The twenty-first century has certainly imposed itself!

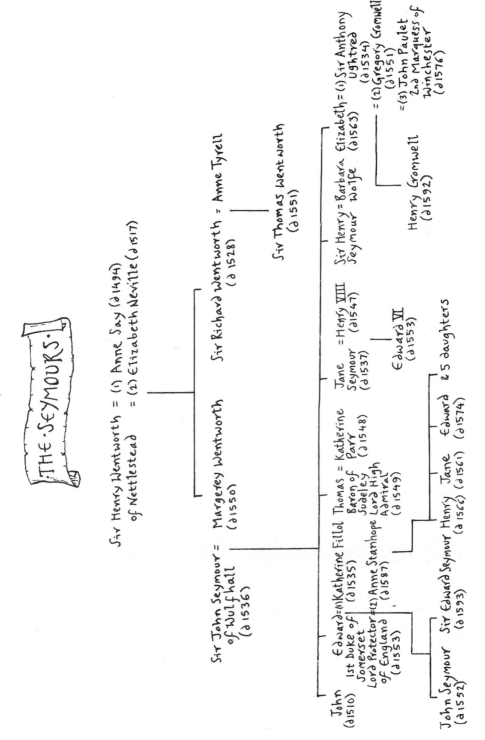

THE·SEYMOURS·

Sir Henry Wentworth = (1) Anne Say (d 1494)
of Nettlestead   = (2) Elizabeth Neville (d 1517)

Sir Richard Wentworth = Anne Tyrell
(d 1528)

Sir Thomas Wentworth
(d 1551)

Sir John Seymour = Margery Wentworth
of Wulfhall   (d 1550)
(d 1536)

Jane   = Henry VIII
Seymour   (d 1547)
(d 1537)

Edward VI
(d 1553)

Sir Henry = Barbara   Elizabeth = (1) Sir Anthony
Seymour   Wolfe   (d 1563)   Ughtred
                                 (d 1534)
                               = (2) Gregory Cromwell
                                 (d 1551)
                               = (3) John Paulet
                                 2nd Marquess of
                                 Winchester
                                 (d 1576)

Henry Cromwell
(d 1592)

John   Edward = (1) Katherine Fillol   Thomas = Katherine
(d 1510) 1st Duke of   (d 1535)   Baron of   Parr
          Somerset   Sudeley   (d 1548)
          Lord Protector = (2) Anne Stanhope   Lord High
          of England   (d 1587)   Admiral
          (d 1553)   (d 1549)

John Seymour   Sir Edward Seymour   Henry   Jane   Edward   & 5 daughters
(d 1552)   (d 1593)   (d 1566?) (d 1561) (d 1574)

this was undoubtedly her greatest achievement, one not shared by the other five queens. She was never crowned; her coronation was planned for October 1536 but postponed, ostensibly because of an outbreak of the sweat, but perhaps because she was not yet pregnant.

Jane was the eldest daughter of Sir John Seymour and Margery Wentworth, who were married in 1494 and lived at **Wulfhall,** in Wiltshire. Sir John was hereditary forester of Savernake Forest and of modest gentry status. He became a courtier and soldier, having fought against the Cornish rebels at Blackheath in 1497. Sir John is buried in **Great Bedwyn** Church.

Margery was a huge catch for Sir John – her family were considerably wealthier, with lands in Suffolk and Yorkshire. Their principal residence was at **Nettlestead**, and they were retainers of the Duke of Suffolk. Margery was cousin to the 3rd Duke of Norfolk and Anne Boleyn's mother, Elizabeth Howard. Furthermore, she was a noted beauty, who attracted the attention of the poet John Skelton. **Wulfhall** is a long way from **Nettlestead** so Sir John must have cut a particularly dashing figure.

In the early years of Henry's reign, Margery was lady-in-waiting to Catherine of Aragon, but then she concentrated on her own family, having ten children with Sir John. Their first four were sons. John, the eldest, died in his teens and is buried in **Great Bedwyn**. The second, Edward Seymour (1501–ex. 1552), was Jane's favourite. He was pushed on by the king, and eventually rose to be Lord Protector to his nephew, Prince Edward, on Henry's death, only to be overthrown and executed by John Dudley. Edward was intelligent, and an outstanding soldier, but seen as proud and haughty (see **Berry Pomeroy**).

The third son, Henry, preferred to remain on the local scene, while Thomas Seymour, the youngest, was ambitious and something of a ladies' man. He married Dowager Queen Katherine Parr, but flirted dangerously with Princess Elizabeth. He appeared jealous of his brother Edward's success, and was eventually executed by him (see **Sudeley Castle**). One way and another the religious reformers picked out and pushed forward by Henry VIII to protect and guide Edward VI (the Seymour brothers and Dudley) made a complete mess of things after the old king's death in 1547. This allowed Mary to take the throne after her brother's premature death in 1553.

Jane was the fifth child. She received only a basic education but excelled at needlework. She enjoyed country pursuits, particularly hunting. All commentators agree that she was no beauty, but rather mousy and pale. She was the antithesis of Anne Boleyn – quiet, softly spoken and submissive, with little wit. Her motto was 'Bound to obey and serve' – sounds ideal for Henry?

Around 1528, Jane arrived at court aged 19 years – quite late for the time. She attended Catherine of Aragon until Catherine was forced to move to Buckden in 1533, with a reduced staff. Jane did not secure a position with the new queen, Anne Boleyn, and returned to **Wulfhall**. During her stay at court, she met and befriended Princess Mary and was clearly in the camp of religious conservatism.

Jane returned to court, in the household of Queen Anne, in early 1535. It is most likely that she accompanied the king and queen on their celebrated summer progress that year, when they stayed at **Wulfhall** for five days in September. Tradition has it that Henry and Jane were first linked romantically during this visit. Perhaps it is, in fact, more likely that Henry's motive was to check out the family background and highlight her brother, Edward, for future promotion?

Jane's place in the king's affections does not become apparent until after New Year, 1536. The way was now open for Jane. The conservative faction at court got behind her – Sir Nicholas Carew, Sir Francis Bryan and even Princess Mary providing valuable coaching on how to handle the king. In late March, Jane's brother Edward was appointed to the Privy Chamber. By the end of the month Henry was writing to Jane. While she was staying at Greenwich but the king was elsewhere, she received a note from him which probably included an invitation to his bed and some gold sovereigns. She deigned to open the note and kindly refused the money, thus escalating their affair to a potential marriage. She had played a 'blinder' – but, had she been coached? During this time, Jane and Queen Anne had actually come to blows over a locket containing Henry's image, so it had become a desperate struggle.

All commentators agree that Jane was not a beauty, nor especially attractive, and she was 27 years old (virtually 'on the shelf' in Tudor times). So Henry was, perhaps, acting this time like a traditional king regarding his bride – she represented good breeding material since her mother had had ten children (the first four of which were male), whilst her father was one of eight. A dead cert for a baby boy, maybe?

The whole campaign to supplant Queen Anne received a huge boost when Anne had a big row with Thomas Cromwell in early April, and he put his weight behind the conservative faction. Jane took no part in the subsequent downfall of Queen Anne, or rather of the whole of the Boleyn family (it was a change of regime, really). She stayed away from court, at **Beddington**, the home of Sir Nicholas Carew.

On 30 May, Jane and Henry were married by Bishop Stephen Gardiner of Winchester, at York Place. On 4 June she was formally declared queen, and two days later her brother, Edward, was ennobled as Viscount Beauchamp. During the summer of 1536, the pace of life at court gradually subsided. Jane was instrumental in achieving a reconciliation between the king and her friend Princess Mary. It took some doing and was achieved entirely on Henry's terms. Mary had to be pressured by the conservatives to sign a written acceptance that her parents' marriage was never valid and that she was illegitimate. After all, even Henry could not live for ever.

Jane did try to intervene to halt the Dissolution of the Monasteries, but got short shrift from the king, and possibly the most chilling rebuke from a monarch in English history: 'Remember Queen Anne's fate – do not meddle in state affairs.' Once Jane was pregnant in the spring of 1537, Henry did concede a few favours for her; for example, he re-established **Bisham** as an abbey.

It is generally believed that Henry's desire to be buried in **St George's Chapel, Windsor**, alongside Jane, indicates her special position amongst his wives. Henry intended to build a splendid tomb and effigy in Jane's memory, but it never happened. Neither was the tomb for Henry built, so as a result they lie in a vault marked only by a black marble slab. Jane's premature death deprived Henry of the chance of a 'reserve' heir, who could have been very useful two decades later.

Actually, had she lived, Jane might have found life very difficult as mother to Prince Edward, since she was conservative in religious matters and had been pushed forward by the conservative faction. In the event, Henry ensured that Edward was brought up in a strong Protestant environment and to support this, gradually eliminated the religious conservative faction at court. The Seymour brothers made a successful transition to reformist views, but could Jane have coped?

ANNE OF CLEVES (1515–57) was the fourth wife of Henry VIII, and the least successful. She was queen for only six months, from January to July 1540. Her marriage was never consummated, and was annulled by Henry in the July. She was never crowned. However, she received a handsome settlement from him and became a very successful King's Sister until her death in Mary I's reign.

Anne and her younger sister, Amelia, were the daughters of the Duke of Cleves, a conglomeration of states centred on Düsseldorf in Germany. In 1540, Anne's brother, William, became duke. He was a Lutheran, although the dowager duchess (Anne's mother) was Catholic. It appears that Anne had been brought up at her mother's knee, and thus received a minimal education and spoke no foreign languages. She enjoyed needlework and playing cards, but had no musical accomplishments (some worrying negatives here).

After Jane Seymour's death the court remained in mourning until February 1538. Cromwell's thoughts had already turned to the next wife. He pushed the idea of an alliance with the Duchy of Cleves to end England's isolation in Europe. Anne came with good recommendations as to her beauty from Henry's ambassadors, Dr Nicholas Wotton and Christopher Mont. Negotiations with the duchy got under way, and Holbein was sent to Germany to produce Anne's portrait. By October 1539, the marriage treaty was signed. Anne left Düsseldorf in November and travelled through the Netherlands to Calais, arousing much interest on the way. She was formally received there by Lord High Admiral Fitzwilliam, a childhood companion of Henry VIII's, and an accompanying party. Fitzwilliam sent a stream of favourable reports to Henry about Anne and her behaviour.

Adverse winds delayed their departure from Calais until after Christmas, but finally the party landed at **Deal** and proceeded, via **Canterbury** and Sittingbourne, to **Rochester,** arriving on New Year's Eve, 1539. Henry was spending New Year at Greenwich, so, when he heard that Anne had arrived at **Rochester**, he decided to pay her a surprise visit on New Year's Day, even though their formal meeting was to take place at Blackheath on 3 January. Accompanied by a small group of horsemen, he rode to **Rochester** disguised as one of the king's servants. The party gained access to Anne's apartments in the **Old Bishop's Palace**, and Henry proceeded to test Anne with a courtly charade. She failed miserably, and even when he dropped his disguise she did not recognise him and concentrated more on the bull-baiting going on in the courtyard outside!

Was Henry checking out her courtly sophistication and worldliness? He did not find whatever he was looking for, and that was it – Anne was written off. Even on the journey back to Greenwich, the king was complaining to Sir Antony Browne that she was not as the other men had reported her. From then on, he complained to anyone who listened about Anne's looks – especially Cromwell, whom the king blamed for the fiasco. Some men, like Browne, guessed right when asked about her looks, as did Russell; some, like Fitzwilliam, got it wrong.

The Blackheath reception went off well – Henry was never anything less than courteous to Anne in public. However, Henry's lawyers were already searching for a way out of the marriage. The wedding was delayed for two days, but on 6 January they were married in the Chapel Royal at Greenwich Palace, by Archbishop Cranmer.

The wedding night did not go well, and in fact Henry never consummated the marriage, claiming Anne did not excite him because of the 'looseness of her breasts' and her 'displeasant airs'. (Their bedhead, dated 1539 and bearing the initials 'HA', survives in the Burrell Collection in Glasgow Museum.)

Things never improved, and so much detail survives in the public domain about Anne's physical limitations (of course it couldn't be Henry's fault!). He talked to his doctors, he talked to Cromwell. Even Anne, who had made great efforts to learn English, had discussions with some of her maids, including the Countess of Rutland and the odious Lady Rochford, which have also become public and in which Anne blamed her own naivety. It seems that the couple may have chastely shared a bed for four months! Inevitably, Henry's eye began to wander. By Easter, he was observed being rowed across the Thames day and night to Lambeth, the home of the Dowager Duchess of Norfolk and her step-granddaughter, Katherine Howard.

On 24 June, Queen Anne was ordered to leave court and move to **Richmond Palace**. Meanwhile, Cromwell had been arrested and condemned by Act of Attainder for treason. Proceedings were slowed so that he could assist in the process of annulling the Cleves marriage and Bishop Tunstall came out of retirement to lend a hand.

In early July, Anne and her Cleves agent were told of the king's intention to proceed to divorce. Not surprisingly, at first she was very upset and broke down. However, by the next day she had recovered her composure and agreed to the 'deal' that Henry was offering – she would cease to become his wife but she would become the 'King's Sister', with court precedence over all women except the king's wife and king's children; she would be given **Richmond Palace**, **Hever Castle** (the former Boleyn property) and **Bletchingley Place** as residences; she would receive £4,000 p.a. and she would be welcome at court. This was a very generous settlement and not bad for six months' 'work'!

Anne showed no desire to return to Cleves – she feared her brother would not have taken kindly to the fiasco acted out in England. Henry forbad her from writing home as another condition. She seemed to like her adopted country, despite the humiliations of early 1540 – presumably, given the level of her English at that time, she might have been oblivious to much of the detail.

Henry was surprised at the ease of the settlement, and relieved. He moved on to another botched marriage. Anne spent most of her time at Richmond and Bletchingley. She attended court often, and the king paid visits to her at Richmond where they played cards together! She seems to have managed her estates well. Anne had shown kindness to both of Henry's daughters while queen. They remained firm friends, and Princess Elizabeth was a frequent visitor to Richmond. When Edward VI died, Anne was in London to greet Queen Mary and her sister, Elizabeth, as they arrived. Anne had a prominent place at Mary's coronation.

She died a rich woman, in July 1557, at the age of only 42 years – probably of cancer. On the queen's orders, she was laid to rest in **Westminster Abbey**, the only one of Henry VIII's queens to be so buried. She died a Catholic. You feel immediate sympathy with Anne – brought to a foreign country, and then having to endure in a foreign language a farce which was not of her making. Frankly, she 'played a blinder' and was rewarded for it. She was the last of Henry's wives to die, and she died in her own bed. A woman to admire.

KATHERINE HOWARD (c. 1523–ex. 1542) was the fifth wife of Henry VIII. She was queen for less than two years before her execution for adultery early in 1542. She was never crowned. While there were elements of farce in the demise of Anne of Cleves, the demise of Katherine was an unmitigated tragedy.

She was the fourth child of Lord Edmund Howard and Joyce *née* Culpepper (widow of Ralph Legh), and thus the most aristocratic of Henry's English wives. The eldest three children were all boys, just like the Seymours above.

Lord Edmund (*c.* 1478–1539) was the younger brother of the 3rd Duke of Norfolk and, although well born, struggled throughout his life for money and for the opportunity to make a contribution. In the 1530s, he was made Comptroller of Calais. His sister, Elizabeth Howard, was mother to Anne Boleyn, making Katherine and Anne first cousins. Katherine's mother came from a substantial gentry family based in Kent, but she died when Katherine was only 2 or 3 years old. Katherine was, therefore, brought up largely in the household of Agnes Tilney, the Dowager Duchess of Norfolk, and second wife and widow of the 2nd Duke. Agnes was thus Katherine's step-grandmother. The dowager, a wealthy woman, lived mainly at Lambeth and **Horsham.**

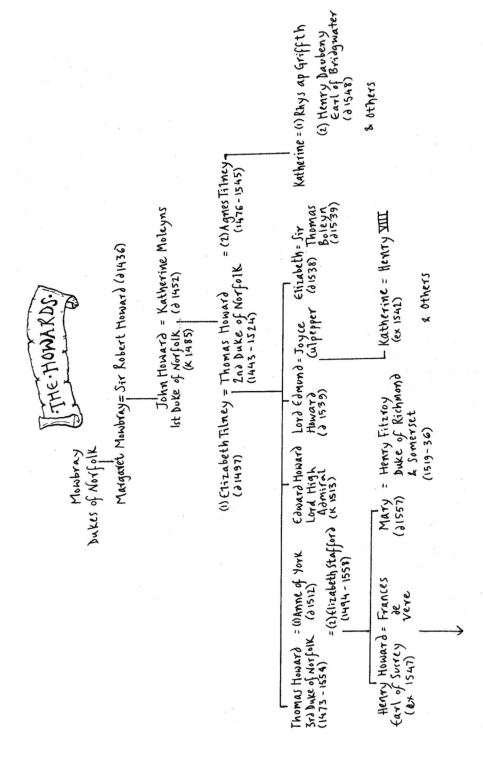

·THE·HOWARDS·

Mowbray
Dukes of Norfolk

Margaret Mowbray = Sir Robert Howard (d 1436)

John Howard = Katherine Moleyns
1st Duke of Norfolk   (d 1452)
(k 1485)

(1) Elizabeth Tilney = Thomas Howard = (2) Agnes Tilney
(d 1497)   2nd Duke of Norfolk   (1476-1545)
                    (1443-1524)

Thomas Howard = (1) Anne of York   Edward Howard   Lord Edmund = Joyce   Elizabeth = Sir   Katherine = (1) Rhys ap Griffith
3rd Duke of Norfolk   (d 1512)   Lord High   Howard   Culpepper   (d 1538)   Thomas   (2) Henry Daubeny
(1473-1554)   Admiral   (d 1539)   Boleyn   Earl of Bridgwater
        = (2) Elizabeth Stafford   (k 1513)   (d 1539)   (d 1548)
             (1494-1558)
                                                                                                                              & others

Henry Howard = Frances   Mary = Henry Fitzroy   Katherine = Henry VIII
Earl of Surrey   de   (d 1557) Duke of Richmond   (ex 1541)
(ex 1547)   Vere   & Somerset   & others
                                        (1519-36)

As was usual at that time, Katherine's date of birth is unknown but is most likely between 1523–25, making her only 15–17 years old when she became queen. Katherine's strongest suit was her looks. She was pretty and plump with auburn hair, and rather sexy. She was kind-hearted. Her disrupted childhood meant, however, that she had little education. In early 1540 she was given a place in Anne of Cleves' household as a maid of honour. She was coached by the conservative faction at court, including Norfolk and the dowager duchess, on how to attract the king's attentions. Given his well-known views on his current wife, Anne of Cleves, this was not going to be a difficult task! By Easter, 1540, Henry had been seen crossing the Thames to Lambeth by boat, both day and night. They must have made an interesting sight together – Katherine, the young, attractive and shapely damsel, still on the cusp of womanhood, and 49-year-old Henry playing the 'sugar daddy', with a 54in waist!

Henry was smitten, and showered gifts on his new paramour. Two weeks after his marriage to Anne of Cleves was annulled, and on the very day Cromwell was executed, Henry married Katherine at Oatlands Palace, Weybridge on 28 July 1540. At first the marriage seemed to go well; Katherine proved the ideal 'trophy' wife, suitable for showing off and indulging. Henry was besotted to an extent not seen with his previous wives. Howard relatives were favoured at court – Katherine's eldest brother, Charles, was appointed to the Privy Chamber, and Norfolk's brother-in-law, the Earl of Sussex, became Lord Great Chamberlain.

Katherine's kindness began to show through. At New Year, 1541, Anne of Cleves was invited to **Hampton Court**, and she and Katherine got along very well with each other and with the king; Katherine and Anne ended up dancing together. Then, Sir Thomas Wyatt, Ralph Sadler and Sir John Wallop were all arrested and sent to the Tower, accused of holding subversive religious views. Katherine interceded with the king, and all three were freed – Wyatt on condition that he took back his first wife! Later in the year, the new queen also orchestrated a degree of reconciliation amongst the royal children (even though Princess Mary was eight years older than Katherine!). In early May, the king and queen visited Prince Edward at Waltham Holy Cross, with both princesses present, and Mary was given permission to reside permanently at court.

However, from February there were signs of strain in the marriage. Henry fell into a depression (perhaps because of his ailing leg) and barred his door to Katherine for ten days. Nonetheless, by mid-March he was much recovered as Katherine made her delayed formal entry into London by river. There are suggestions that Katherine thought she was pregnant in early April but it turned out to be a false alarm, or she had a miscarriage, and by early May it was Katherine who was now depressed, owing to a rumour that Henry wished to reinstate Anne of Cleves!

At the end of June, Henry and Katherine embarked on the king's only progress to the north. It was to have momentous consequences. The huge royal party travelled north via Dunstable, Ampthill, Grafton, Stamford, **Grimsthorpe**, **Lincoln**, Boston, Newcastle and returned via **York**, Hull, Kettleby, Collyweston, Ampthill and **Windsor**.

They were held up in York, because King James V of Scotland did not show up for the planned meeting with his uncle Henry. They returned to **Hampton Court** at the end of October. On All Saints' Day, 1 November, Henry ordered special services to be held around the country to celebrate the good life the king led and, in particular, his wife, 'this jewel of womanhood'. That same day, however, Archbishop Cranmer left Henry a letter in the royal pew which contained information that was dynamite.

While Henry had been away on progress, Cranmer had been approached by one John Lascelles, a waiter at the king's table and a Protestant reformer. Lascelles' sister, Mary Hall, had been a servant in the Dowager Duchess of Norfolk's household in Lambeth and had revealed to him that, before she became queen, Katherine had compromised herself with her music teacher, Henry Manox, and then with a Francis Dereham. Apparently, discipline in the household was so lax that Katherine had shared a bed with Dereham on more than 100 occasions. She had been no more than 15 years old at the time.

At first Henry refused to believe the insinuations, but nevertheless asked Cranmer to investigate in detail. The queen was placed under house arrest in the sole company of the odious Jane Boleyn, Lady Rochford, but not told why. At this, she became hysterical, already fearing the worst. Four trusted councillors were appointed to investigate the matter – Fitzwilliam, Russell, Sir Antony Browne and Wriothesley. Together with Cranmer (who had now determined that Katherine must go because she was too sympathetic an ear to the conservative faction), the four questioned Mary Hall, John Lascelles, Manox, Dereham and other ladies of the dowager duchess' household. They quickly established the truth of Mary Hall's accusations. Henry was devastated, and broke down in front of the council, which by now included Norfolk himself.

Of course, pre-marital sex was a sin, but not a crime. The trial of Anne Boleyn had established, however, that adultery by a queen was a crime of treason. Cranmer now interviewed Katherine, from whom he obtained a confession; but he was not happy with it. Manox, Dereham and members of the dowager duchess' household were sent to the Tower.

In fact, Katherine had made a mistake during the summer progress by offering Dereham a job in her household. The council suspected that the two had continued to have sexual relations, which would now constitute adultery. Under questioning and torture, Dereham let slip that he had been supplanted in the queen's affections by Thomas Culpepper, Katherine's maternal cousin. The queen and Lady Rochford were now questioned on this new revelation. Katherine admitted to three meetings with Culpepper during the summer progress at Lincoln, Pontefract and York – on occasion using the stool house for an assignation! She tried to put the blame on Culpepper's persistence, and on Lady Rochford's encouragement of the affair. Lady Rochford, of course, blamed Katherine (it is impossible to fathom Lady Rochford's motives in this sad story – after all, she had already been through the whole adultery story with her sister-in-law, Anne Boleyn).

The queen was moved to Syon Abbey, whilst Lady Rochford went to the Tower. An incriminating letter from Katherine to Culpepper was found (and survives). Culpepper was arrested and sent to the Tower. Dereham and Culpepper were tried for treason, in the Guildhall, and found guilty. The council attempted to obtain confessions to adultery while Katherine was queen, but were unsuccessful. Manox was not prosecuted, as the council were persuaded that he did not achieve full intercourse with Katherine. He testified at the trial.

In mid-December, Culpepper was beheaded at Tyburn. Dereham, not being of gentle birth, suffered the full horrors. Later that month, the Dowager Duchess of Norfolk, her daughter the Countess of Bridgewater (another Katherine Howard – see **Barrington Court**), and Lord William Howard and other members of the household were tried for misprision (aiding and abetting) of treason, and found guilty. They were imprisoned, but later released. The Duke of Norfolk escaped punishment by dint of disowning everybody involved.

During the many interviews it had become apparent that, before she married Henry, Katherine had made enough promises to Dereham to constitute a pre-contract to marriage. She did not have the wit to grasp at this straw – if her marriage to Henry was invalid, then she could not be guilty of treason. The king chose to ignore the issue because he wanted rid of her. An Act of Attainder was passed by Parliament in February, 1542, which convicted Katherine and Lady Rochford of high treason. Accompanied by Fitzwilliam, Suffolk and others, Katherine was received at the Tower by Sir John Gage, the Lieutenant. The queen had, early on, been hysterical about the charges against her, but at the end she managed to compose herself. Aged no more than 19 years, she was beheaded by axe – not for her the special French sword allowed to Anne Boleyn.

Lady Rochford had been so distressed about the position she found herself in, that she is said to have gone mad. It was illegal to execute such mentally ill prisoners in Tudor England, but Henry was so keen to execute Lady Rochford that, in one of the low points in his reign, he asked Parliament to pass an act allowing the execution of such prisoners. She followed Katherine to the block, but at the last recovered her reason. Quite what this shadowy woman was about is very difficult to comprehend. This was, indeed, a tawdry affair and stretches credulity. Katherine's first cousin, Queen Anne, had been executed for the same offence only six years previously. Perhaps the Howards were just a completely dysfunctional family?

KATHERINE PARR (1512–48) was the sixth and last wife of Henry VIII. She was queen for three and a half years, from 1543–47, and outlived Henry. She was the most successful queen after Jane Seymour, but was never crowned.

Katherine was the eldest child of Sir Thomas Parr and Maud Green, who later had a son, William. Sir Thomas came from a powerful gentry family from **Kendal** (his grandfather, Sir William, was a great favourite of Edward IV's). In 1507, Thomas and his widowed stepfather married the Green sisters, co-heiresses of Sir Henry Green, a very wealthy landowner from Northamptonshire. Sir Thomas and Maud settled into **Green's Norton,** near Towcester, which is where Katherine was brought up rather than in Kendal (there was a London house as well).

Sir Thomas died of the sweat in 1517, but Maud, who was still in her twenties, did not remarry. She brought up the two children herself and, in fact, provided Katherine with a strict and religious upbringing, and a fine education. She also managed Katherine's marriage prospects, with the result that, in 1526, Katherine married Edward de Burgh, Lord Borough, who lived at **Gainsborough Old Hall**. It has recently been established that Borough was not elderly, as traditionally thought, but probably in his twenties. Mental instability dogged this family, and Edward himself may have suffered illness. He died two years later.

Before 1533, Katherine married for a second time to John Neville, Lord Latimer (1493–1543), a member of the once all-powerful clan associated with Warwick the Kingmaker, but who destroyed themselves in the Wars of the Roses. Lord John, a widower, lived at **Snape Castle** and **Danby Hall** in North Yorkshire, and became embroiled in the Pilgrimage of Grace in 1536. He played a somewhat equivocal role in the uprising, but was eventually pardoned by the king. The couple were welcomed at court, attended often and got on well with Henry.

By early 1543, the king had recovered from the traumas of the downfall of Katherine Howard. In February, unusually, he sent Katherine Parr a gift – even though she was already married. In fact, Latimer had been ill for some time (his will dates from September 1542) and he died in March 1543. Henry had seen something to interest him in Katherine. However, convention demanded he respect her widowhood. Katherine's heart had already been captured by Sir Thomas Seymour, Jane's brother, and Henry dealt with that threat by appointing Seymour ambassador in Brussels. After abiding by conventions with a suitable delay, Katherine and Henry were married in July, at **Hampton Court**. Bizarrely, Anne of Cleves was a witness. The king celebrated his wedding at Windsor by having three Protestant heretics burned in the Great Park – as you do!

What attracted the king to Katherine? After the disaster with the previous queen, her double widow status and her mature years – she was around 30 years old at this time – will have been welcome. She was not seen as a beauty, though. Rather, she was comely, with auburn hair and had a warm and friendly personality. Henry will have appreciated her intellect and her interest in religious matters. She published two books on religion, which were well received. Katherine loved conversation, especially religious discourse, as did the king (this was to get her into trouble with him later). In short, this was a companionate marriage. We have no clues regarding the physical side of the marriage, but there were no children, although Katherine later conceived with Thomas Seymour. During her marriage to Henry, Katherine had no option but to suppress her feelings for Seymour, which, as an intelligent woman, she succeeded in doing.

Katherine's achievements as queen started with the dysfunctional royal family. She was very keen to be a loving stepmother, and encouraged both Princess Mary and Elizabeth to come to court. She quickly became great friends with Mary, who was about the same age. She took on the task of supervising Elizabeth's education, a rewarding job because the princess was precocious and highly intelligent. The king was sufficiently impressed to ask Katherine for advice when appointing new tutors for Prince Edward, when he was 6 years old. Eventually, Edward came to love his stepmother, and so harmony prevailed in the royal family.

In July 1544, Katherine was appointed regent while Henry laid siege to Boulogne. She was assisted by Cranmer, Wriothesley, Hertford, Thirlby and Petre. She acquitted herself well, avoiding the sweat by travelling with her stepchildren in the Midlands, and ensuring that church bells were rung throughout the land when Boulogne fell in mid-September.

Katherine came to be surrounded by Protestant sympathisers – Katherine Willoughby, Dowager Duchess of Suffolk; Anne Stanhope; Lady Hertford and Lady Dudley – and the conservative faction at court grew suspicious. Katherine had become too confident in her religious debates with the king. Henry hated being contradicted in debate, and became somewhat frustrated with her. Bishop Gardiner and Chancellor Wriothesley obtained his agreement to have her investigated for heresy. Katherine received an early warning of the intended coup and, after initially becoming hysterical, calmed herself, went to the king and argued her way out of trouble. Given that two previous queens had gone to the block, this must have been a terrifying experience, especially since heresy would incur being burned at the stake.

Katherine's final contribution was to nurse the king during his final illnesses; something which perhaps came naturally. By the end of Henry's reign, Katherine had become well liked in the country. Although Henry's will did not make her regent, or even give her a place on the Regency Council for Edward VI, it did lay down that she be given the status of a reigning queen, not a dowager. He also granted her a massive income of £7,000 p.a. for life – at the top end of the scale for that period.

On the day of Henry VIII's funeral, the Regency Council conferred on Thomas Seymour the post of Lord High Admiral and made him Baron Seymour of **Sudeley Castle** – some recognition at last for his efforts. Emboldened, he began a correspondence with the Princess Elizabeth, now of marriageable age. However, she knew full well that she would need the council's permission to marry so she turned him down. In March 1548, Seymour turned back to Katherine, whom he knew had affections for him and now had a large income to boot. Katherine, who was unaware of Seymour's earlier approach to Elizabeth, responded favourably. Seymour knew that the council would not sanction this marriage, so he went straight to the child king, who gave his blessing. They were married in secret, at the end of April, while she was still in official mourning for Henry. Normally such an upright woman, Katherine seemed to have thrown all caution to the wind as far as the handsome, but impulsive,

Seymour was concerned. He was the love of her life, but her heart had chosen badly – he was a scoundrel!

By May, Katherine had informed Lord Protector Somerset, Seymour's brother, of the marriage. He was put out, but the council somewhat reluctantly approved it. However, when it was made public there was considerable offence taken, especially by Princess Mary and by Somerset's wife, Anne Stanhope. The latter launched a feud with Katherine over who should take precedence at court. Katherine had reigning queen status, but was married to the younger Seymour brother, while the Duchess of Somerset was the wife of the Lord Protector, the elder brother. Katherine lost and withdrew from court.

At New Year, 1548, Katherine invited Princess Elizabeth to come and live at their Chelsea home, where she could oversee the rest of her education. Soon afterwards, they were joined by Lady Jane Grey, daughter of the Marquess of Dorset and another promising intellectual, and by Lady Margery Seymour, Thomas' ageing mother. All went well, and in March Katherine found she was pregnant for the first time in her life at the age of 35 years. With Elizabeth in the house and a pregnant wife, it was not long before Seymour returned to his pursuit of the princess. Early morning romps became regular. Wrapped up in her own personal happiness, Katherine did not, at first, spot the danger. However, her suspicions were eventually aroused and Katherine caught them alone together in each other's arms. Katherine's illusion of perfect love was shattered, and Elizabeth, who had very clearly abused her hospitality, was asked to leave.

Katherine's warm personality ensured that, before her baby was born, she had re-established relations with Elizabeth and with her husband, and been reconciled to the Lady Mary. Katherine and Lord Thomas travelled to Sudeley for the birth. She was delivered of a healthy girl, Mary, but disaster struck. Katherine died nine days later, probably of puerperal fever. Her last hours were unpleasant for all concerned, as she was delirious for much of the time and frequently railed against her husband. She was buried in the chapel at **Sudeley Castle**. Her funeral service was taken by Miles Coverdale, her confessor. It was the first royal Protestant service.

Seymour tried one more time to woo Elizabeth, but she had at last learned her lesson and did not respond to his letter. A year later he went to the block – caught trying to kidnap Edward VI!

Mary, Katherine's daughter, was looked after by Katherine's good friend, Katherine Willoughby, but probably died while still young.

THE REST OF THE TUDOR ROYAL FAMILY

HENRY VII (Henry Tudor) (1457–1509, king from 1485) was the only child of Edmund Tudor and Lady Margaret Beaufort. He was born after his father had died in Yorkist captivity in Carmarthen Castle. Edmund and his brother, Jasper, were the sons of Owen Tudor, a member of the Welsh gentry, and Dowager Queen Katherine of Valois (Henry V's widow), who had married in the late 1420s.

Owen had been keeper of Katherine's wardrobe before the marriage, and was thrown into prison for a while after her death. He was released, but executed by Edward IV after the Battle of Mortimer's Cross in 1461. His sons had become members of Henry VI's very small royal family, being made Earls of Richmond and Pembroke respectively. However, any claim to the English throne possessed by Henry Tudor came only from his mother, Lady Margaret Beaufort, the sole heiress to the primary line of this illustrious family who were the legitimated descendants of John of Gaunt and his mistress, Katherine Swynford. In 1407, Henry IV had seemingly barred the Beauforts from the crown itself. Henry Tudor was an unusual mix of Welsh, French and English blood. On the execution of Henry, Duke of Buckingham by Richard III in 1483, Tudor became the prime Lancastrian claimant. The saintly Henry VI, in earlier years, is said to have shown much favour to his namesake and to Lady Margaret, and to have predicted Tudor's eventual accession to the throne.

In the summer of 1483, Henry's mother secured a deal with the Dowager Queen, Elizabeth Woodville, in which Henry would marry Elizabeth of York, Edward IV's eldest daughter and heir now that the princes in the Tower were presumed dead. It secured the support of many of Edward IV's former household members. Henry Tudor was not a fighting man in the traditional sense but, with covert backing now in place in England, he was prepared to invade from France with a small force and very much against the odds, at least on paper. Bosworth was his reward.

A naturally cautious but intelligent man, Henry worked closely with his mother and secured his dynasty. He built on the good work of Edward IV by transforming the finances of the crown – he rivals Henry I as England's greatest 'accountant king', and in many ways was the first modern monarch. Although he froze out his Yorkist wife politically, their marriage seems to have been harmonious. It was his decision, in 1488, to pursue the marriage alliance between Prince Arthur and Catherine of Aragon, suggested by the Spanish, which underpins everything in this book. After Elizabeth of York's death in 1503, Henry VII spent much time in argument with his son and heir Prince Henry.

QUEEN ELIZABETH OF YORK (1466–1502) was Henry VII's queen, and Henry VIII's mother. As the eldest daughter of Edward IV and Elizabeth Woodville, she had been brought up to royalty, and her whole life was spent within the royal family. In 1475, she was betrothed to Charles, the Dauphin of France, but the French pulled out in 1482. When her father died unexpectedly in 1483, her whole world was turned upside down. Her uncle, Richard III, usurped the throne, her brothers (the princes in the Tower) disappeared and she became hot political property as the heir of Edward IV.

Bizarrely, at one time, Richard III considered marrying his niece, but he was talked out of it by his advisors, who felt that the north of England would not wear the marriage. It was Henry Tudor's declaration, at Rennes Cathedral at Christmas 1483, that *he* would marry Princess Elizabeth of York which secured the support of former Yorkist retainers in the south. This promise was fulfilled in mid-January 1486, after the appropriate papal dispensations had been obtained. This classic political union was vital to the success of the fledgling Tudor regime.

Elizabeth went one better and produced an heir, Prince Arthur, within eight months. The marriage appears to have been loving – the couple had eight children, of whom three survived to adulthood. Elizabeth spent much time at **Eltham Palace** with Prince Henry and his sisters, with Arthur's household being located at **Ludlow** from 1492.

Elizabeth is said to have been the only person that Henry VIII truly loved. However, there was a darker side to Elizabeth's life. Politically she was completely shut out of the decision-making process of the Tudor monarchy, largely because, in this sphere, there were three in the royal marriage – Lady Margaret Beaufort was very close to her son, and spent much time with him on political matters. Lady Margaret even interfered in the running of the queen's household; for example, laying down ordinances on royal childbirth for Elizabeth to follow. On formal occasions, Lady Margaret would walk very closely behind the queen. David Starkey has described Lady Margaret as 'the mother-in-law from hell' (Starkey, *Six Wives*, p. 28) – I am sure Elizabeth would have agreed!

From 1502, events went rapidly downhill for the queen. Firstly, Prince Arthur died aged 15 years at Ludlow, in the company of his new wife, Catherine of Aragon. Then, in 1503, Elizabeth herself died following childbirth in the Tower. She was the first reigning Queen of England to die in childbirth since the Norman Conquest (interesting that 'the mother-in-law from hell' had written the royal ordinances for childbirth!). Her body lay in state in **St John the Baptist Chapel in the Tower**, and she was buried in the magnificent **Chapel** in **Westminster Abbey** – to be joined in 1509 by her husband.

MARGARET TUDOR (1489–1541) was Henry VIII's elder sister. In 1503 she was married to King James IV of Scotland. They had seven children, only one of whom, James, survived to adulthood.

James IV was killed in the disastrous defeat by the English at **Flodden** Field in 1513, and Margaret acted as regent until she foolishly married Douglas, Earl of Angus. She spent a year back in England in 1517, and in 1524 she succeeded in getting her son, James, now aged 12 years, elevated to full kingly powers as James V. He married Mary of Guisnes, and fathered Mary Queen of Scots.

Carvings at Haddon Hall said to be Henry VII and Elizabeth of York.

The effigy of Elizabeth of York in Westminster Abbey.

When Elizabeth I died childless in 1603, Mary Queen of Scots' son, James VI, became James I of England. Henry VIII's Act of Succession had excluded Margaret Tudor's Scottish line of descent from the English throne, but by that time there were no sensible alternatives left. Margaret was the founder of the new Stuart dynasty in England.

MARY TUDOR, Dowager Queen of France and Duchess of Suffolk (1496–1533) was Henry VIII's younger sister and, in childhood, his favourite. In 1514, she was married to Louis XII, the aged King of France, as part of Henry's new pro-France policy. Louis was 52 years old, and Mary only 18 years. Within 3 months, the bridegroom was dead. His successor, Francis I, was a notorious rake and attempted to seduce Mary.

She needed to be escorted back to England, so Charles Brandon, one of Henry VIII's closest companions, went over to Paris. Actually, Mary was attracted to Brandon, and they were secretly married in France. Cannily, Mary had already negotiated with her brother that, after Louis, her next marriage would be to a man of her own choice. She had chosen very quickly! When Henry found out he was extremely angry, but eventually agreed to the union on payment of a very large fine by Brandon. He organised a splendid wedding at Greenwich.

Charles and Mary had three children who, of course, featured in the succession in Henry's will. Frances, the elder daughter, married Henry Grey, son of the Marquess of Dorset. Their daughter was Lady Jane Grey, who became the 'Nine Day Queen', put on the throne by John Dudley, Duke of Northumberland in 1553.

Mary had befriended Catherine of Aragon before she married Henry VIII. Not surprisingly, therefore, Mary quickly developed a serious dislike of Anne Boleyn, and the Brandons began boycotting court from 1529. Relations with Henry were only restored once Mary had become terminally ill with cancer in 1533. Mary and Charles lived at **Westhorpe** and she is buried in nearby **Bury St Edmunds**.

LADY MARGARET BEAUFORT (1443–1509) was the mother of Henry VII, and it was through her that he possessed any sensible claim to the throne (see **Henry VII** biography).

She was the only child of John Beaufort, Duke of Somerset and Margaret Beauchamp. Her father returned from Normandy in disgrace in 1443, having led an unsuccessful expedition against the French. He died in 1444, probably by his own hand. Lady Margaret inherited his vast estates, particularly in the West Country, and became one of the wealthiest heiresses of the fifteenth century.

At the age of 7 she was married to John de la Pole, the son of the Duke of Suffolk. After the latter's fall from power and his death in 1450, the marriage was annulled and she married Edmund Tudor, Henry VI's half-brother. In January 1457, aged only 13 years, she gave birth to Henry Tudor in Pembroke Castle. Unfortunately, the birth was very difficult so Margaret was unable to have any more children. Even worse, Edmund had died of the plague in Carmarthen three months earlier.

The austere Lady Margaret Beaufort. (National Portrait Gallery)

Another husband was quickly found for Lady Margaret, Sir Henry Stafford, younger son of the Duke of Buckingham. Stafford had been pardoned by Edward IV after Towton in 1461, and thus fought for him at Barnet in 1471. Unfortunately, he died later of wounds received at the battle. Within the year, Margaret married for the fourth time to Thomas, Lord Stanley, a major player in the Wars of the Roses. This was to be the great political marriage of the age, whose outstanding achievement was the Tudor conspiracy behind the Battle of Bosworth. These remarriages unfortunately meant long separations from her son, Henry. Initially he was made the ward of William, Lord Herbert, and lived at Raglan Castle. After the Battle of Tewksbury, Henry fled to France and into exile with his uncle Jasper.

Lady Margaret and Lord Stanley maintained a low profile for the rest of Edward IV's reign. However, after Edward's death, Margaret played the central role in plotting opposition to Richard III. In particular, she established contact with Dowager Queen Elizabeth Woodville, who was in sanctuary in Westminster Abbey. After the princes in the Tower were presumed dead, a rapprochement was achieved by an agreement between the two women that Henry Tudor would marry Elizabeth of York, Edward IV's eldest daughter. This agreement enabled many Yorkists to support Henry Tudor, especially in the south.

After Bosworth, Lady Margaret quickly became her son's closest confidante, both politically and domestically. Not surprisingly, she is said to have shed tears of joy at his coronation. The new Queen Elizabeth was frozen out and kept in the background. I have an inkling that Lady Margaret would be the most awesome of the women in this book to meet. She was highly intelligent, determined and cunning, but easily underestimated by political opponents, especially men, since she was small, reserved and highly religious. Her achievement was to have outwitted virtually everyone on her march to power – Edward IV, the Duke of Buckingham, Richard III, Elizabeth Woodville and her daughter, Elizabeth of York.

Lady Margaret played a leading part in the campaign to have Henry VI made into a saint, but without success. In 1499, in a move rarely used, she took a vow of eternal chastity which enabled her to establish a separate household from her husband, Lord Stanley, but not to divorce. She lived in splendour at Collyweston in Northamptonshire. She died just five or six days after the coronation of her grandson, in 1509, apparently poisoned by a cygnet which she ate at the coronation banquet! She is commemorated by a fine effigy in **Westminster Abbey**.

PRINCE ARTHUR OF WALES (1486–1502) was the eldest son of Henry VII and Elizabeth of York. He is the surprise package in our story – even his birth being a surprise, as he was born only eight months after his parents' wedding.

His name is also a surprise. It was not a common name in medieval England – the only precedent in the royal family was Edward IV's acknowledged bastard, Arthur Plantagenet (1462–1542). A fledgling dynasty like the Tudors would have been expected to choose the name Henry, in order to link to Henry VI, their Lancastrian forebear. As a girl, Lady Margaret Beaufort, Henry VII's mother, was very fond of Henry VI, and the feeling was mutual – the name of course was eventually chosen for the second son.

When Arthur was just 2 years old, Henry VII incredibly concluded a marriage alliance with the Catholic Kings of Spain, Ferdinand and Isabella, for the hand of their youngest daughter, Catherine. In 1492, Arthur was sent to Ludlow in the Welsh Marches in order to obtain the proper training for kingship. This arrangement exactly matched the example of Edward V, who had also been sent to Ludlow by his father, Edward IV.

Arthur received a thorough education, and proved studious and thoughtful.

He also spent time at Tickenhill Palace in Bewdley (this was also known as Beaulieu – see **New Hall, Boreham**) and at **Haddon Hall** in the Peak District, which was the home of his treasurer, Sir Henry Vernon. After 1492 he did not spend much time at court in London.

In mid-November 1501, Arthur was married to Catherine of Aragon in St Paul's Cathedral. A conventional bedding ceremony ensued, and the royal couple were despatched by Henry VII, in the middle of winter, to Ludlow so that Arthur could resume

Tudor emblem based on the Beaufort portcullis.

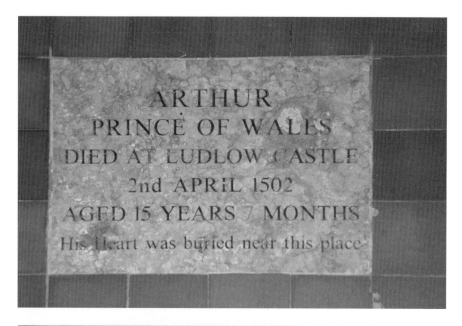

ARTHUR
PRINCE OF WALES
DIED AT LUDLOW CASTLE
2nd APRIL 1502
AGED 15 YEARS 7 MONTHS
His Heart was buried near this place

Floor plaque of Prince Arthur in Ludlow church.

The splendid chantry tomb of Prince Arthur in Worcester Cathedral.

his role as Prince of Wales. However, in spring of 1502, the couple fell ill. Catherine survived, but Arthur did not. The cause of death is not known, but is thought to have been consumption or sweating sickness. Arthur is buried in a beautiful tomb in **Worcester Cathedral**.

Although he died so early in our story, surprisingly, Arthur was to become a central figure in the King's Great Matter as it developed in the 1520s and 1530s. Arthur's brother, Henry VIII, had become increasingly uncomfortable about the fact that he had married his dead brother's widow. He thought that God obviously disapproved, and so had not blessed Henry's marriage with sons. Negotiations with the Roman Church established that it was critical to canonical law to ascertain whether Arthur had actually consummated his marriage to Catherine. Catherine admitted they had slept together seven or eight times, but was adamant that she was still a virgin when Arthur died. (See **Catherine of Aragon**.)

PRINCE EDWARD, later EDWARD VI (1537–53) was the ultimate objective of Henry VIII's quest, and a central figure in this book. Henry wanted a son to ensure the future of the Tudor dynasty, and the history of the monarchy since the Norman Conquest fully supported that objective. Henry I died in 1135, with only a legitimate daughter, Matilda, to succeed him. Her succession was disputed by Stephen, and twenty years of civil war ensued (the Anarchy). After Stephen, the succession passed through Matilda to her son, Henry II, the first Plantagenet king.

After twenty-eight years of trying, Henry VIII finally achieved his objective when Jane Seymour gave birth to a boy who, somewhat surprisingly, was named after his maternal grandfather, Edward IV – we might have expected a Henry.

From birth, Edward was surrounded by religious reformers – his uncle Edward Seymour, his tutors and, latterly, his stepmother, Queen Katherine Parr. Henry himself was conventionally Catholic, but he made sure that Edward was of a more reforming religion. Edward developed into a rather serious and studious sort of boy, who wasn't particularly precocious. He was neither tall like his father nor as outgoing. Dying at 15 years old, it is impossible to assess him as a king, but his reign is notable for the first real steps taken towards Protestantism in England, for example the introduction of Cranmer's *Book of Common Prayer*.

As he lay dying, he foolishly tried to exclude the technically illegitimate Princesses, Mary and Elizabeth, from the succession. He sought to ensure a Protestant succession by favouring Lady Jane Grey who, unhappily, became the Nine Day Queen, before Mary I staged a well-organised coup from East Anglia. The maverick John Dudley, Duke of Northumberland lay behind the abortive move.

King Edward VI. (Getty Images)

PRINCESS MARY, later MARY I (1516–58) was the only surviving child of six born to Catherine of Aragon and Henry VIII. She was brought up by her mother to be a devout Catholic, and she stayed true to the faith all her life. Henry kept mother and daughter apart in the 1520s and 1530s.

Mary displayed stubbornness, and even bravery, in opposing her father's insistence that she accept the break with Rome. She was still taking mass during her brother Edward's reign. Persistence was her middle name. She found much popular support in 1553, when a well-organised *coup d'état* against John Dudley, Duke of Northumberland and Lady Jane Grey, swept all before it from East Anglia and the south. Her epithet, 'Bloody Mary', stemmed from her over-enthusiastic executions of Protestants and her burnings of two bishops and Archbishop Cranmer in **Oxford**.

In 1554, Mary married King Philip of Spain in **Winchester** Cathedral. He became King of England, she Queen of Spain. However, she was reluctant to have him crowned in this country. Mary did not have children; the best she could manage was a 'phantom' pregnancy in 1556. This was fortunate, because England could have been in peril as an independent nation if the children of a Spanish monarch had succeeded to the throne.

PRINCESS ELIZABETH, later ELIZABETH I (1533–1603). At the age of 2, the baby Elizabeth lost not only her mother, but also her legitimacy, when Anne Boleyn was executed for adultery and her marriage to Henry VIII annulled in 1536. However, Henry did not abandon Elizabeth and she was given a full royal education. She proved a highly intelligent child, but with a more stable temperament than her mother's. She managed to survive everything that was thrown at her, including a spell in the Tower during her half-sister's reign, to be on hand to inherit Mary's throne in 1558.

Much of the story in this book is gloomy and morbid, but here we have a glorious tale where a daughter was able to finish off the work started by her mother a generation earlier, establishing the Protestant religion in England. Anne Boleyn would have been more than proud. Together with the defeat of the Armada and her rapport with Parliament, Elizabeth is recognised as one of the greatest of medieval monarchs. The Tudors finished on a high.

However, Elizabeth never married and never had children. She went somewhat further than flirtation with Thomas Seymour when she was a teenager, and she clearly had strong feelings for Robert Dudley, a son of John Dudley, Duke of Northumberland with whom she had been educated. But no marriage eventuated – see **Cumnor**. Elizabeth was succeeded by James VI of Scotland, who was descended from Margaret Tudor, Henry VIII's elder sister.

HENRY FITZROY, Duke of Richmond and Somerset (1519–36) was the only royal bastard acknowledged by Henry VIII. His mother was Elizabeth (Bessie) Blount, daughter of Sir John Blount of Kinlet, Shropshire, and a maid of honour to Catherine of Aragon. Henry is thought to have begun an affair with Bessie in 1514, when she was around 14 years old. The baby was conceived during Queen Catherine's last pregnancy, which itself resulted in a stillborn daughter.

The boy, Henry, was born at **Blackmore** in Essex, and Wolsey was a godfather. Henry Fitzroy's mother, Bessie, had been married to Sir Gilbert Tailboys in 1522 and the king initially kept the birth under wraps but, in June 1525, the child was given his prestigious titles. The Richmond title had belonged to Henry VIII's grandfather, Edmund Tudor, in the 1450s, while the Somerset dukedom had belonged to the Beauforts. Fitzroy was also granted an annual income in excess of £4,800, very appropriate for such grand titles.

Queen Catherine was, of course, much put out by the elevation of the royal bastard. In that same year, the child, Fitzroy, was appointed Lord High Admiral, Lord President of the Council of the North and Warden of the Marches towards Scotland – clearly, in practice, the roles were fulfilled by others!

The young duke was raised as a prince at **Sheriff Hutton Castle**, near York. At one time it was rumoured that Fitzroy would be married to his half-sister, Princess Mary, but in fact, in 1533, he married Mary Howard, the only daughter of Thomas Howard, 3rd Duke of Norfolk. Fitzroy had been educated alongside her brother, Henry Howard, Earl of Surrey. Under direction, the marriage was never consummated.

Fitzroy died tragically young, at the end of July 1536, just two months after Anne Boleyn's execution, which he had witnessed with his friend Henry Howard. Ironically, at that time a bill was passing through Parliament which would have enabled Henry VIII to nominate Fitzroy as his successor if he so wished, there being no legitimate male heir to the king at that time. He died at **St James's Palace**, and the Duke of Norfolk was instructed by Henry VIII to take his body in a cart covered only by straw to **Thetford Priory** in Norfolk, to the mausoleum of the Howards. The king later chastised the duke for the lack of due ceremony in the funeral – it could not have been easy to work with Henry VIII!

After the Dissolution, Fitzroy's remains were moved to **Framlingham**, where he shares an ornate tomb with his wife, Mary Fitzroy, who is thought to have died of consumption or tuberculosis, the male Tudor disease.

SUPPORTING CAST

ELIZABETH 'BESSIE' BLOUNT (1501–40) was the daughter of Sir John Blount and Catherine Persall, of modest gentry means from **Kinlet**, Shropshire. As a young girl, she became a maid of honour to Catherine of Aragon. It is thought that, from 1514, she became Henry VIII's mistress. She was noted for her beauty and her dancing skills.

In 1519, Bessie gave birth to Henry Fitzroy, the king's only acknowledged bastard (see **Blackmore** and **Framlingham**). For this reason, she is the only woman who we can be sure was Henry's mistress. Her relationship with Henry came to an end during her pregnancy, and she was not involved with Fitzroy's upbringing.

Kinlet is only 6 miles from Bewdley, where Prince Arthur and Catherine of Aragon had stayed during their short marriage. Her family were rewarded with the keepership of Tickenhill Palace in Bewdley, where Arthur had lived.

In 1522, Bessie was married off to Sir Gilbert Tailboys of South Kyme, Lincolnshire, who received grants of extra land for his pains. They had three children of their own. Sir Gilbert died in 1530, predeceasing his father. Fortunately, Bessie had been given a dowry from Tailboys lands so was still comfortably off. She remarried, in 1534, to her younger neighbour, Edward, Lord Clinton, and had three more daughters. Bessie became a lady in waiting to Anne of Cleves, but died in 1540 and is commemorated at **South Kyme**. Lord Clinton is buried in St George's Chapel, **Windsor**.

Charming wall brass of 'Bessie' Blount and her husband, Gilbert Tailboys, who has disappeared!

MARY BOLEYN (c. 1499–1543) was the elder daughter of Sir Thomas Boleyn and Elizabeth Howard. Sir Thomas claimed that his wife produced a child a year for ten years, but only three survived to adulthood – Mary, Anne and George. For centuries, there has been confusion over whether Mary or Anne was the elder. It is now generally accepted that Mary was. She was probably born at Blickling Hall, in Norfolk, and educated by a French governess at Hever with her siblings. In 1514, her father secured her a place as maid of honour to Mary Tudor, Henry's sister, who was going to France to marry King Louis XII. The aged Louis died after only three months, and the dowager queen left France in early 1515, but Mary stayed on at the court of the new king, Francis I.

Thomas Boleyn had just been appointed ambassador to France and he joined Mary in Paris, as did her younger sister Anne. Mary seems to have become embroiled in a series of affairs during her stay in Paris, including one with King Francis, a notorious womaniser. The king later referred to Mary as 'the English mare' and '*una grandissima ribalda, infame sopra tutte*' ('a great whore, infamous above all others'). In 1519, Mary returned to England as maid of honour to Catherine of Aragon. The next year she was married to William Carey, an up and coming courtier from Chilton Foliat in Wiltshire (just a few miles from the Seymour residence at **Wulfhall**, interestingly). The king attended the wedding, and it is thought that Mary became his mistress shortly after, in 1521.

From 1522–26, Mary's husband, William, received grants of manors and keeper-ships from the king, including keeper of **New Hall**, or Beaulieu, near Chelmsford. Their first child, Catherine, was born in 1524, followed by Henry in 1526. Although the affair with the king was never publicised, rumours did emerge that Henry had fathered one or both of the children but, unlike Henry Fitzroy, the king never acknowledged either child. Alison Weir is of the opinion that Catherine was Henry's but, by the time the boy had been born, the affair had finished (Weir, *Mary Boleyn*, p. 147).

William died of the sweating sickness in 1528, but Mary's sister, Anne Boleyn, was already close to the king and was able to help out with finances. Mary accompanied Anne on a state visit to Calais with Henry in 1532. However, she once again blotted her copybook by secretly marrying beneath herself to William Stafford, a soldier and second son of a modest Essex landowner. Anne, by now queen, was furious and banished the couple from court – they were also disowned by the rest of the Boleyn family. Mary had married for love but she was now pregnant and short of money. Anne eventually sent a golden cup and some money, but the sisters never met again.

In 1528, the king had obtained a papal dispensation to marry the sister of a woman with whom he had previously had sexual relations – i.e. Mary. Incredibly, he rejected the Pope's authority to dispense on the issue in 1536, in order to annul his marriage to Anne Boleyn, just days before her execution. The logic was the mirror image of that which he had used to annul his marriage to Catherine of Aragon. Princess Elizabeth became a bastard, as well as losing her mother! Mary lived out her days as a social outcast at Rochford Hall in Essex, but she did outlive her parents and her unfortunate siblings.

Fortunately, Elizabeth I was very kind to her Carey cousins. Catherine married Sir Francis Knollys and was Elizabeth's chief lady of the bedchamber (see **Rotherfield Greys**), and her brother, Henry, was ennobled by Elizabeth as Lord Hunsdon, and has a huge monument in **Westminster Abbey**.

Mary's seems a strange life – early on, the mistress of two powerful kings, but then followed by life as a social outcast in Essex. The pitfalls of marrying for love in the sixteenth century perhaps?

CHARLES BRANDON, Duke of Suffolk (c. 1484–1545) was the son of Sir William Brandon, a hero of Bosworth Field. Richard III's death-or-glory charge at the end of the battle drove straight at Henry Tudor; Brandon, as standard bearer, blocked the charge, thus saving Henry Tudor's life but succumbing to Richard's blows. The infant, Charles, was brought up at court by Henry VII and educated with Prince Henry. Brandon became Henry VIII's oldest friend and, with one or two hiccups, they remained close. In the early days, Brandon was a boon companion and jousting opponent, but he was also an accomplished soldier. He distinguished himself at the sieges of Therouanne and Tournai, in 1513, and led armies in France in 1523 and 1544.

He also played a leading part in suppressing the Pilgrimage of Grace, in Lincolnshire, in 1536.

Brandon had a chequered marital history. He had two short-lived marriages in the early years of the sixteenth century. In 1515, he was sent by Henry VIII to France to collect the king's sister, Mary, who had been recently widowed as dowager queen. Mary held a torch for Brandon and they secretly married – see **Mary Tudor**. When Mary died in 1533, Brandon promptly married Katherine Willoughby, who was actually betrothed to his son. He was 47 years old and she was 13 years! They lived at **Grimsthorpe Castle**.

Charles had been made Duke of Suffolk in 1514, and held a variety of public offices, from master of horse to Lord President of the council. He was also given various specific tasks by Henry, including Lord High Steward at Anne Boleyn's coronation in 1533, despite his and Mary's dislike of Anne and his celebrated attempt to evict Catherine of Aragon from Buckden in the same year.

Brandon was not the most industrious of courtiers, and not the brightest, but he did succeed in keeping his head on his shoulders while many around Henry were losing theirs. The king paid for Brandon's burial in **St George's Chapel, Windsor**, where his funeral helm can still be seen.

THOMAS CRANMER, Archbishop of Canterbury (c. 1489–ex. 1556, archbishop from 1533) is one of the central figures in our story, and one of the founders of the Church of England. Born into minor gentry stock in **Aslockton**, Nottinghamshire, Cranmer studied at Jesus College, Cambridge, which is one of Lady Margaret Beaufort's foundations. He became an evangelical Church reformer and humanist, but never a Lutheran.

As a young man he married, but his wife died during her first childbirth. While teaching at Cambridge, he developed the idea that Henry VIII should put aside the legal case being pursued in Rome for the King's Great Matter, and instead undertake a general canvassing of opinions from university theologians throughout Europe. When the king heard about this idea from Cranmer's colleague, Stephen Gardiner, he took to it and implementation followed. Cranmer joined Henry's team and was involved in embassies to the Holy Roman Empire. However, he failed to persuade the Emperor, Charles V, who was Catherine of Aragon's nephew, to support Henry's cause – a losing wicket if ever there was one!

Henry also used him as an ideas generator. It will, however, have come as something of a surprise when Cranmer heard, in October 1532, that he had been appointed Archbishop of Canterbury on the death of William Warham – the Boleyns had lobbied hard on his behalf. Since Anne Boleyn was already pregnant with the future Elizabeth I, much had to be done, and quickly. Cranmer married Henry and Anne in late January 1533, annulled the marriage of Henry and Catherine of Aragon in May, crowned Queen Anne on 1 June and baptised Princess Elizabeth in September (and acted as her godfather) – some workload!

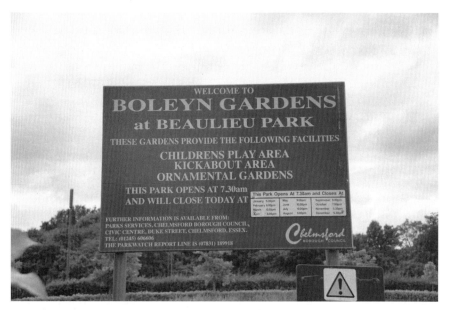

Good work by Chelmsford Council.

With Cromwell's help as vice regent, Cranmer established the new *modus operandi* of the Church of England. As prelate he was, of course, involved in most of the state occasions during Henry's reign. In addition, he visited Anne Boleyn in the Tower and heard her confessions, during which she reiterated her innocence of the charges. He had also, just a day or two before her execution, to annul Anne's marriage to Henry on the grounds that it was within the forbidden degrees of affinity, because of Henry's earlier liaison with Mary Boleyn – Anne thus died as Marquess of Pembroke, not as queen. Henry's cruelty knew few bounds!

Cranmer instigated the legal investigations into Katherine Howard's sexual exploits by leaving a letter for the king in the Chapel Royal. It was also Cranmer who administered the last rites to Henry VIII. Cranmer had given the king everything he could have desired, but it was really as he became a member of the regency council in Edward VI's reign that his greatest contribution to English life started. The reforming majority on the council were able to begin the process of Protestant Reformation. Cranmer was at the forefront of the movement, and left his personal and greatest legacy in the form of the *Book of Common Prayer*, still in use in the Church of England today.

After the success of Mary I's coup in 1553, Cranmer bravely did not flee the country. He was arrested and imprisoned for two years, during which he recanted his Protestantism. When it became clear that he was going to die anyway, he withdrew the recantation and died a Protestant martyr in the flames at **Oxford**, on the same spot that Latimer and Ridley had been burned a year earlier.

THOMAS CROMWELL, Earl of Essex, (c. 1485–ex. 1540) came from humble origins in Putney. His grandfather had moved from Norwell, in Nottinghamshire, whose adjacent village is called Cromwell. His father, Walter, ran a number of enterprises, including fulling, and owned a brewery, although not always successfully. Very little is known about his mother, whose surname was Glossop.

Interestingly, his uncle was cook to William Warham, Archbishop of Canterbury. One of Cromwell's sisters, Katherine, married a Welshman called Morgan Williams, from a prosperous Putney family. Their son, Richard, changed his surname to Cromwell, and went on to found the branch of the family from which Oliver Cromwell was descended. (So, that quintessentially English politician actually had a fair amount of Welsh blood in him!) Morgan was a kinsman of John Williams – see **Thame**.

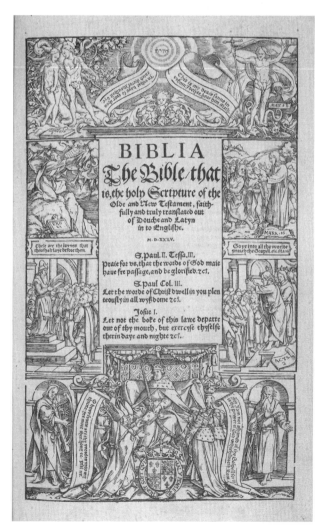

Cromwell persuaded Henry VIII to introduce the Great Bible in English in 1539. (British Library)

The mature Thomas Cromwell by Holbein. (Getty Images)

Thomas Cromwell's father was a brute and they did not get on, so, around 1502, the young man left home and travelled around Europe to Italy and the Low Countries. He even fought for the French Army in their defeat at the Garigliano River. There is an air of mystery attached to these travels, during which Cromwell may have picked up ideas for Church reform. Thomas returned to England around 1515. The next year he married Elizabeth Williams, a widow of a wealthy Yeoman of the Guard. By 1520, with no formal education, he had managed to establish himself as a lawyer and money lender. He came into contact with Cardinal Wolsey and entered the Commons. He came to the fore by undertaking, on Wolsey's behalf, the land conveyancing needed to dissolve the thirty monasteries being used to finance Wolsey's college in Ipswich. This work became Cromwell's speciality, and was used to good effect during the more widespread dissolutions in the late 1530s.

Cromwell joined Wolsey's council in 1526, and became the go-between for Wolsey and the king. He survived the fall of his mentor, and joined Henry's council in 1530. He supervised all the king's legal and parliamentary affairs through the Reformation Parliament and, in 1534, was appointed principal secretary and chief minister to Henry. Two years later he became keeper of the Privy Seal, vicar-general and vice regent in matters spiritual – an astonishing achievement in medieval times for the son of a fuller.

Cromwell's success was based on high intelligence, a prodigious work rate and attention to detail, a certain ruthlessness and a willingness to give the king what he wanted. These traits are seen to good effect in his organisation of the Dissolution of the Monasteries, which was undertaken with chilling speed and efficiency. A second area of achievement was government administration, where Cromwell laid down the foundations for today's departments of state. He also introduced poor-relief legislation for the first time in England, making parishes responsible.

Cromwell was a religious reformer, who helped to move England towards Protestantism. He instigated attacks on Catholic pilgrimages, shrines, ceremonies, images and purgatory. However, perhaps his greatest achievement in matters spiritual was to persuade a somewhat reluctant king to introduce the official *Great Bible* in English, in 1539. Every parish was to have one.

Cromwell, thus, has many positive achievements to his name – so why is he so controversial? Serving Henry was not a job for the faint-hearted! One of Cromwell's strengths was that he gave the king what he wanted. However, Henry's goals were often morally questionable, whilst the means adopted by Cromwell were equally so. One such 'achievement' was his destruction of Anne Boleyn and her family. Anne and Cromwell fell out spectacularly at Sunday mass in early April 1536. He proceeded to put together the judicial case against her, alleging multiple adultery, incest and treason – no doubt with Henry's support. Modern research by Alison Weir and others has shown that the dates of key meetings between Anne and her lovers do not stack up, and could not have occurred. In other words, Cromwell's case was a stitch-up.

By modern standards of public service, Thomas was highly corrupt in the financial arena as well. At the time of his fall in 1540, he had become, from nothing, the second wealthiest man in England after the Duke of Norfolk, by expropriating for himself land and buildings as the monasteries were dissolved – see **Lewes**, **Melton Mowbray** and **Launde**. Of course, at that time most of the aristocracy were similarly corrupt, but the scale of Cromwell's gains made him vulnerable to his enemies once the king's support was withdrawn. Perhaps his biggest mistake was to push on too quickly with religious reform, a field where he had the freedom to have gone more slowly. In 1539, he really pushed Henry to complete the 'Great Bible' project. In fact, in June of that year the king, assisted by the Duke of Norfolk, issued the Six Articles which stopped Cromwell's religious reforms in their tracks. The writing was on the wall.

Finally, the arrival of Anne of Cleves, in early 1540, and the king's bizarre rejection of the new queen, sealed Cromwell's fate by generating a climate of blame against him and enabling the king to strike. Cromwell took the full force of the king's wrath, summed up in his own words as 'She is not as other men have reported her'.

In April 1540, despite this climate, Cromwell was made Earl of Essex and Lord Great Chamberlain, which surely enraged his enemies at court. Out of the blue he was arrested in the Privy Council in June. Norfolk and the Earl of Southampton tore off his garter insignia as he was removed to the Tower. He was condemned by parliamentary attainder, not by any judicial process, and found guilty. The bill accused him of corrupt financial gain, heresy because of his religious reforms, of treason and it made a good deal of his humble origins. There were also suggestions that Cromwell had leaked secrets from the marriage bed of Henry and Anne of Cleves.

Henry had one final task for his chief minister, however – to sort out the annulment of the marriage, which was duly achieved. One gets the feeling that Cromwell had done all that Henry wanted from him, and that it was time for him to go, or perhaps, after a decade of service, he simply knew too much?

Cromwell was beheaded by axe at the end of July 1540, the axe-man making a complete hash of the job. His recent earldom had enabled the king to commute the full horror for a treason conviction to that of decapitation. Oddly, five months later, his son, Gregory, was ennobled even though he was a much less able man. Gregory was a member of parliament and was knighted at the coronation of Edward VI (see **Launde**).

JOHN DUDLEY, Lord Lisle, later Duke of Northumberland (*c.* 1502–ex. 1553) was the eldest son of Edmund Dudley and his second wife Elizabeth Grey, daughter of Viscount Lisle. Edmund had been a councillor and financial enforcer for Henry VII, but was famously executed by Henry VIII soon after his accession in 1509.

In 1512, John became the ward of Sir Edward Guildford, whose daughter, Jane, he later married. The attainder against his father was also lifted. John had a conventional upbringing, and he became a successful soldier fighting under the Duke of Suffolk in France. John Dudley leant towards religious reform, he attended the christenings of Princess Elizabeth and Prince Edward, and was master of horse to Anne of Cleves (although not for long!). In 1542, he was granted his maternal grandfather's title of Viscount Lisle.

Alongside Edward Seymour, he fought successfully against the Scots and, as Lord High Admiral, helped repel the French fleet at the Battle of the Solent in 1545 (despite the total loss of the *Mary Rose*). Seymour and Dudley were championed by Henry VIII as religious reformers, and came to dominate the council as the king ruthlessly purged the conservative faction at court. Upon Henry's death in early 1547 all, therefore, looked straightforward for the accession of the young Edward VI, supported by Seymour and Dudley.

Unfortunately, the arrogant Seymour was not liked by his fellow councillors so Dudley broke with Seymour, ousted him from his position as Lord Protector, had him executed and, in effect, replaced him as president of the council. It was a betrayal in the grand manner, because the two had been friends as well as political allies – even sharing an interest in Renaissance architecture (which survives in stone at **Berry Pomeroy** and **Dudley Castles**).

The split in the reforming party proved catastrophic when Edward VI died in 1553, aged only 15 years. Dudley, now the Duke of Northumberland, tried to engineer the accession of Lady Jane Grey who had married, much against her better judgement, Dudley's fifth son, Guildford. Jane, who reigned for only nine days, was the granddaughter of Mary Tudor, Henry VIII's sister, through her mother Frances Brandon. Dudley's coup had little popular support, whereas the other Mary Tudor, Henry VIII's daughter, received widespread support in East Anglia and the south.

John Dudley was captured by Mary's forces and later executed, despite abjuring his Protestantism. Lady Jane Grey followed not long afterwards, beheaded on **Tower Green**. Ironically, perhaps, despite all the political mayhem from 1549 onwards, the reign of Edward VI is marked by some really important achievements. The question is – why did Henry VIII actively promote the career of a man whose father he had so dramatically executed in 1509? Was Dudley in some way out to obtain revenge on Henry?

THOMAS HOWARD, 3rd Duke of Norfolk (1473–1554) was the eldest son of his namesake, the 2nd Duke, and his first wife, Elizabeth Tilney. Although the dukedom is ancient, the Howards were the great *arrivistes* of the fifteenth century. John Howard, the 1st Duke, was born into wealthy Suffolk gentry stock and was ennobled by Edward IV during the Wars of the Roses. The Howards gave great support to Richard III's coup in 1483, and were rewarded with the Norfolk dukedom because John's mother had been the last surviving Mowbray, the previous ducal family.

At Bosworth Field, the Howards were again Richard III's greatest supporters. John, the 1st Duke, led the vanguard, but was killed in the melee against the troops of the peerless John de Vere, Earl of Oxford. Howard's son, Thomas, probably saved his own life by ordering his men to lay down their arms. Nevertheless, Thomas was imprisoned by Henry VII and the dukedom confiscated – Thomas reverted to their junior title of Earl of Surrey.

Thomas junior also turned into another highly effective soldier. He fought against the Cornish rebels in 1497, and against the Scots, and then went to Spain with the

Marquess of Dorset in 1512. He became Lord High Admiral in 1513. That same year he played a prominent part in the stunning victory over the Scots, orchestrated by his father at **Flodden Field**. As a result, the dukedom was restored to the family by Henry VIII, and Thomas junior became Earl of Surrey. The family was now the wealthiest in England, with vast estates in East Anglia and elsewhere and, conveniently for Henry VIII, they had no possible claim to the throne.

In 1495, Thomas junior had been married to Anne Plantagenet, daughter of Edward IV and next youngest sister to Queen Elizabeth of York. They had four children, all of whom died young. Anne died around 1512, and Thomas married the equally prestigious Elizabeth Stafford (1497–1558), daughter of the Duke of Buckingham. By her, Thomas had three children, including his son Henry, the poet who became Earl of Surrey, and daughter Mary, who married Henry Fitzroy.

In 1516, Thomas became a member of the council and, in 1522, he took over from his father as Lord Treasurer. Two years later he inherited the dukedom. As the King's Great Matter unfolded over the next ten years, Thomas was to play a central, if rather unsavoury, role. He seems to have been ruthlessly ambitious and unscrupulous, with a violent temper and a tendency to take offence. Not an easy man to deal with, and in a modern context certainly not a man to have as your line manager!

Thomas was also religiously conservative, being quoted as claiming 'he had never read the Bible and never intended to' – that was the job of the clergy. Nevertheless, for twenty years or more he gave sterling service to Henry VIII. He was made Earl Marshal in 1533. In 1536 he was given the odious task of presiding at the trials of Anne Boleyn and her brother, George, who were his niece and nephew. He played the leading part in suppressing the Pilgrimage of Grace, and the next year he was godfather for Prince Edward and organised the funeral of Jane Seymour. His religious conservatism came through when he played a big part, in 1539, in pushing through the Six Articles as Henry VIII put the brakes on religious reform.

Thomas and his family's standing, however, suffered badly during the Katherine Howard debacle. As he had done with Anne Boleyn, he repudiated the queen (who was, once again, his niece) by issuing an abject apology to the king and thus avoiding punishment. Nevertheless, two years later, Henry required his military abilities to fight the French and so he was back in favour.

Finally, in late 1546, just before the king died, the duke and his son, Henry, were arrested and sent to the Tower. Thomas confessed and, in true style, repudiated his son, who was executed. The warrant for Thomas' own execution was prepared, but Henry died before he could sign it. Edward VI's Regency Council did not enforce the warrant, although Thomas was kept in the Tower until Mary I's coup in 1553. He showed no such clemency when, for one last time, acting as Lord High Steward at the trial of John Dudley, Duke of Northumberland.

Thomas is buried at **Framlingham** alongside his first wife, Anne, and the tombs of his son, Henry, and daughter, Mary.

EDWARD SEYMOUR, Earl of Hertford, later Duke of Somerset and Lord Protector (1501–ex. 1552) was the eldest surviving son of Sir John Seymour and Margery Wentworth, and the eldest brother of Jane, Henry VIII's third wife.

There were two distinct halves to his career. For the first thirty years, he played the conventional role as heir to a distinguished but modest baronetcy in Wiltshire, together with roles at court culminating in his appointment as master of horse to Henry Fitzroy, Henry VIII's acknowledged bastard. He was also Esquire of the Body to Henry. However, in the early 1530s, it is almost as if he had some sort of 'call from above'. He discarded his first wife, Catherine Filliol, and their two sons, and traded up to a more aristocratic model in Anne Stanhope, starting a second family of sons, most of whom were called Edward – see **Wulfhall** and **Berry Pomeroy**.

In March 1536, two months before the fall of Anne Boleyn, he was appointed to the more prestigious Privy Chamber, probably so that he and his wife could chaperone his sister, Jane, in whom Henry was now taking great interest. On the day Jane was proclaimed queen, Edward was created Viscount Beauchamp and from then on he became an increasingly important figure in Henry VIII's government – especially after the birth of Prince Edward, his nephew, in 1537. Only three days after the birth, he was created Earl of Hertford and then became a member of the Privy Council.

He was a religious reformer, which fitted in easily with the king's choice of the Protestant religion for Prince Edward. Seymour was a fine soldier, and led expeditions into Scotland in 1544 and in 1547, when he won the Battle of Pinkie. He took over command from the disgraced Henry Howard, Earl of Surrey, in France in 1546, where he successfully defended Boulogne. By the end of Henry's reign in early 1547, Edward Seymour and his close companion, John Dudley, Lord Lisle (who was also a reformer), dominated the council – thanks largely to the ruthless purging of the conservative faction undertaken in the last ten years of Henry's reign. Even the Howards fell in late 1546.

After Henry's death, Seymour grabbed the initiative, distributed patronage to other councillors and had himself declared Lord Protector and Duke of Somerset. He had reached the top of the tree – leading the government of his 9-year-old nephew, Edward VI. Unfortunately, however, he had developed into a rather arrogant, haughty individual who did not relate well to other members of the council. The young Edward also found him restrictive and overbearing, along with his equally haughty wife. By contrast, John Dudley, now Earl of Warwick, got on well with both the council and with the king. The council had Seymour arrested in October 1549 and, by early 1550, Dudley had emerged as leader of the council. Seymour was briefly reinstated to the council, but was executed – on largely fabricated charges – for attempting to overthrow Dudley in early 1552. Dudley then made himself Duke of Northumberland.

THOMAS SEYMOUR, Lord Sudeley (*c.* 1502–ex. 1549) was one of Edward's younger brothers who always seemed envious of his elder brother's success. At the beginning of the Protectorate in 1547 he was ennobled and appointed Lord High Admiral with a seat on the council.

He was personally closer to the young king than his brother (he bribed him with pocket money!) and so was able to secretly marry Dowager Queen Katherine Parr, whose household included the young Princess Elizabeth. Seymour could not resist flirting with the teenager, until Katherine found them in an embrace and banished Elizabeth from her home. After Katherine's death in childbirth, Seymour persisted with Elizabeth by letter, proposing marriage. She showed some interest, but was not prepared to proceed without the council's authority, which was unlikely to be granted.

Finally, Seymour was arrested after a madcap attempt to kidnap the young king, and was beheaded with his brother's reluctant agreement in March 1549. Elizabeth, in true style, later provided the definitive assessment of Seymour: 'This day died a man of much wit but little judgement.'

WILLIAM WARHAM, Archbishop of Canterbury (c. 1460–1532, archbishop from 1503). Unlike his successor, Thomas Cranmer, Warham is not a household name despite being archbishop for nearly thirty years. However, he did play a key part in the dramas of the King's Great Matter in the 1520s and 1530s.

Warham came from very ordinary gentry/yeoman farmer stock from **Oakley**, but acquired a first class education at Winchester College and New College, Oxford. He became a successful lawyer and diplomat. From 1496, he led the negotiations with the Spanish ambassador over the proposed marriage of Prince Arthur to Catherine of Aragon. In 1501, he became Bishop of London and was involved in the marriage ceremony of Arthur and Catherine. In 1503, he translated to Archbishop of Canterbury, and the following year he became Lord Chancellor. He married and crowned Henry VIII and Catherine. Warham was chancellor of Oxford University from 1506 and delighted in the company of scholars. He was a friend of Erasmus whose *Greek Testament* he sponsored. He was also a great builder – see **Otford**.

Warham was appointed by Henry VII, so it came as no surprise that he fell out with Henry VIII in 1515 and resigned the chancellorship in favour of Wolsey. He fell further behind Wolsey when the latter was made up to cardinal, the leading ecclesiastical position in England. Nevertheless, as the King's Great Matter got underway in the 1520s, Warham was thoroughly involved alongside Wolsey because of his prior involvement in the marriage negotiations in the 1490s. Initially, Warham acquiesced with Henry's break with Rome, including the submission of the clergy in 1531, which established King Henry as the head of the Church with a special clause inserted by Warham: '… so far as the law of Christ allows'. However, in February 1532, in a change of heart, Warham repudiated all that had changed since 1529, and upbraided the king in the Lords, revealing his true religious conservatism.

He was now a real nuisance to Henry, who was ready to move forward to the annulment of his marriage with Queen Catherine. In 1531, two of his servants were poisoned! Furthermore, Warham had expressed his desire to be buried in the **Martyrdom** in **Canterbury Cathedral**, the area where Becket had been hacked to death. Did he feel threatened? At any rate he duly obliged Henry by dying in August 1532 and he was replaced by the evangelical Cranmer, Henry's marriage to Catherine was annulled and Anne Boleyn became queen. With the benefit of hindsight, is there perhaps a suggestion that for some reason Henry could not proceed to annulment with Warham at the helm? And yet Warham had, all along, had doubts about the papal dispensation issued to allow Henry to marry Catherine. One of the many puzzles in our story?

CARDINAL THOMAS WOLSEY (*c.* 1473–1530) was the son of Robert Wolsey of Ipswich, butcher and cattle dealer (although there are hints he may have latterly become a wealthy cloth merchant). He attended Ipswich School and Magdalen College, Oxford.

In 1507, Wolsey entered the service of Henry VII and became Royal Chaplain. On Henry VIII's accession he was appointed almoner, which included a seat on the Privy Council. This rise to power from relatively humble origins is attributed to his intelligence and drive. The war with France, in 1513, gave Wolsey the opportunity to demonstrate both his diplomatic and logistics skills. In 1514, he was appointed Bishop of Lincoln and then Archbishop of York. In 1515, Archbishop Warham of Canterbury resigned as Lord Chancellor and the post was given to Wolsey. In the same year, he was made a cardinal – his rise to the top of the pile had been meteoric. He achieved

Public house near Hampton Court.

major success in the diplomatic arena with the Treaty of London in 1518, and the Field of the Cloth of Gold in France in 1520.

Wolsey's duties for the king were varied – he arranged the secret birth of Henry Fitzroy, Henry's acknowledged bastard, in 1519 and became his godfather. In 1526, he reorganised the royal household in a series of announcements called the 'Eltham Ordinances', and he prosecuted Sir William Compton and Lady Anne Hastings for adultery through the ecclesiastical courts (see **Stoke Poges**). Wolsey founded a grammar school in **Ipswich** and Cardinal College in Oxford, which Henry VIII renamed Christchurch. He also acquired land at **Hampton Court** in 1514, where he built the magnificent Tudor mansion which, in 1526, he gifted to the king while retaining a suite of rooms for his own use.

Wolsey was never popular with the peerage because of his humble origins, so when the annulment proceedings against Catherine of Aragon began to founder, his position became increasingly isolated. He had managed to obtain papal agreement to hold the proceedings in England, and he jointly chaired them at the Blackfriars in London with Campeggio, his fellow legate. But Campeggio 'played for time', and the case was suspended indefinitely in July 1529. This effectively sealed Wolsey's fate – he had already made an enemy of Anne Boleyn, and she had become convinced that he was not putting his heart into the annulment proceedings. He was stripped of his government offices and property. He was allowed to remain archbishop and decided to visit his see for the first time. He travelled north, but then Henry Percy, Earl of Northumberland, was sent to arrest him at Cawood, near York. Under guard, he headed back towards London, but died at **Leicester Abbey**. See also **Sheffield**.

FOUR

The Guide by Region

VISITING THE SITES

- It is usually better to go in summer since many houses, castles and even churches are often closed to the public in winter.
- Afternoons are best, until 4.30 p.m.
- Access to churches can be difficult, even in summer, because of problems of theft and vandalism. Parish churches in urban or semi-urban environments are often likely to be locked. Churches in very isolated rural environments may also be locked. Cathedrals and large town churches are usually open, with supervision. A phone call or letter before your visit is the best idea. Alternatively, a phone number is usually given on the board in the churchyard or in the church porch, and a key is sometimes available locally.
- Phoning clergy and parish offices in the morning is better.
- Most cathedrals ask for visitors' donations.
- Most of the sites in this guide are open to the public.
- Directions are given to each site, and are designed for use with modern motoring atlases. Where there is more than one church in a town (tower) or (spire) is indicated.

Ratings System for Sites

★	Standard monuments to an aristocrat/person involved in the drama.
★★	More detail known of involvement, or some architectural interest.
★★★	A significant participant in the period.
★★★★	Outstanding historical interest.
★★★★★	Truly of national importance.

Rating System for Battlefields

+   Site known but little survives.

++   Site known and some interesting survivals.

+++   Plenty to see or key battle with some survivals.

++++   Key battle with much to see.

+++++ Decisive battle with plenty to see.

Pound Symbol

£ Entrance fee charged.

££ Higher entrance fee charged.

Abbreviations

NT   National Trust property.

EH   English Heritage property.

Cadw   Welsh Historic Monuments.

KAL   Key to church available locally (check porch/board).

PO   Parish office phone number.

Underlining

<u>Underlining</u> is used to highlight the person(s) involved in the period being celebrated at a particular site.

Bold Type

Bold type is used in site descriptions in three ways:

1 To highlight locations in a building, e.g. **chancel**.
2 To indicate a secondary site, e.g. **East Barsham**.
3 To highlight a memorial at a site to a person who features in Chapter 3, 'The Main Characters', where biographical information is given, e.g. **<u>Jane Seymour</u>**.

Site Categories

Sites are split into primary sites and secondary sites. Secondary sites are conveniently close to primary sites, but do not necessarily warrant a long-distance visit on their own merit. They are 'while you are in the area do also visit' sites. Full directions are not necessarily given for secondary sites.

MOST REWARDING SITES TO VISIT

★★★★★ Canterbury, the Tower of London, Hampton Court, Westminster Abbey, Hever, Windsor, Ludlow.

★★★★ Framlingham, Peterborough, Haddon Hall, Sudeley Castle, National Portrait Gallery, Worcester, Oxford.

++++ Battle of Flodden.

SOUTH EAST

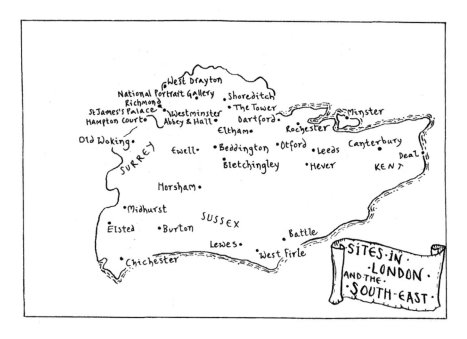

BATTLE, St Mary's Church ★★★
Situated in the town centre, across from the abbey gatehouse but not in the abbey.

Between the **Lady Chapel** and the **altar** there is a marvellous, highly coloured **tomb chest** with **effigies** celebrating Sir Antony Browne (*c.* 1500–48) and his first wife, Alice Gage (d. 1540), daughter of Sir John Gage (see **West Firle**).

Sir Antony was the son of Sir Antony senior and Lucy *née* Neville, who was the widow of Sir Thomas Fitzwilliam and mother of Sir William Fitzwilliam (therefore Sir Antony's half-brother – see **Midhurst**). Lucy was one of the daughters of John Neville, Marquess Montagu, who was the brother of Warwick the Kingmaker.

The fine tomb of Sir Antony Browne at Battle.

Sir Antony junior was multi-talented – as a young man, he excelled in the tiltyard and was famously subject to a furious sword assault by the king at Greenwich in 1524. He was sent on embassies to France, and made ambassador in 1527. Within the royal household, he progressed from Esquire of the Body, in 1525, to Master of the Horse in 1539. He became King's Standard Bearer, following in the footsteps of his father. Politically, he leaned towards the conservative faction, supporting Jane Seymour. He came under suspicion when an attempt at reconciliation with Princess Mary was being made in 1536, and he was interrogated but survived.

He and his wife are most famous for the role they played when Henry first met Anne of Cleves incognito, at the Bishop's Palace at **Rochester**. Lady Browne had been appointed as Mother of the Maids – a rather severe one, as befitted a daughter of the Lieutenant of the Tower of London! They were as unimpressed with Anne as Henry was, unlike some of the other courtiers who did not catch the royal mood early (see **Rochester**). They accompanied Anne to Blackheath, where she formally met Henry, who was never anything but courteous to her in public.

After Alice's death, Antony married Elizabeth Fitzgerald, the Earl of Surrey's 'Fair Geraldine' (see **Windsor**). He was over 40 years old – she was 15, and a noted beauty! Browne inherited Cowdray House from his stepbrother in 1542 (see **Midhurst**). As Henry's health declined, Browne became increasingly close to him and he was appointed guardian to Prince Edward and to Princess Elizabeth, and made an executor of Henry's will. It was he who rode to Hertford to inform Edward of his father's death in January 1547.

BEDDINGTON, St Mary's Church ★

Situated next to a school in Beddington Park, between Carshalton and Beddington, just north of A232, Carshalton–Croydon road.

The **Carew Chapel** contains monuments to the Carew family, who lived here in the late Middle Ages. In particular, a **tomb chest** and **brasses** to Sir Richard Carew (d. 1520) and his wife, Malyn *née* Oxenbridge, the parents of Sir Nicholas Carew. Sir Richard was Captain of Calais.

Also here is an **alabaster monument** to Sir Francis Carew, son of Sir Nicholas, who managed to recover his father's lands in 1554, after the latter's execution and attainder.

Immediately next door to the church, on the north side, lies **Beddington Place**, which now houses a school in a building which survives from the reign of Henry VIII. It was rebuilt in the 1530s by Sir Nicholas Carew (c. 1496–ex. 1539) and rebuilt again in the eighteenth century.

Sir Nicholas was the classic Tudor courtier. At the age of 6, he was picked out to be a member of Henry's household and shared the prince's education. He became a renowned jouster, and performed at the Christmas revels in 1514. During that year, he married Elizabeth *née* Bryan, a noted beauty and daughter of the vice chamberlain to Catherine of Aragon. He was associated with the rakish group dubbed the 'King's Minions'. In 1518, he and others were purged from court by Wolsey, but this did not stop the king from staying in Beddington the following year. In 1522, Carew was appointed Master of the Horse. As a member of the Privy Chamber, he was again barred from court by Wolsey as part of the Eltham Ordinances.

Sir Nicholas did have a serious side – he had good French, became ambassador to France and was well-liked by the French king, Francis I. He was also a soldier and attended the king at the Field of the Cloth of Gold. He was restored to favour in 1527/28 because of the rise of his cousin, Anne Boleyn. In fact, he did not care for her and, from 1529, was a supporter of Catherine of Aragon and Princess Mary, perhaps influenced by his old friend, Henry Courtenay, Marquess of Exeter. Despite this, the king and Anne visited Beddington in early 1531 and June 1533. Carew acted as Queen's Champion at Anne's coronation.

In April 1536, Cromwell allied with Sir Nicholas and other conservatives in order to bring about the downfall of Anne and the Boleyns. That same month, Carew was, surprisingly, made a Knight of the Garter instead of George Boleyn – an early sign that things were not looking good for Queen Anne.

In May 1536, Jane Seymour stayed here while the trial and execution of Anne Boleyn were taking place. Everything changed around so that, by the spring of 1538, Cromwell had his hooks into the conservative faction. Carew was keen to see Princess Mary restored to court and became implicated in the 'Exeter Conspiracy'. The first inkling that he was in trouble was when the king made derogatory remarks to Carew during a game of bowls. Carew unfortunately reacted angrily – never a sensible plan with Henry. He was tried and executed in early 1539.

BLETCHINGLEY, St Mary's Church ★
Located in the village centre, just north of A25, Redhill–Godstone road. Access the church by turning north on a minor road to Merstham.

A plain **tomb chest** in the **south chancel arcade** commemorates Sir Thomas Cawarden (d. 1559), who was steward to Anne of Cleves at nearby Bletchingley Place. In 1547, Sir Thomas became her tenant there, and then inherited upon her death in 1557. She obviously thought a lot of Cawarden, who had provided her with a loan to buy a house in Dartford.

Thomas Cawarden came from an ordinary background, but he certainly sounds a lively character whose roles included Master of the Revels and Tents – the latter were used for festivals, royal progresses and military expeditions. Given Henry VIII's love of revels, this position sounds demanding! He must have done a good job because he was knighted by Henry at Boulogne in 1544. He was also keeper of **Nonsuch Palace** 1553–56. He was a religious reformer, and personally helped to abolish or deface the idolatry in this church. He was implicated in Wyatt's Revolt in Mary's reign and imprisoned, but survived into the reign of Elizabeth I who remembered an earlier readiness to serve her, so he became, briefly, joint Lieutenant of the Tower of London, before retiring. Sir Thomas married a woman called Elizabeth, but nothing else is known of her and they had no children.

Continue on the minor road, north towards Brewer Street; after 1 mile go round a sharp left-hand bend and on the right you will see **Place Farm**, formerly the site of **Bletchingley Place**, one of the properties given to **Anne of Cleves** as part of her divorce settlement with Henry VIII. It had formerly been owned by the Duke of Buckingham, who was executed in 1521. Now a private residence, intriguingly, a medieval **brick arch** can be seen at the front of the house near the doorway. Pevsner thinks this was the base of a **Tudor gatehouse**. The scale of this residence will have been massive.

BURTON (West Sussex), Parish Church ★★
Located next to the main house (private) in Burton Park, 3 miles south of Petworth. Turn off A285, Petworth–Chichester road in Duncton, onto a private road to the main house for ¾ mile.

Probably the most charismatic site in this volume, set in lovely surroundings. On the **north wall** of the **nave**, a **monument** and **brass** to Sir William Goring (d. 1554) and his wife Lady Elizabeth Covert (d. 1558). Only her brass survives, but do not worry, because she will have been involved in most of what follows!

In 1533, Goring attended the coronation of Anne Boleyn acting as a server. He became a member of the royal household and attended the christening of Prince Edward. Goring was an early Protestant, and helped uncover the Pole 'conspiracy'

Lovely wall tomb of Sir William Goring and his wife Elizabeth at Burton. His brass has gone missing.

in the late 1530s – the Poles lived locally (see **Warblington**). He was also involved in demolishing St Richard's shrine in Chichester Cathedral. Cromwell then assisted Sir William in securing the post of chamberlain to Anne of Cleves in 1540 – he would have acquired a few stories there! Surviving Cromwell's fall, he stayed on with Anne until 1546 when he became a gentleman of the Privy Chamber. He was also a soldier and served in the Commons for Sussex.

CANTERBURY, Cathedral ★★★★★ £

Located in the city centre.

Christchurch Gate

The medieval gate through which you enter the cathedral grounds, and where you pay your entry fee, is one of the most important and intriguing monuments in this book. Its significance is easily missed, but Pevsner tells us that it commemorates **Prince Arthur**, based on the heraldry (Pevsner, *North and East Kent*, p. 221). He also tells us that the date in Latin is 1507, but that this has been altered at some stage during maintenance! Looking at the architectural style, he estimates construction to have started in 1517 and finished 1520/21 – almost twenty years after Arthur died.

Arthur had no particular connection with Canterbury; he spent most of his time at Ludlow or Bewdley. However, Arthur's brief marriage to Catherine of Aragon became the hotly debated subject of the King's Great Matter in Henry VIII's reign during the 1520s. William Warham, Archbishop of Canterbury had been involved in the early negotiations about this marriage from 1496 and was a key player in the later debates with Henry. Could the construction of this gate have been a not-so-subtle way of reminding Warham that Arthur had also been married to Catherine?

One of the most important and mysterious historic sites in this book.

Tomb of Cardinal Reginald Pole in Canterbury Cathedral.

Once in this magnificent cathedral, head for the **north-west transept**, or **Martyrdom**, where Thomas Becket was murdered. A **tomb chest** and **effigy** commemorates **William Warham (c. 1450–1532)**. Warham acquiesced in much of Henry's break with Rome in the late 1520s but, in the last year or so, began to resist the king's demands. Fortunately for Henry, Warham died in August 1532, aged 82 years.

At his own request, the archbishop was buried in the **Martyrdom**. Did he consider himself likely to be martyred like Becket? Two members of his household had already died of poisoning in 1531, whilst Warham probably survived the incident because he was abstemious. Henry responded to the outrage by haranguing Parliament for ninety minutes on the horrors of poisoning!

In the **north choir aisle**, note the splendid **tomb chest** of Archbishop Bourchier (1411–86), who married Henry VII and Elizabeth of York in Westminster Abbey in January 1486. Bourchier came from a powerful Yorkist family, and was prelate for over thirty years.

In the **Trinity Chapel** lies the **tomb chest** and **effigy** of Dr Nicholas Wotton (c. 1498–1567), who was a younger son of Sir Robert Wotton, from Boughton Malherbe, near Ashford. He was educated at Oxford, and had spent time at Perugia. He was a diplomat and churchman. In 1529, he was sent by Henry to secure a favourable response from the French universities to the King's Great Matter. In 1536, he was, briefly, proctor for Anne Boleyn. In the spring of 1539, Wotton was one of the ambassadors sent by Henry VIII to negotiate with the Duke of Cleves for marriage to his daughter Anne. He arranged for Holbein to go out to Cleves to paint his famous portrait of Anne. Wotton reported favourably on Anne to Henry, if in a somewhat low-key fashion. He escaped any blame from the king for the subsequent fiasco. At the end of the year, Wotton escorted Anne to England to meet Henry. After refusing bishoprics, he was appointed the first post-Reformation Dean of Canterbury, followed by Dean of York. Wotton continued his diplomatic career in France, the Netherlands and the Holy Roman Empire, becoming one of the most able and respected practitioners. He was still in his post in 1566, a year before he died. His sister, Margaret, married Thomas Grey, second Marquess of Dorset.

In the **Corona** is the white **tomb chest** of Cardinal Reginald Pole (1500–58), who was Archbishop of Canterbury during the reign of Mary I, and therefore the last Catholic archbishop here. That the authorities were prepared to allow him to be buried in the cathedral emphasises that the break with Rome was essentially a political not doctrinal event. Pole was the third son of Sir Richard Pole and Margaret Plantagenet, daughter of George, Duke of Clarence who was brother to Edward IV and Richard III.

Reginald was destined for the church and received considerable financial support from Henry VIII during his studies at Oxford and Padua. Henry sent him to win over the Sorbonne University to the king's cause in 1529. He even offered Pole the archbishopric of York if he would support the King's Great Matter, but Pole refused.

In 1536, Pole sent Henry his published treatise which contained strong denunciation of Henry's policies. The king was livid, and blamed the whole Pole family for their opposition. Three years later his eldest brother, Henry, was executed. His mother, Margaret, followed in 1541. She had been restored to her ancestral earldom by Henry VIII in 1512. In the king's eyes, her subsequent behaviour showed that she had been most ungrateful (see **Warblington**). By association, Pole shares some of the blame for the burning of Protestants in Mary I's reign, although there is evidence that he favoured a more lenient approach. He died within twelve hours of Mary's death in 1558.

St Augustine's Abbey (remains)
Situated outside the city walls, on the south side. Signposted.

While in Canterbury, do visit the remains of the other great abbey in the city (the cathedral was also once an abbey). Founded in AD 598, this one did not fare so well at the Dissolution. Much of the stone was removed, and then the **north-west corner** of the church's nave was converted into a **royal palace** for Henry VIII, as one of a series between London and Dover (see **Dartford** and **Rochester**). The palace later fell into disuse, but the surviving **brickwork** can be seen. Anne of Cleves may have stayed here on her way to London in early 1540.

CHICHESTER, Cathedral ★★
Located in the city centre.

In the **choir, south aisle**, there is a brightly coloured **effigy** and **tomb recess**, celebrating Bishop Robert Sherbourne (c. 1454–1536), who was bishop from 1508. Sherbourne went to Winchester College and New College, Oxford, and became a councillor to Henry VII in 1496. He was Dean of the Chapel Royal and, in 1499, made Dean of St Paul's, being involved in the wedding ceremony for Prince Arthur and Catherine of Aragon in 1501. He was envoy to the papal court and became much involved in the negotiations surrounding the marriage of Prince Henry to Catherine after Arthur's death. In 1504, he was successful in obtaining the infamous papal dispensation which allowed the marriage to go ahead.

In 1505, he was made bishop of St David's, before coming to Chichester. In 1528, as the King's Great Matter began to take shape, Sherbourne was interviewed by Fitzwilliam regarding his involvement in the negotiations twenty-five years earlier.

In the **south transept**, don't miss the **painted portraits** of English kings and bishops of Chichester. They were commissioned by Sherbourne in the early sixteenth century. Additional paintings, also commissioned by Sherbourne, can be viewed at the **East Pallant Gallery,** about 400m east of the cathedral. In the **retrochoir**, one of the two plain **tomb chests** commemorates <u>Bishop George Day (d. 1557)</u>. He was chaplain to Bishop John Fisher of Rochester, and then almoner to Queen Katherine Parr. He was a religious conservative who, perhaps, kept Katherine's evangelical tendencies in check. While you are in the cathedral note the **effigy** of Bishop Story (d. 1503). He left Chichester a tremendous legacy – he paid for the lovely market cross just to the east of the cathedral, and founded the Prebendal School which continues its good works to the west of the cathedral.

DARTFORD, the Manor House *

Located in Priory Road (South), at the north-west corner of the inner ring road (A226). If you can see B&Q you are there!

An oasis in a desert of downtown sprawl. It is now a stylish wedding venue, so an interesting place for a history buff to get married!

The **gatehouse** is the only survival of a much larger Tudor palace, built by Henry VIII on the site of the recently dissolved priory, around 1541–44, and commemorates **Anne of Cleves**. When her marriage to Henry was annulled in mid-1540, Anne received a more than generous settlement from the king which included **Richmond Palace** and **Bletchingley Place** in Surrey. After Henry's death, Edward VI's government wanted to reward Sir Thomas Cawarden, Anne's steward, for his reforming zeal. Anne was asked to swap Bletchingley for the now completed Dartford Palace and the former was given to Cawarden in 1553. Anne used the property until her death in 1557. There are good information boards and, if there is no ceremony being held, do pop inside.

DEAL, Castle ** £

On the seafront, ½ mile south of the town centre on A258, Dover road. (EH)

Superbly located in front of the shingle beach, this castle, or fort, was built by **Henry VIII** in 1539–40. Henry left England many legacies, but perhaps the least controversial was his construction of a chain of forts around the coast of southern England, as protection against seaborne invasion from France/Spain when the expected backlash against Henry's break with Rome occurred. Deal and nearby Sandown and Walmer together protected the Downs, the safe anchorage within the Goodwin Sands to the east of Deal.

The original structure of the castle survives, although some later modifications have been made externally. Internally it survives intact. It was here, in late December 1539, that **Anne of Cleves** landed in England after a Channel crossing much delayed by contrary winds. She and her entourage from Calais were met by Charles Brandon,

Duke of Suffolk and his wife, Katherine Willoughby, and by Sir Thomas Cheney, Lord Warden of the Cinque Ports. Although the castle was still under construction, Anne was given her first meal on English soil and then escorted to Dover Castle for the night. Deal is a hidden gem of Kent – enjoy a day out and bring the children!

ELSTED, 'The Three Horseshoes' ★

At the east end of the village, up from the Midhurst–South Harting road, 4 miles west of Midhurst.

There are many late Tudor structures surviving as public houses from the Elizabethan building boom. However, far fewer are dated to 1540 – towards the end of Henry VIII's reign – as this one is, and even fewer are located in such marvellous surroundings! Come for lunch in summer and enjoy the far-reaching views of the Downs, or come for dinner in winter and revel in the Tudor beamed interior and log fires. In short, get in period and, over a pint or a meal or both, ponder over the fact that in 1540, local girl Katherine Howard (she lived at Horsham) was Queen of England – but not for long. Alternatively, repair here after visiting Cowdray House in nearby Midhurst to celebrate the two half-brothers who lived there, both of whom were intimate friends of Henry VIII yet kept their heads – unlike so many other of his 'friends'.

EWELL, Nonsuch Palace ★

Located 1 mile north-east of Ewell Station, on and to the south of A24, Mordon–Epsom road. From the junction of A24 with A240, Kingston–Reigate road, proceed for ⅓ mile. On a left-hand bend turn into the car park. Signposted.

From the car park, walk south for 400m down the entrance avenue to a **plaque** marking the site of modern excavations of the foundations of the medieval **palace**.

Set at the south-west corner of a 2,000-acre deer park, the building was essentially a hunting lodge, plus private house based around two Tudor courts. **Henry VIII** adopted the very latest architectural styles of West Europe to produce the most exotic palace ever built in England – hence the name. Begun in 1538, this became Henry's favourite building project in his later years. However, although the inner court was virtually complete by 1541 and the house was therefore habitable, the outer court was unfinished at his death. **Elizabeth I** much enjoyed the house. It was demolished in the late seventeenth century, and the park reduced in size. Even today, though, the scale of the surviving park impresses – plenty of room for a picnic and/or the dog. It really does not feel hemmed in by the suburbia of Surrey.

HAMPTON COURT ★★★★★ ££

On the north bank of the River Thames, at the junction of A308 Kingston-upon-Thames and A309 Thames Ditton roads. Signposted.

This iconic Tudor palace does not disappoint. It is one of the very finest Tudor buildings in this book.

In 1514, **Cardinal Wolsey** acquired the lease from Henry Daubeny, later the Earl of Bridgewater (see **Barrington Court**), and started building. Henry VIII visited regularly in the 1520s, by which time Wolsey had converted it into a palace. In 1526, he handed over this palace to the king while retaining a suite of rooms for his own use. **Henry VIII**, of course, started to refurbish and rebuild. The surviving Tudor rooms are a mixture of Wolsey and Henry builds. In the late seventeenth century, William and Mary completely rebuilt the private royal apartments, but the heart of the old Tudor palace survives. The palace is associated with Prince Edward's birth in 1537, followed quickly by the death of his mother, Jane Seymour; with Henry's divorce from Anne of Cleves; with Katherine Howard's infidelity; and also with Henry's marriage to Katherine Parr.

Clock Court and the great hall of Henry VIII at Hampton Court.

Henry VIII constructed a tilt yard at Hampton Court later in his reign. This tower remains next to the cafe.

The following should not be missed:

The Great Hall
Anne Boleyn Gate
The Chapel Royal
Henry's Kitchen
Henry VIII exhibition
Royal portraits
Haunted Gallery (look out for the ghost of Katherine Howard)
Council Chamber
Fountain Court
Astronomical clock
Real tennis court
Tiltyard Tower (adjacent to the cafe)

HEVER, Castle ★★★★★ ££
Set in deep countryside south of B2027 Edenbridge–Tonbridge road. Signposted.

Actually more a fourteenth-century, fortified manor house than a castle, this is a splendid site. A beautiful setting and lovely building with period rooms and some interesting exhibits.

The manor was bought by Sir Geoffrey Boleyn, Anne's great-grandfather, in 1462. Upwardly mobile and rich, he had been Lord Mayor of London in 1459, and afforded to buy a new manor house in Norfolk, at Blickling, as well. The property was inherited by **Sir Thomas Boleyn (1477–1538), Earl of Wiltshire**, Anne Boleyn's father, in 1505. He undertook much interior remodelling, including the **Long Gallery** and other rooms which survive. The **Anne Boleyn** bedroom is very interesting. When the family were in the south of England this was the childhood home of Anne and her elder sister Mary. Henry VIII courted Anne here, staying at nearby Penshurst Place, which had belonged to the Duke of Buckingham before his execution in 1521.

Do not forget to visit **St Peter's Church**, just outside the castle's entrance. There is a fine **tomb chest** and **brass** to **Sir Thomas Boleyn**, but no sign of his wife, Elizabeth *née* Howard (Anne's mother) – as invisible in death as she seems to have been in life. She died in 1539 and was buried in the Howard vault in Lambeth Parish Church, but nothing survives. These parents surely will have died heartbroken – Elizabeth produced around ten children, of whom only three survived to adulthood, Mary, Anne and George. Anne and George were executed in 1536 and Mary, after having been mistress to the French king, Francis I, and to Henry VIII, married beneath herself and was disgraced.

The lovely Hever Castle.

HORSHAM, Chesworth Farm ★★

Located just 1 mile due south of the railway station, but a little tricky to find. Take A281 Henfield/Brighton road out of the town centre. After 1 mile turn right on a minor road to Southwater/Sedgewick. After ½ mile, park at the bend and take the public footpath right (north-west) for ½ mile to Chesworth Farm. Keep left on the path round the moat.

This private house is set in lovely countryside, with the remains of a moat. The **south wing** is a Tudor survival and can be viewed from the footpath on the southern side (go in winter for better viewing). This is part of the medieval house was owned by the Dukes of Norfolk.

It is the country house where **Katherine Howard** grew up, under the direction of her step-grandmother, the Dowager Duchess of Norfolk, Agnes Tilney. Her life here alternated with time in London at the Duke's Lambeth home. Katherine's mother died when she was young. Although assisted by other family members, like Katherine's aunt and namesake (Countess of Bridgewater from 1538), the dowager duchess appears to have kept very slack discipline. This property is most likely, therefore, to have been the scene for some of Katherine's supposedly wild exploits in the late 1530s, before she married Henry VIII. It's not much of a memorial but Katherine, being so young when she was executed, has left little for posterity. It makes for a good walk in pleasant country.

LEEDS (near Maidstone), Castle ★★ ££

Located 1 mile south of Junction 8 on M20. Signposted off A20, 5 miles east of Maidstone.

This most picturesque of castles was, for centuries, in the possession of the queen consort. From 1422–37 it belonged to Dowager Queen Catherine of Valois, Henry V's widow. In 1517–23, **Henry VIII**, in typical fashion, transformed the castle into a true royal palace. Henry used it as a stopover on his way to the channel ports. A **display** celebrates the stopover by Henry and **Catherine of Aragon** in 1520, on their way to meeting the French king, Francis I, at the Field of the Cloth of Gold. The **Gloriette** retains a medieval/Tudor atmosphere in the **Queen's Room** and **Gallery** (look out for Catherine of Aragon's pomegranate emblems), **Henry VIII's Banqueting Hall**, **Fountain Court** and the **chapel**.

LEWES, Anne of Cleves House ★★ £
In Southover High Street, south and below the main street in Lewes.

Anne of Cleves did very well out of her divorce settlement with Henry VIII. She acquired **Richmond Palace**, **Hever Castle** and **Bletchingley Manor** as her main residences, plus a number of other manors to generate income. This property was one of them.

At the Dissolution, Thomas Cromwell appropriated this manor from nearby Lewes Priory for the use of his own family. His attainder led to the manor being available in the Crown's portfolio at the time of Anne and Henry's divorce. In total, Anne's income reached about £4,000 p.a., enabling her to maintain an appropriately aristocratic lifestyle right up to her death in 1557. This house, now a local museum, is a fine example of a Wealden hall house, built in the fifteenth century with later additions. The garden is also very nice. It is not known whether Anne ever visited the manor – she spent most of her time at Richmond or Bletchingley when not at Court.

LONDON

Eltham Palace ★★★ £
Situated ½ mile off Eltham High Street, and west of Court Road (A208 to Mottingham). Take the Tilt Yard.

From 1475–83, Edward IV had rebuilt the old medieval royal palace here, so the early Tudor monarchs were happy to use it, especially as the royal nursery. In fact, it was largely in this palace that **Prince Henry** grew up in the 1490s, surrounded by his sisters and his mother, **Elizabeth of York**. In contrast, his elder brother, Prince Arthur, was brought up with his own household in faraway Ludlow.

It was not until 1504 that Henry entered a man's world. He continued to stay here as king, especially in the first half of his reign, and carried out his own refurbishment in the 1520s. In turn, **Princess Elizabeth** was brought up here as a baby and received regular visits from Queen Anne. At this time the palace was one of only six possessed by the monarch that were big enough to feed 800 people! It had a brick bowling alley and gained a reputation for staging drama. Wolsey was a regular visitor, and it was here that he drew up his royal household reforms in 1526, known as the Eltham Ordinances.

The splendid **Great Hall** and hammer beam roof survive from the fifteenth-century rebuilding. Part of the premises were converted into a beautiful art deco house in the 1930s by members of the Courtauld family.

National Portrait Gallery ★★★★
Located in St Martin's Square, off Trafalgar Square, behind the National Gallery.

The gallery houses a superb collection of original paintings of Tudor royalty and aristocrats in the **Tudor Room**. Don't miss the **queens' annex** at the far end of the room. A great place to start your study of Henry VIII and his queens.

Shoreditch, St Leonard's Church ★★★
Situated at the north end of Shoreditch High Street on the corner of Hackney Road.

Inside this church is a modern **monument** to actors of the late medieval era. This includes the name of Will Somers (d. 1560). We are interested in this man because, for over twenty years, he was Henry VIII's fool, or court jester. Born in Shropshire, with presumably modest parentage, he was brought to court in 1525 by Richard Fermor, a merchant of the Calais Staple.

The king enjoyed the banter and repartee generated by the fool, and he became a fixture at court, being afforded much leeway in ribald remarks about just about anybody. In Henry's later years, he and Somers became very close. The fool was said to be the only man who could distract the king from his ulcerated and painful leg. Somers appears in a number of Tudor family portraits with Henry and his children – very surprising considering his lowly status. Oddly he called the king 'uncle' – perhaps a looser term in Tudor times, in the same way 'cousin' was? After Henry's death, Somers continued in post through the reigns of Edward VI and Mary I. He retired in 1560, not long after Elizabeth had come to the throne. He was the last court jester. But, who was the real Will Somers? (See **Haddon Hall**.)

The Tower ★★★★★ ££
Access from Tower Hill tube station, or by river boat.

There is a lot to see here, but the following locations should not be missed:

Traitors' Gate / St Thomas's Tower
The watergate where, traditionally, distinguished prisoners were brought by river and disembarked into the care of the Constable of the Tower.

St Peter ad Vincula Chapel on Tower Green. The saddest place in England?

Queen's House
Not open to the public.

This half-timbered building was so named in Queen Victoria's reign, but it is where Anne Boleyn resided before her execution. It overlooks **Tower Green**, the site of the scaffold used when executions needed to be private. Commemorated here are:

> Anne Boleyn (ex. 1536)
> Margaret Pole, Countess of Salisbury (ex. 1541)
> Katherine Howard (ex. 1542)
> Jane Boleyn, Lady Rochford (ex. 1542)
> Lady Jane Grey, the Nine Day Queen (ex. 1554)

Note also that William, Lord Hastings, Edward IV's friend and companion in arms, was executed nearby on a log, in 1483. He had been hauled out of the council chamber by Richard III, and summarily executed before lunch without any semblance of a trial.

Beyond the memorial lies the **Chapel Royal of St Peter ad Vincula**. To gain access you will need to join a tour group. The chapel was rebuilt in 1519–20 by **Henry VIII**. It is the burial place of those executed on Tower Green and Tower Hill. Originally, most executed bodies were buried quickly without record. However, during restoration work in Queen Victoria's reign a number of bodies were identified and reburied. **Anne Boleyn**, **Katherine Howard** and <u>Lady Jane Grey</u> lie beneath the **chancel pavement** in front of the altar.

The White Tower

The display of medieval **armour** in this building is worth a look, and don't miss **Henry VIII's** armour in all its glory in the bookshop! However, the most moving place in the tower is the beautiful Norman **chapel** of St John the Evangelist. Here lay in state the body of **Queen Elizabeth of York** after her death following child-birth in 1503, the first reigning queen consort to die due to childbirth since the Norman Conquest.

Tower Hill Memorial

On the west corner of Trinity Square Gardens, just north of, and across the road from, the Tower.

Tower Hill was the location used for the public execution of peers and other gentle-men. The crowds were often large and unruly (hence the use of Tower Green within the confines of the Tower for the more sensitive executions). Some 125 men met their deaths on this hill, and a selection are commemorated on a series of dignified **plaques** covering the period 1292–1750.

Of particular interest are <u>Edward Stafford, Duke of Buckingham (1478–ex. 1521)</u>, executed for plotting treason against Henry (see **Thornbury**); <u>Henry Courtenay,</u>

Just a few of Henry's victims on Tower Hill.

Marquess of Exeter (*c.* 1496–ex. 1538), Henry's nearest male relative through his mother's family, executed for plotting treason with the Pole family (see **Tiverton** and **Warblington**); **Thomas Cromwell (*c.* 1485–ex. 1540)**, Henry's chief minister; Henry Howard, Earl of Surrey (1516–ex. 1547), son of the Duke of Norfolk, who was executed days before Henry VIII died (see **Framlingham**); and **Edward Seymour, Duke of Somerset (1501–52)** who was Lord Protector to Edward VI for two years before being ousted by his rival John Dudley.

Also commemorated on the plaque is Edward Plantagenet, Earl of Warwick (1475–ex. 1499), son of the Duke of Clarence, Edward IV's brother, who was executed when Henry VII needed to clean up the succession before Prince Arthur's marriage to Catherine of Aragon. A cruel act, since this Edward Plantagenet was probably not of sound mind. Amongst the others who died here were Smeaton, Norris, Brereton and Weston – all found guilty of adultery with Anne Boleyn along with George Boleyn, Anne's brother.

Westminster Abbey ★★★★★ ££

Access via Westminster tube station.

There are so many church monuments and tablets here that it can seem like looking for the proverbial needle in a haystack. After entering the Abbey via the **north transept**, turn left into the **north ambulatory** and proceed in a general clockwise direction, but detour to visit Henry VII's Chapel. Monuments are listed in the order they will be encountered.

Chapel of St Andrew

A poignant, alabaster **monument** to Henry, Lord Norris of Rycote (d. 1601), and his wife, Margaret *née* Williams (d. 1599). Henry was the son of Sir Henry Norris, who was executed in 1536 for adultery with Queen Anne Boleyn. Henry VIII offered Sir Henry, who was a close and long-standing friend, a pardon provided he confessed but, gallantly, he refused and paid the ultimate price. His wife was the daughter of John, Lord Williams, who was much involved in the Dissolution of the Monasteries, and then a prominent courtier in Mary I's reign (see **Thame**).

Chapel of St John the Baptist

A stone **tomb** with **effigy** commemorates Thomas Ruthall, Bishop of Durham (d. 1523). Oxford educated, he became a leading administrator and diplomat in the reigns of both Henry VII and Henry VIII. The latter promoted him to Bishop of Durham just two days after his own accession. Ruthall was thus involved in the final negotiations with the Spanish ambassador around Henry's marriage to Catherine of Aragon. He rose to be principal secretary and, although of cautious disposition, was a leading councillor to Henry VIII in the early years of the reign.

In 1513, he strengthened the defences of Norham Castle on the Tweed (which was owned by the Bishops of Durham) ahead of the Battle of Flodden against the Scots, but the castle was still overrun. He worked alongside Wolsey and was present at the Field of the Cloth of Gold.

The tallest **monument** in the Abbey commemorates <u>Henry Carey, Lord Hunsdon</u> <u>(c. 1525–96)</u> and his wife, <u>Anne *née* Morgan</u>. Henry was the son and younger child of William Carey and Mary Boleyn, Queen Anne's sister. In fact, given his likely date of birth, there is some chance that Henry was the son of Henry VIII, who is reputed to have had an affair with Mary Boleyn at this time. The king, however, never acknowledged the child as his own. His father, William, was a rising courtier but died of the sweat in 1528. Elizabeth I was very generous to her two maternal cousins, Henry being elevated to the peerage and made Lord Chamberlain.

Chapel of St Paul

Note the **tomb** of <u>Giles, Lord Daubeny (1452–1508)</u> and his wife <u>Elizabeth Arundell</u> <u>(d. 1500)</u>. Giles fought at Bosworth and became one of Henry VII's closest confidants. See **Hampton Court**, and **Barrington Court** built by his son, Henry, in Somerset.

Chapel of Henry VII (or Lady Chapel)

The centrepiece of the Abbey for the Tudor historian, this chapel ranks with King's College, Cambridge, and St George's Chapel, Windsor, as one of the glories of medieval English architecture. It was consecrated in 1519. At its heart is the splendid black marble **tomb** and gilt bronze **effigies** of **Henry VII** and **Queen Elizabeth of York**. At the head of the tomb lies **Edward VI**, his grave is marked by a **floor stone** placed there by Christ's Hospital in 1966. Edward was their founder.

In the **north aisle** of the chapel lies the white marble **tomb** of **Elizabeth I (1533–1603)**. Beneath Elizabeth's coffin lies the coffin of **Mary I**, her elder sister. In the **south aisle** of the chapel lies the magnificent bronze **effigy** of **Lady Margaret Beaufort**, the mother of Henry VII. A marble **tomb** and alabaster **effigy** commemorates <u>Margaret Douglas, Countess of Lennox (1515–78)</u>. She was the daughter of Margaret Tudor, Henry VIII's sister, and her second husband, Archibald Douglas, Earl of Angus. Margaret had first been married to King James IV of Scotland, who was killed at the Battle of Flodden in 1513. Margaret junior was born in Northumberland, and spent most of her childhood at the English court with her cousin, Princess Mary.

Margaret was appointed lady-in-waiting to Anne Boleyn but, soon after Anne's execution, she fell in love with Lord Thomas Howard and they were secretly engaged.

When the king found out he was furious because, at that particular time, Margaret was next in line of succession to the English throne, Henry having bastardised both his own daughters! This changed, of course, when Prince Edward was born the following year.

Margaret and her lover were sent to the Tower. Margaret was released in October 1537, but Lord Thomas died there. In 1540, Lady Margaret was in trouble again for having an affair with Katherine Howard's brother, but she was forgiven. She was a witness at Katherine Parr's wedding to Henry VIII, and became her lady-in-waiting. The two women had met in the 1520s at Court. In 1544 she was finally married to Matthew Stewart, Earl of Lennox. Their son Henry Stuart, Lord Darnley married Mary Queen of Scots, thus uniting two claims to the throne of Scotland. Matthew was regent of Scotland but Darnley was murdered without issue.

South Ambulatory – Chapel of St Nicholas

In this chapel lies the standing **monument** and **effigy** of <u>Anne Seymour (*née* Stanhope), Duchess of Somerset (*c.* 1510–87)</u>, and wife of Edward Seymour, Duke of Somerset who was uncle to and Lord Protector of Edward VI after Henry VIII's death. In 1534/35 Seymour ditched his first wife, Catherine Filliol, disowned his two sons by her and traded up to Anne, who was descended from Thomas of Woodstock, the youngest son of Edward III.

Anne was intelligent and determined and a religious reformer. The couple had ten children. Queen Jane Seymour, Princess Mary and Thomas Cromwell were godparents to their first child – not exactly auspicious? The child died young. However, Anne proved as arrogant and haughty as her husband. After Henry VIII's death and Dowager Queen Katherine Parr's marriage to Edward Seymour's younger brother Thomas, Anne fought a furious and protracted battle with the dowager queen over precedence at Court. After her husband's fall from power and execution in 1550, she herself was imprisoned until 1553. By now, however, she was not too proud to marry her husband's steward, Francis Newdigate. (Wealthy Tudor women had a tendency to marry a more junior man second time around.)

Note also in this chapel, <u>William Dudley, or Sutton, Bishop of Durham (d. 1483)</u>, who was uncle to Edmund Dudley, executed by Henry VIII right at the beginning of his reign.

Chapel of St Edmund

There are two mural **tablets** here. One commemorates <u>Lady Jane Seymour (d. 1560)</u>, daughter of Protector Somerset and Anne Stanhope, and a maid of honour to Elizabeth I and author. The other is to <u>Catherine Knollys (d. 1569)</u> who was the daughter of Mary Boleyn and William Carey (or just possibly of Henry VIII) and therefore cousin to Elizabeth I – see **Rotherfield Greys**. She was Lady of the Bedchamber to her cousin and died in service.

On the **east** side of this chapel is a **tomb chest** and **effigy** of <u>Frances Grey, Duchess of Suffolk (1517–59)</u>. Frances was the daughter of Charles Brandon, Duke of Suffolk and Mary Tudor, Henry VIII's younger sister. She married Henry Grey, who was made duke. When Edward VI died without issue in 1553, Frances was Mary Tudor's heir but specifically excluded from the succession in Edward's will. John Dudley, Duke of Northumberland married his son, Guildford, to Lady Jane Grey, Frances' daughter, in order to ensure a Protestant succession and keep Princess Mary from the throne. Jane did not want to be queen, and didn't even like Guildford. Her reign lasted just nine days. Jane and her father were executed in 1554. Frances married her Master of the Horse, Adrian Stokes.

South Transept

Note the **floor stone** to <u>Owen Tudor</u>, younger brother of Edmund Tudor, Henry VII's father. Owen was, for a time, a monk at Westminster in the later fifteenth century.

Sacrarium

On the **south** side, a stone **tomb** commemorates **Anne of Cleves** and lies beneath an **altarpiece** by the Florentine painter Bicci di Lorenzo. After the humiliations of her marriage to Henry VIII, Anne secured a generous divorce settlement from him and built a pleasant and comfortable life in England. She befriended Princess Mary and converted to Catholicism. She died during Mary's reign and is the only one of Henry's queens to be buried in the Abbey.

South Choir Aisle

Note the modern **tablet** to <u>William Tyndale (1494–1536)</u>, who translated the New Testament into English in 1525, and whose fine prose was incorporated, virtually unchanged, in the King James Bible a century later. He was burned at the stake in Belgium after being pursued by agents of Sir Thomas More, Lord Chancellor.

The Undercroft Museum

This contains the funeral **effigy** of <u>Dowager Queen Catherine de Valois (1401–37)</u>, Henry V's wife. After Henry's death, she married her Master of the Wardrobe, Owen Tudor. Through her son, Edmund, she was the grandmother of Henry VII but conveyed no claim to the throne. Also here is a bronze **bust** of <u>Sir Thomas Lovell (d. 1524)</u>, who fought for Henry Tudor at the Battles of Bosworth and Stoke Field, then became Chancellor of the Exchequer, which, at the time, was a role in the royal household. He was implicated in Henry VII's financial extortions orchestrated by Empson and Dudley, but was left untouched by the new king, Henry VIII, when he moved against the other two. Lovell continued to serve Henry in a variety of roles including Lieutenant of the Tower, but was rather edged out by Wolsey's rise to power.

Westminster Hall ★★★ £

Part of the Palace of Westminster. Access via a tour of the Houses of Parliament from Parliament Square.

This huge building survives from the medieval palace. It was built by William II, Rufus, as long ago as 1097, and was used for coronation banquets, public trials and other public events. It has thus witnessed much English history. Until 1825, its regular function was to house the Courts of King's Bench, Chancery and Common Pleas.

The hall's stonework is original Norman, but the tremendous hammer beam roof was added by Richard II at the end of the fourteenth century. So, in this building were held the coronations of Henry VIII and Catherine of Aragon together in 1509, and Anne Boleyn alone in 1533 (by tradition a king did not attend his queen's coronation if it was a separate event). None of the rest of Henry's wives received a coronation.

The more menacing use for the hall was for public trials. Here in May 1536, Norris, Smeaton, Weston and Brereton were condemned for adultery with Queen Anne. Anne and her brother, George, as peers, were tried in the Tower. In December 1541, in a sickening rerun, Culpepper and Dereham were condemned here for adultery with Queen Katherine Howard, Anne's first cousin. Katherine Howard received no trial but was condemned purely by the use of the dreaded Parliamentary attainder.

St James's Palace ★★

Located at the western end of Pall Mall, at the junction with St James's Street. Not open to the public but can be viewed externally.

This site is a rare survival of a royal **Tudor palace** in Central London, and is a mixture of original Tudor buildings and later work. It is still the official residence of the monarch. The fine **gatehouse** and **chapel** were built by **Henry VIII** in the early 1530s, and can be viewed externally from the bottom of St James's Street. The streetscape is open and the palace abuts the street. It was first built for **Henry Fitzroy, Duke of Richmond and Somerset (1519–36)**, whom Henry VIII acknowledged as his illegitimate son. After Fitzroy's death in 1536, the palace became the home of **Edward, Prince of Wales (later Edward VI)**.

MIDHURST, Cowdray Ruins ★★★ £

Situated ½ mile north-east of the town centre. Access is via a splendid walk from the council car park at the end of North Street (the main street). Signposted.

Only a ruin now, following a fire in the late eighteenth century, but the view of this magnificent Tudor mansion as you approach from the car park takes some beating. Words like gaunt and haunting come to mind.

Sir David Owen (1459–1535) was the illegitimate son of Owen Tudor, who was the grandfather of Henry VII. By 1485, the Tudor family comprised only Henry, his mother Lady Margaret Beaufort and Henry's uncle, Jasper Tudor. Sir David was, therefore, a very welcome supporter in exile with Henry in France, and at Bosworth. On Henry's accession it was arranged for Sir David to marry the local heiress in Midhurst, Mary de Bohun. Around the turn of the century, Sir David started to build this Tudor **house** and in 1529, it was bought by William Fitzwilliam, Earl of Southampton (*c.* 1490–1542). Unusually, Sir David continued to live here until his death in 1535 (his **effigy** can be seen in nearby **Easebourne Church**). Fitzwilliam then extended and modified the house so that it very much celebrates his life as well.

He came from an unusual background and did very well for himself. His mother was Lucy Neville, one of the four daughters of John Neville, Marquess Montagu, who was the Kingmaker's younger brother. John was killed at the Battle of Barnet alongside his brother. In the 1460s, John had been a Yorkist stalwart who contributed much to their military successes, but changed sides in deference to family loyalty. His daughters were subsequently married off to gentry of modest means.

William was a third son but, around 1500, he was chosen as a companion for Prince Henry. Was it because of his brains, his mother's splendid pedigree or the fact she had just married for a second time to Sir Antony Browne, Henry VII's standard bearer? His father, Thomas Fitzwilliam, hailed from South Yorkshire. William seems to have got on well with the Prince and, by 1509, was the new king's cupbearer. Contemporary observers claimed that Fitzwilliam understood Henry's 'nature and temper better than any man in England' – although not when it came to judging Anne of Cleves' beauty, clearly!

Both of William's elder brothers were killed at Flodden, whilst he was injured in the naval engagement off Brest. He was knighted in France. He was made Esquire of the Body in 1513 and was married in that year to Mabel Clifford, daughter of Lord Clifford. She was a Yorkshire lass, but a number of notches up socially. They had no children. Fitzwilliam began a long and highly successful administrative career. He was multi-talented – as well as being a military man, he was a diplomat (he was ambassador to France) and had a talent for interrogation. He started as a member of Wolsey's household and then became a member of the Privy Council. In early May 1536, he interrogated Sir Henry Norris, one of Anne Boleyn's accused adulterers, and managed to extract a confession out of him (Norris later alleged he was deceived). He was present in the Chamber with Norfolk and Paulet when Anne Boleyn was charged formally with adultery. Surprisingly, however, later in 1536 Fitzwilliam was suspected of siding with the conservative faction at Court and put in the Tower. He survived, and was ennobled as Earl of Southampton.

In 1540 he helped to arrest Cromwell in the Chamber. He was appointed Lord Privy Seal after Cromwell's execution. He was one of four councillors involved in interrogating the Dowager Duchess of Norfolk in late 1541, once Katherine Howard had come under suspicion. He also led the party which escorted Katherine from Syon Abbey to the Tower.

William very nearly came a cropper with Anne of Cleves. Sent by Henry to Calais to head up the welcoming party for Anne, he sent reports praising Anne's beauty and deportment, unlike some of his colleagues. After the fiasco at **Rochester** once Anne had crossed the Channel, the king was not pleased with Fitzwilliam.

Always an active man, Fitzwilliam died at Newcastle on his way to fight the Scots. On his death in 1542, Cowdray passed to his half-brother <u>Sir Antony Browne</u> <u>(c. 1500–48)</u>, whose mother was also Lucy Neville (see **Battle** for Sir Antony's biography). Browne made further improvements to the property.

MINSTER-IN-SHEPPEY, St Mary and St Sexburga's Church ★★
Located 4 miles south-east of Sheerness, on B2008 Eastchurch Road at the village centre.

Under an arch of this ancient religious foundation, in the centre of the 'two churches', lies the **tomb chest** with **effigy** of <u>Sir Thomas Cheney (c. 1485–1558)</u>, son of William Cheney of Shurland. He was a local boy made good, but probably given a head start by his uncle, Lord John Cheney, one of the heroes of the Battle of Bosworth.

His career began as a henchman to Henry VII, then Esquire of the Body to Henry VIII and rising to be constable of a number of castles in the area, including nearby Queenborough, his father's position. In 1536, he was appointed Lord Warden of the Cinque Ports and, by then, had achieved the status of a 'kinglet' of the Isle of Sheppey and the most powerful man in Kent. However, Sir Thomas was much more than just a soldier; he had good French and thus was given diplomatic commissions and was a successful household servant, becoming Treasurer of the Royal Household in 1530.

Unfortunately, Cheney had a reputation for being somewhat proud and cantankerous. He had a long-running dispute with Sir John Russell over the wardship of the latter's two step-daughters in 1527/28, which was taken up by Cardinal Wolsey, Anne Boleyn and finally, the king! The issue defined the break between Anne and Wolsey in 1529. From 1528, this put Cheney firmly in the pro-Boleyn faction, along with Sir John Wallop. He was banned from Court for a while and very much out of favour. However, by 1532 he was restored to Court.

Shurland was the Tudor home of Sir Thomas Cheney.

Actually, Sir Thomas was a religious conservative, and was even charged with treason by his own son before the Privy Council for having images in his chapel in 1540. But he did manage to navigate his way through service to all five Tudor monarchs, so he can't have been awkward all the time – he must have been a very subtle trimmer. He attended the christening of Prince Edward in 1537, and then formally greeted Anne of Cleves and her entourage at Christmas 1539 at Deal, when she first arrived in England. His role as Lord Warden was to escort her to Deal Castle. I wonder if he realised that the subsequent journey to London would be quite so disastrous? (See **Deal** and **Rochester**.)

Three miles east, in Eastchurch, on the sharp right-hand bend in the A250 (Leysdown road) can be seen **Shurland**, the surviving parts of the large **Tudor mansion** built by Sir Thomas. In a gesture designed to signal his reacceptance at court, he was visited here twice in 1532 by Henry VIII and Anne Boleyn. The second time, in the autumn, was when they were en route to France where their relationship was finally consummated. Cheney had recently upgraded the house. This site is now a private residence, but the survivals are genuine.

OLD WOKING, Palace Ruins ★★

Old Woking village is situated 2 miles south of Woking, on the A247 Woking–Send road. At the roundabout in the village, on a sharp bend, head north on the B382 to West Byfleet. After ¼ mile, turn right on an unmetalled road for ¾ mile, passing a sewage works on the left. Follow the road round to the right. Park and follow the footpath to the south for 200m.

This is probably the most unlikely historical site in this book! You are presented with the scant remains of one of Henry VIII's many palaces in the Home Counties – plenty of **moat** and trees and a little **Tudor brickwork**. Despite the immediate approach, and despite the closeness of true suburbia, this is a real haven especially in summer.

The site commemorates **<u>Lady Margaret Beaufort</u>**, mother to Henry VII. A fifteenth-century structure, the palace was owned by the senior branch of the Beaufort family, but lost by attainder during the Wars of the Roses in the 1460s. In 1466, Edward IV rather generously returned the property to Lady Margaret, by now heir to the senior branch. She lived here during the late 1460s with her second husband, Sir Henry Stafford, a younger son of the Duke of Buckingham.

In 1468 she entertained Edward IV here (oh, to have been a fly on the wall). In the 1470s, she stayed here with her third husband Thomas, Lord Stanley, whose principal residence was Lathom in Lancashire. All in all, Woking represented home for Lady Margaret, a beacon of continuity in her otherwise much disturbed life. However, in 1503, Henry VII insisted his mother hand over the property and, in a rare show of family disunity, she showed some reluctance to do this. He converted it into a splendid palace at considerable cost – well, Henry is bound to have thought it expensive! On Henry's death in 1509, Lady Margaret made sure she regained possession, but she died a few months later.

Henry VIII undertook two upgrades, in 1515 and 1532. The palace was of standard Tudor design – gatehouse, courtyard plan and great hall, all on a grand scale. The hunting in the park here was good, so the palace was popular with Henry. He visited alone in 1510 and 1534 when his wives were pregnant, and in late 1540 with his new

The moat of Old Woking Palace, Lady Margaret Beaufort's favourite residence.

wife, the ill-fated Katherine Howard. Elizabeth I visited, but James I sold off the property. The site was fed by water courses from the nearby River Wey, and surviving ditches can be made out in some of the surrounding fields.

OTFORD, Archbishop's Palace ★
Located at the village centre, 300m south of the parish church next to a small park.

This is an odd one! Nearby Knole had been established as a palace for the archbishops of Canterbury in the fifteenth century. However, quite soon after the start of his tenure, **Archbishop Warham of Canterbury** began to build here in around 1514, even though there was another large palace only 3 miles away. It was in use by 1518. He was something of a builder, but his motive is unclear – just extravagance?

Only the **partial ruins** of a tower and other buildings remain, but this was once one of the most splendid and vast palaces in England. The ruins are rather unusually, and pleasantly, intertwined with later cottages.

Warham entertained Henry VIII, Catherine of Aragon and Henry's sister Mary here in 1514, while Mary was on her way to France to marry the elderly King of France. In 1520, Henry and Catherine again stayed here on the way to the Field of the Cloth of Gold, reputedly with as many as 5,000 followers. On Warham's death, Henry demanded that the new archbishop, Cranmer, hand over both Otford and Knole, claiming that the archbishop, who owned sixteen houses, had too many in Kent! Actually, Henry claimed that he didn't like Otford because it is too low lying, by the River Darent, so he decided he would stay at Knole on higher ground while most of his household would stay at Otford. By 1537, Henry owned both properties but, by 1547, after his death, Otford was in decay.

RICHMOND, Palace ★★
Located on Richmond Green, with frontage onto the Thames. Follow signs to the town centre, green or theatre. There is parking at the far end of the green (signposted).

This was one of the most sumptuous of Tudor palaces. It was **Henry VII's** *pièce de résistance*, built in the late 1490s on the ashes of the old medieval palace of Sheen, which had burned down in 1497. It occupied a splendid site between what is now Richmond Green and the bank of the Thames. Unfortunately, only a limited amount remains. However, there are good information boards on the west side of the green, with the remaining Tudor **gatehouse** behind you. As usual, the palace was surrounded by a large deer park (as in the Old Deer Park to the north). This palace was popular with most of the Tudors. Henry VIII celebrated his first Christmas here with Catherine of Aragon in 1509. It was marked with a joust in front of the palace

One of the few survivals of Henry VII's masterpiece at Richmond.

on Richmond Green. Elizabeth I died here in 1603, marking the end of the great Tudor dynasty.

Enjoy the splendid, but much later, architecture around the green and make sure to head west down Old Palace Lane in order to view the palace site from the riverbank. En route you will pass one of Richmond's hidden gems, the **White Swan** pub. It's not in period, and the food is not in period, but don't miss it.

ROCHESTER, Old Bishop's Palace ★★

Located in the city centre, immediately to the south of the cathedral, near its south-west corner. Follow the signs for the cathedral, head south past the western door, and the palace is a long, three storey building on the left.

The **western** side (right) of this building incorporates the Old Palace. A **plaque** on the garden wall commemorates <u>Bishop John Fisher (1475–ex. 1535)</u>, who earlier in his career had been confessor to Lady Margaret Beaufort and had given her funeral oration. He was executed by Henry VIII in 1535, for refusing to take the oath to the Act of Succession.

However, we are not here for this reason; instead, here on New Year's Day, 1540, occurred one of the most bizarre incidents in our story. **Anne of Cleves** had been delayed by contrary winds across the Channel. Her party, led by William Fitzwilliam, Earl of Southampton and Lord High Admiral, arrived at Deal on 27 December, and by 31 December had reached Rochester. On New Year's Day, the king, on hearing of her arrival at Rochester, set out from Whitehall with five companions to visit her here, unannounced. All six were dressed in similar coats and hoods. Henry embraced Anne, saying that he brought gifts from the king (he had brought furs with him).

The charade continued, but Anne ignored Henry and certainly did not recognise him. Finally Henry had to reveal himself, much to Anne's chagrin. At that stage she lacked the English to greet Henry adequately or explain her *faux pas*. On the way back to Whitehall, Henry was already complaining to Sir Antony Browne, his Master of the Horse, that Anne was not as men had reported her. He had taken against her on sight, and it seems that was that – he took the furs back to Whitehall! By the time Anne was formally received at Blackheath, Henry's lawyers were already casting around for grounds for an annulment.

Why had Henry aped his feeble-minded predecessor, Henry VI, and carried out such a silly prank? He already had a Holbein portrait of Anne so he knew what she looked like, and medieval kings married for political gain – not for love. Perhaps he wanted to test her sophistication in reacting to his revelation? She seems to have failed the test. Henry blamed everyone but himself for the error, but particularly Cromwell. He complained to anyone who would listen, and there followed a short period where courtiers had to guess which way to jump in regard to their opinion of Anne's attractiveness. Antony Browne and his wife, Alice, got it right; Fitzwilliam and Cromwell got it wrong.

WEST DRAYTON, Old Manor Gatehouse ★

Located south of the railway station, and immediately south of St Martin's parish church. Access is from junction 4 of M4 (Heathrow) north side. Take the first minor road, turn left to West Drayton, off A408 Uxbridge road. After 1 mile on Sipson Road, as it becomes Station Road, turn left into Church Road. The manor is on the right.

Rather overwhelmed by suburbia, this private house commemorates Sir William Paget (1506–63), who was one of a small band of brilliant administrators who graced the English court in the later sixteenth century, along with Petre, Paulet and Sadler.

From modest beginnings in Staffordshire, Paget managed to acquire a first-class education at St Paul's School, and Cambridge and Paris Universities. He befriended Stephen Gardiner at Cambridge, and probably through him secured diplomatic work in the 1530s. By 1537, he was secretary to Queen Jane Seymour, and then Anne of Cleves and Katherine Howard – here was a man who could tell us a thing or two! He was ambassador to France from 1541–43, before becoming Henry VIII's principal secretary, alongside Wriothesley in 1540. At this time, Paget became a close friend and something of a mentor to Edward Seymour, Lord Hertford, later to become the Duke of Somerset.

By the end of Henry's reign, Paget was one of the king's closest confidantes, and was highly influential in the handover to the minority of Edward VI. Paget became uneasy with Somerset's increasing aloofness from the council. With amazing adeptness, he detached himself from Somerset just as the latter was toppled from power.

He then reasserted himself to arrest the Protector on behalf of John Dudley, Earl of Warwick, who had replaced Somerset as principal councillor! Paget was ennobled by Dudley for this fine piece of footwork.

While at Cambridge, Paget had been a deserving scholar maintained by Thomas Boleyn. His studies reflected the Protestant sympathies of his patron. However, throughout his long career Paget managed to keep his own religious views to himself. This enabled him to make his peace with Mary I in 1553, although on Elizabeth I's accession he retired from public life. In fact, his immediate descendants became recusants. Later the family went from strength to strength as Earls of Uxbridge and Marquess of Anglesey, where they live to this day.

WEST FIRLE, St Peter's Church ★★

Situated 5 miles east of Lewes. Turn off A27 Lewes–Eastbourne road on a cul-de-sac to the village. Take the second fork left up to the church.

Nestling under the Downs in lovely countryside, the **vestry** contains monuments of the Gage family. We are interested in the fine **alabaster effigies** and **tomb chest** for Sir John Gage (1479–1556) and his wife Philippa Guldeford (dates not known).

Sir John had an incredible fifty-year career, in and around the royal household, gaining a Knight's Garter in 1541. He was Esquire of the Body to both Henry VII and Henry VIII. In 1526, he became Vice Chamberlain of the Household, but blotted his copybook by questioning the Anne Boleyn marriage, and was banned from Court. He attended both the christening of Prince Edward and the funeral of Jane Seymour in 1537. Back in favour in 1540, he became Comptroller of the Household, a Privy Counsellor and Constable of the Tower of London – a busy portfolio? It fell to Sir John to escort Katherine Howard into the Tower in 1542, and to arrange and supervise her execution on Tower Green. He reported to the Privy Council that, beforehand, she wept and cried 'without ceasing'.

Sir John Gage lived at West Firle, near Lewes – a delightful place.

In 1542, he was made Chancellor of the Duchy of Lancaster, and then organised the logistics for the invasion of France in 1544. He was one of Henry VIII's executors, attended his funeral and, surprisingly, was made a member of Edward VI's Regency Council, even though he was a staunch Catholic. He lost his offices during Edward's reign but regained them under Mary. She appointed him Lord Chamberlain, and he carried her train at her wedding to Philip of Spain. As Constable of the Tower, he guarded Princess Elizabeth in his seventy-sixth year! He died at West Firle in his bed. Holbein has left us a lovely line portrait of Sir John – his face looks far too kind for a Constable of the Tower, more that of an academic!

SOUTH

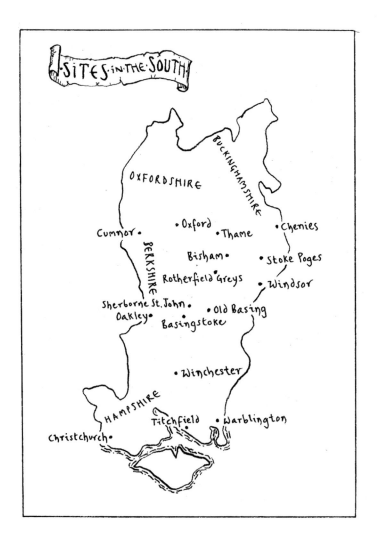

BISHAM ★★

Situated 1 mile south of Marlow, on the first of two sharp bends just before the village of Bisham. Next to the Thames.

All Saints Church

Unusually situated right on the bank of the Thames, this church also contains one of the most delightful monuments in this book.

In the **Hoby Chapel** is a complex **tomb chest** commemorating two half-brothers, <u>Sir Philip Hoby (c. 1505–58)</u> and <u>Sir Thomas Hoby (1530–66)</u>. The Hoby family hailed from Radnorshire. Sir Philip was a linguist who became a protégé of Cromwell. In 1535 he was sent as an envoy to Spain and Portugal. In 1538 he was despatched by Cromwell with Hans Holbein to obtain portraits of possible queen consorts for Henry, including one of Anne of Cleves. In 1540 he attended the reception for Anne of Cleves at Blackheath.

Before 1540, he married Elizabeth *née* Stonor, widow of Sir William Compton, Henry's Groom of the Stool who had died in 1528. In 1543, he was accused by the conservative lobby as part of the Windsor scheme, and imprisoned along with his wife in the Fleet prison. His staunch Protestantism, however, saved him and they were both soon released. In the 1540s, he secured much monastic land and became a wealthy man. From 1543 he was a member of Katherine Parr's council and he was later ambassador to Emperor Charles V, 1548–50. He was a firm supporter of Lord Protector Somerset until, in 1549, he joined John Dudley, Duke of Northumberland.

Sir Thomas followed his half-brother in being a linguist, diplomat and translator. Their monument was erected by Thomas' wife, Elizabeth *née* Cooke, who composed the lengthy poem and features in the tomb design. The monument includes representations of Hobby hawks – the family emblem (the name has the same pronunciation). She later married Lord John Russell.

However, the most interesting tomb in the chapel is the very unusual **obelisk,** celebrating <u>Lady Margaret Hoby (1560–1605)</u>. Lady Margaret was a Carey, the daughter of Henry Carey, Lord Hunsdon, and thus the grand-daughter of William Carey and Mary Boleyn. Given the uncertainty over Henry Carey's parentage, Margaret may have had royal blood in her veins! The four swans on the monument are the family crest of the Careys. Lady Margaret was married to Sir Edward Hoby and she was a close friend of Queen Elizabeth.

Abbey

At the south end of the village, just off A404 High Wycombe–Bray road. Right next to the Thames.

The abbey survives at Bisham amongst the National Sports Centre amenities.

Bisham Abbey now houses the National Sports Centre, but it is still possible to visit the site. The surviving abbey buildings provide accommodation and catering facilities. The Augustinian priory was dissolved in 1537 but as a special favour to his wife, Jane Seymour, Henry reconstituted it as a Benedictine abbey. Perhaps surprisingly and rather bravely, Jane had lobbied the king against dissolving the monasteries. With her early death the abbey itself was soon dissolved in 1540. Sir Philip Hoby was granted the property in 1553. He began the job of converting the main building straight away. On his death in 1558 the work was continued by his half-brother Sir Thomas. A lovely building, in a lovely spot.

CHENIES ★★

St Michael's Church
Located in the village centre, north of A404 Rickmansworth–High Wycombe road.

The traditional burial place of the Earls and Dukes of Bedford. To quote Pevsner, 'The **Bedford Chapel** has as rich a store of funeral monuments as any parish church of England.' The chapel is not normally open to the public but can be viewed from inside the church.

The earliest monument on view is to John Russell, 1st Earl of Bedford (c. 1485–1555) and his wife Ann, *née* Sapcote (d. 1559). Russell was of modest gentry stock from

Dorset, with involvement in wine shipping. His career took off in a classic case of being 'the right man, in the right place, at the right time'.

In 1506, Duke Philip of Burgundy and his Spanish wife, Juana the Mad (Catherine of Aragon's sister), were shipwrecked near Weymouth on their way up the Channel to Burgundy. They were met by local dignitaries, who couldn't speak Spanish. Young Russell was sent for to interpret. He did such a good job that the duke and his wife were thrilled, and insisted they introduce him to Henry VII's court when they reached London. Russell duly became a gentleman of the Privy Chamber. Henry VIII employed him on diplomatic missions, before he took part in the war against the French in 1513. He lost an eye at the siege of Morlaix, in Brittany, in 1522. In 1526, late in life, he married Ann who was the heiress to Chenies Manor.

He managed to make an enemy of Anne Boleyn in 1528 because of a long-running row he was having with her cousin, Sir Thomas Cheney. He is said to have celebrated when she was later executed. At the end of 1536, he was made a Privy Councillor. After the execution of the Marquess of Exeter, later in the decade, he became a leading power in the south-west. He gained a peerage and was Lord High Admiral, and then Keeper of the Privy Seal. In 1540, he was with Henry at Rochester when they welcomed Anne of Cleves. Next day, Henry was anxious to know what Russell thought. As usual, Russell gave the right reply, he 'took her not to be fair but of a brown complexion'. Oh, to be a courtier at the court of King Henry VIII!

Russell gained many monastic lands in Devon and the south-west. He was also granted the kitchen garden of Westminster Abbey, which became Covent Garden. He supported the new religion, and was Lord High Steward at Edward VI's coronation.

The very distinctive lines of Sir John Russell's Tudor house at Chenies.

In his will, Henry VIII had stipulated that Russell should be made up to earl (still controlling beyond the grave!). This duly happened in 1550 – reward for a long and distinguished career at court. The Dukes of Bedford descend from John and his wife, and Ann built the Bedford Chapel.

Manor House £
Situated next to the church.

Ann Sapcote brought this delightfully mellow house to the Bedford marriage. It is a fascinating mix of an early Tudor west range and a later south wing added by the Russells in the mid-1520s – all in brick. A tour of the gardens gives a fine view of the outside of the house.

CHRISTCHURCH, Priory ★★★
Located on the quay, close to the town centre. Signposted to the adjacent car park.

This delightful church, with its lovely Norman nave, contains, in its **north aisle**, the superb **Salisbury Chantry** commemorating Margaret Pole, Countess of Salisbury (1473–ex. 1541) and her son, Reginald Pole, Archbishop of Canterbury (1501–58).
The chantry stands empty, however. Margaret was imprisoned in the Tower and eventually executed by Henry VIII with appalling brutality in 1541. She is buried in the Tower, in the Chapel of St Peter ad Vincula. Her story rates as one of the most tragic of the era (see **Warblington** and the **Tower of London**). Reginald died the same day as Mary I, which was very convenient for everyone – especially Reginald (see **Canterbury Cathedral**).

CUMNOR, St Michael's Church ★★
Located on the north-west edge of the village, which is just west of A420 Oxford–Farringdon road.

Here, in effect, we come to the end of our story of the Tudor dynasty. In 1560, the manor house next to the church was lived in by Antony Forster, steward to Robert Dudley, later Earl of Leicester.

Robert Dudley, fifth son of the recently executed John Dudley, Duke of Northumberland was a long-term favourite of the new queen, Elizabeth. In the 1530s and 1540s they had shared in much of the education of Edward VI and enjoyed each other's company. Dudley was with Elizabeth at Hatfield when she heard that she had become queen, and he was soon appointed her Master of the Horse, which meant they spent a lot of time together.

It is not much but this fireplace was part of Cumnor Place, where Amy Robsart was found dead in 1560.

Tongues began to wag, and then Amy Robsart, wife of Robert Dudley, was found dead here, in Cumnor Place, in an empty house in September 1560, at the foot of a shallow flight of steps with her neck broken. The incident developed into one of the most celebrated murder mysteries in English history. Amy was reported to have been depressed and probably suffering from breast cancer, so suicide could have been possible. The coroner returned a verdict of accidental death, which saved Dudley's reputation and his neck, but which was not believed by many contemporaries. It seemed much more likely to them that she had been murdered by Dudley, so that he would be free to marry Queen Elizabeth. In fact, this whole incident now made it impossible for Dudley to marry the queen and, with the advantage of hindsight, we can see, perhaps, that if Elizabeth couldn't marry her true love she wasn't marrying anyone and the Tudor dynasty ground to a halt here.

Antony Forster came under suspicion, but was vindicated. Modern historians have raised the possibility that Amy was murdered on the orders of William Cecil, specifically to prevent the marriage to Elizabeth I. Cecil was Dudley's main political rival and he was losing influence with the queen. Dudley, the widower, waited another eighteen years – just in case marriage became possible. It didn't, so he married Lettice Knollys, who was promptly exiled from court by Elizabeth. Elizabeth clearly liked her men to herself, even if she didn't marry them! (See **Rotherfield Greys**.)

The manor house was very close to the west end of the church, but was pulled down in the nineteenth century. However, the remains of a **fireplace** can still be seen in situ in the churchyard, beyond the **west door** of the church, a humble

The Bear and Ragged Staff emblem of the Earls of Warwick at Cumnor.

monument to such a notorious affair. Inside the **church** is a fine, life-size statue of **Queen Elizabeth I**, brought here from nearby Wytham. The tomb of the 'villainous' <u>Antony Forster (d. 1572)</u>, who, in fact, followed a perfectly respectable parliamentary career after 1560, can also be seen.

Mull over the 'whodunit' in the excellent **Bear and Ragged Staff**, just ¼ mile west of the church. Not only is it in period (sixteenth to seventeenth century), but it also celebrates the distinguished emblem of the Earls of Warwick, made famous by Richard Neville, who was earl during the Wars of the Roses. Stay the night if you need more time to crack the mystery!

OAKLEY ★

Malshanger House

Situated 1½ miles north of Oakley village. From B3400 Basingstoke–Overton road, head north from the railway viaduct just west of Oakley village on minor roads, via Summer Down Farm, leading to the rear of property (which used to be a school).

From the rear of this private house is visible a large but thin **brick tower**. This is what remains of the huge Tudor house built by **Archbishop Warham of Canterbury (c. 1450–1532)**. Warham was a great builder (see **Otford** and **Canterbury**). He was archbishop from 1503, and so played a major part in the King's Great Matter. In fact, it was only after his death that Henry was able to proceed to divorce. His parents owned the manor here.

Interestingly, two other important players in Henry's reign come from the Basingstoke area – William, Lord Sandys (see **The Vyne**), Lord Chamberlain of the Household, and Sir William Paulet (see **Old Basing**). Sandys and Paulet were visited by Henry VIII and Queen Anne in late summer 1531.

The remaining tower of a large Tudor house built by Archbishop Warham at Malshanger, near Basingstoke.

St Leonard's Church
Located on the west side of the village, on a minor road south of B3400 Basingstoke–Overton road. From Basingstoke turn left off B3400, just after the railway viaduct. (KAL)

This church was rebuilt in the nineteenth century, using parts from the medieval Malshanger Chapel associated with the Warham family. There is a **brass** to Robert Warham (d. 1487) and his wife Elizabeth, the archbishop's parents. They were tenant farmers here, so surely could not have foreseen their son's involvement in the heady religious issues occurring in the English Reformation?

OLD BASING ★★
Situated 1½ miles east of Basingstoke, signposted off the eastern bypass.

House £
Originally a Norman Conquest castle, the medieval house was rebuilt in the early Tudor style by Sir William Paulet (d. 1572), from 1531. It was largely in brick and had four towers. Many modifications followed, until Sir William built a second house on the site called the New House. By his death, Basing had become one of the most splendid houses in England. It was regularly visited by royalty – Henry VIII in October 1535; Edward VI plus Mary and Philip of Spain; and Queen Elizabeth I, a renowned scrounger, came five times during her reign!

The lovely Tudor barn built by Sir William Paulet at Old Basing.

Unfortunately, the house was besieged a number of times in the Civil War and, in 1645, almost destroyed. Some **brickwork** remains on the well-laid-out site, but the main survival from 1535 is the **Great Barn**, until 1984 a fully working agricultural store.

St Mary's Church
In the centre of Basing village, ½ mile east of the house.

In the **chancel**, **south side**, are **tomb chests** and **arches** to <u>Sir William Paulet, Marquess of Winchester, (c. 1485–1572)</u> and his first wife, <u>Elizabeth Capell (d. 1558)</u>, and to his son, <u>Sir John Paulet, 2nd Marquess of Winchester</u> and possibly his second wife <u>Elizabeth *née* Seymour</u>, sister to Queen Jane.

The branch of the Paulet family moved here from Somerset in the fifteenth century – the grandfather and father of the 1st Marquess are commemorated by **tomb chests** on the **north side** of the chancel. His father, Sir John, had fought against the Cornish rebels in 1497.

The 1st Marquess was an extraordinary man – he died 'in harness' as Lord High Treasurer at the age of 87 or 88 years, a massive age for the time. He held national office under four Tudor monarchs, which required a remarkable ability to adapt his religious views. He attributed his career success to his being 'a willow not an oak'. He also lived to see 103 of his own descendants.

His father lived until 1525, so William's career did not really get into its stride until he was over 40. He began in 1529, with diplomatic roles in Europe. He became an associate of Wolsey and then Cromwell. In early May 1536, he was one of the four Privy Councillors, led by the Duke of Norfolk, who charged Anne Boleyn with committing adultery. During proceedings, the other three members of the group were less than polite to Anne – Anne thought that only Paulet behaved like a gentleman. He was one of the judges at the subsequent trial of Anne's supposed lovers.

During his long career, he held a whole range of senior household and financial positions. He became Lord Chamberlain in 1543. He was well rewarded from 1539, firstly as Lord St John, then Earl of Wiltshire, before being made Marquess in 1551 by John Dudley, Duke of Northumberland. A few months later, Paulet changed sides and helped to overthrow the duke in favour of Mary – very much the willow!

OXFORD, the Martyrs' Memorial ★★★★
Located in the city centre, at St Giles Street and Broad Street. Close to the Randolph Hotel.

The **cross** in St Giles Street is early Victorian, and is modelled on the Waltham Eleanor Cross. It commemorates the burning, by Mary I in 1555–56, of the three Protestant bishops, Latimer, Ridley and Cranmer, which took place just around the corner in Broad Street.

Archbishop Cranmer (1490–ex. 1556) was, of course, the big prize. Newly appointed to the see of Canterbury in 1532, he not only passed judgement on the validity of Henry and Catherine's marriage in 1533, but also was the driving force behind the sweeping Protestant reforms instigated in Edward VI's reign. Mary succeeded in getting Cranmer to recant his Protestant faith, but once he saw he was not to escape the flames he reneged and died a martyr, thrusting his right hand into the flames.

<u>Bishop Hugh Latimer (*c.* 1490–ex. 1555)</u> was a radical Church reformer who was Bishop of Worcester from 1535–39, until he opposed the counter

The memorial to Cranmer, Latimer and Ridley at Oxford.

reforms of Henry VIII in 1539, known as the Six Articles. Anne Boleyn was very influential in the appointment of reforming bishops at this time. He was the premier preacher of his time, and preached for Anne in her campaign against the king in the spring of 1536. Latimer was restored to favour after Henry's death, and became court preacher to Edward VI. Later he was chaplain to Katherine Willoughby, Dowager Duchess of Suffolk, and a noted reformer.

Bishop Nicholas Ridley (c. 1500–ex. 1555) was Bishop of Rochester from 1547 and assisted Cranmer in writing the *Book of Common Prayer* in 1548. He was much involved in the accession of Lady Jane Grey after Edward VI's death, and preached against the legitimacy of Princesses Mary and Elizabeth at that time. After Mary I's coup he was imprisoned in the Tower.

The **cross** is also a memorial to the English Reformation generally. It was intended as a counterbalance to the slide back to Catholicism initiated by the Oxford Movement in the mid-nineteenth century. Around the corner, in Broad Street, a small **cross** has been inlaid into the tarmac road opposite Balliol College. This marks the spot where the three unfortunates were burnt. At the time it was in the town ditch. See also **Christchurch College** in St Algate's, founded by Thomas Wolsey.

ROTHERFIELD GREYS ★★

St Nicholas's Church
Located 2½ miles west of Henley-on-Thames, on a minor road from Henley to Greys Green.

In the Knollys Chapel is a splendid **monument** to Sir Francis Knollys (1514–96), Lady Katherine Knollys (c. 1524–69) and their fourteen surviving children.

It is Lady Katherine who interests us here. Her maiden name was Carey, and she was the daughter of none other than Mary née Boleyn and her first husband, William Carey, who died of the sweat in 1527. Katherine's younger brother was Henry. Queen Elizabeth was very kind and supportive to her two maternal cousins; Henry was made Lord Hunsdon, named after the royal palace in Hertfordshire, whilst Sir Francis, above, became Treasurer of the Royal Household from 1572–96. Such preferment raised suspicions that Katherine and Henry were, in fact, the illegitimate offspring of Henry VIII from his affair with Mary Boleyn in the early 1520s. However, Henry never acknowledged them and there is no supporting evidence.

The eldest daughter of Katherine, Lettice, wears a coronet to signify she became a countess, twice over. Much to the annoyance of the queen, her second husband was Robert Dudley, Earl of Leicester (see **Cumnor**).

Greys Court £
Located 1 mile north of the church. Keep right at the junction. Signposted.

The Knollys family acquired this property in 1518, and parts of the original four-teenth-century fortified manor house survive. From 1559, Sir Francis Knollys (1514–96), a devout protestant, built this lovely Elizabethan house. He had hoped that the queen would visit but she never did, perhaps because of Lettice's marriage to Robert Dudley.

SHERBORNE ST JOHN, the Vyne ★★ £
Set in deep countryside, 3 miles north of Basingstoke, on a minor road north from Sherborne village to Bramley. Signposted off A339 Basingstoke northern bypass. (NT)

At first sight, the exterior of this elegant country house does not seem to offer much for the Tudor historian. However, although much altered in later centuries, at the heart of the house remains the Tudor structure built by William, Lord Sandys (c. 1470–1540). The **Oak Gallery** (long), **ante-chapel** and **chapel** are particularly rewarding, containing portraits, busts, stained glass and coats of arms of a range of Tudor celebrities – Henry VIII, Catherine of Aragon, Queen Margaret of Scotland (Henry's sister), Wolsey, Bishop Fox of Winchester, Archbishop Warham, Sir William Paulet (these last two both had family estates nearby) and Bishop Tunstall of London.

Sandys was an administrator and diplomat who got to know Henry while the latter was growing up in the 1490s. He is seen as a favourite of the king, who visited the Vyne three times – in 1510 (with Catherine), in 1531 (with Anne) and again, in 1535, with Anne during the summer progress. Another royal visit may have occurred in 1516. Sandys gained lands from the fall of Buckingham in the early 1520s. In 1526 he was appointed Lord Chamberlain in the king's household, as part of Wolsey's shake-up known as the Eltham Ordinances. In 1532, he became Comptroller of the Household. In this role he was a member of the party which escorted Queen Anne from Greenwich to the Tower in May 1536. Sandys married Margaret Bray, half niece to Sir Reginald Bray, a close confidant of Henry VII. He was friendly with his neigh-bour Sir William Paulet (see **Old Basing**).

While you are visiting the Vyne, why not call in at the **Chapel of the Holy Ghost** in **Basingstoke**? It is located immediately north of the railway station. From the station, turn right and turn right again under the railway line, onto Sherborne Road. Turn right tightly up into a cemetery and park. The chapel is actually visible from the up platform in winter. The **ruins** of this chapel stand in two parts – the original thirteenth-century west tower, and the **Guild Chapel of the Holy Trinity** in brick, built on the south side of the chancel by Lord Sandys in 1524 as a family mausoleum. This is his burial place.

STOKE POGES, St Giles Church ★★

On the eastern edge of Stoke Park, 1 mile south of the village centre and on the northern fringes of Slough. Signposted off B416 Slough–Gerrards Cross road.

Delightfully situated, this church has a lovely and well-kept graveyard – quite appropriate, given that the eighteenth-century poet Thomas Gray wrote his famous Elegy here! There is a monument to him in the graveyard.

However, we are interested in the **Hastings Chapel** inside the church. This was built out, in brick, from the south aisle in 1558, by Edward, Lord Hastings of Loughborough (*c.* 1521–71), to house the remains of his parents who had died within a day of one another, in 1544 at Stoke Poges, their principal seat (must be a story there – the sweat?). Although no monuments survive, the chapel therefore commemorates Lord Edward, above, his father George, 1st Earl of Huntingdon (*c.* 1488–1544) and his mother Countess Anne, *née* Stafford (1483–1544). The family were direct descendants of William, Lord Hastings, who was friend and right-hand man to Edward IV during the Wars of the Roses.

Edward was George's second son. A military man, he fought against the French and was an early supporter of Queen Mary in 1553. He became Lord Chamberlain of her household. When she died, he withdrew from public life and became very melancholy. He was imprisoned for hearing mass in 1561, but released. He had no children. His father, George, had succeeded to the peerage in 1508. He was also a military man and a long-time favourite of Henry VIII. He fought in France in 1513 and 1523, and was present at the Field of the Cloth of Gold. He signed the petition to Pope Clement VII regarding the divorce in 1530. He was present at the coronation of Anne Boleyn, but also at her trial in 1536. In 1529 he had been elevated to 1st Earl of Huntingdon, one of the oldest earldoms, known as 'catskin earls' because of the nature of their robes.

But it is Edward's mother, Countess Anne, who is of most interest to us. She was one of the sisters of Edward Stafford, 3rd Duke of Buckingham and was therefore something of a catch for George. They married in late 1509, but very soon there were rumours of an affair with the new king. The duke got to hear of these, and managed to find Sir William Compton in Anne's bedroom! Rumours suggested that Compton was acting as a go-between with the king. A row ensued which, of course, King Henry heard about. Buckingham was summoned to Court where another row broke out – Buckingham was 35 years old to Henry's 18 years, and arguably had a better claim to the throne (and knew it). Eventually, George had Anne sent to a nunnery to cool off!

Henry had certainly succeeded in ruffling Buckingham's feathers – he was to go even further in 1521, and executed him. Oddly, George must have turned the other cheek, since Anne produced five sons and daughters in what, subsequently, looks like a happy marriage. Interestingly though, Anne and Compton were pursued through the courts by Wolsey for adultery. In a further twist, when Compton died in 1527 he left a legacy to Anne in his will. No smoke without fire – but was Henry really involved with Anne?

THAME, St Mary's Church ★★
Situated on the north-west edge of town, north of the main street.

In the centre of the **chancel** there is a very high quality **tomb chest**, with **effigies** to <u>John, Lord Williams of Thame (1501–59)</u> and his first wife <u>Elizabeth Bledlow (1490–1556)</u>. She was actually buried in nearby Rycote Chapel.

We have something of an enigma here. Williams was of Welsh origin, his father, another John, being the first to head east. He settled in Burghfield, near Reading, and married Isabel More, a modest heiress. One is tempted to suggest a Ludlow link? From this ordinary background, John rose to be a peer. He was probably helped by being a kinsman of Morgan Williams, who married Thomas Cromwell's sister, Catherine.

John followed Cromwell into the service of Cardinal Wolsey in the 1520s, and was appointed Clerk of the King's Jewels in 1530. During the 1530s he was much involved in the Dissolution of the Monasteries with Cromwell, acquiring Thame Abbey and generally making a lot of money. His reputation was further helped by his involvement in suppressing the Pilgrimage of Grace in Lincolnshire. He attended the christening of Prince Edward and was knighted in 1537. Later, he attended the reception for Anne of Cleves.

The elegant effigies of Lord and Lady Williams at Thame.

Interestingly, Williams was 'blessed' with a visit by the king and his new queen, Katherine Howard, when they stayed at Williams' house at nearby Rycote on honeymoon in August 1540, just weeks after his kinsman, Cromwell, was executed. One wonders how the dinner conversation went.

Williams steadily increased his lands and properties in the area. He was briefly imprisoned during Edward VI's reign, but really sprang to prominence after Edward's death, when he very quickly raised 6,000 men in the area for Princess Mary. He was ennobled by her in 1553. He held a number of royal positions, including Chamberlain to King Philip. As Sheriff of Oxfordshire he had to organise the notorious executions of Bishops Latimer and Ridley, and Archbishop Cranmer in 1555–56. He was also involved in the house arrest of Princess Elizabeth, who stayed at Rycote in May 1554. However, Williams was so taken with his charge that he rather overdid the lavishness of the entertaining. He was replaced as royal escort by Sir Henry Bedingfield, but Elizabeth I never forgot his kindness and referred to him as her 'favourite uncle'.

In 1558, Williams founded a **grammar school** which was built in 1569. It still stands on the south side of Church Lane, west of the church. It now houses commercial offices. Williams' **coat of arms** survives.

TITCHFIELD ★★

St Peter's Church
Located in the village centre, on the east side. 1⅓ miles south of A27 Portsmouth–Brighton road.

In the **south chapel** is a splendid monument to <u>Thomas Wriothesley, Earl of Southampton, (c. 1505–50)</u> and his wife, <u>Countess Jane (*née* Cheney)</u>.

Wriothesley (pronounced Risley) was one of a large number of highly effective bureaucrats who feature in Henry VIII's government. He came from an upper middle class background in London, and was educated at St John's College, Cambridge. He became a protégé of Thomas Cromwell, and profited greatly from the Dissolution of the Monasteries, acquiring Titchfield, Hyde and Beaulieu Abbeys in Hampshire.

He was ambassador in Brussels in the 1530s. Despite supporting the Anne of Cleves marriage, Thomas survived the fall of Cromwell in 1540 to become one of Henry's two principal secretaries (Sir Ralph Sadler was the other). He was much involved with the annulment of the Cleves marriage, and the transfer of the ex-queen to Richmond Palace. He was a key member of the four-man team which investigated Queen Katherine Howard's behaviour in 1542, and he escorted her by barge down the Thames to the Tower.

He received a peerage in 1544, becoming successively Lord Privy Seal and Lord Chancellor. Notoriously, in this role Wriothesley, supported by Richard Rich, undertook the torture of Anne Askew, a Protestant heretic. Before her execution, she was interviewed and claimed that during her racking both Wriothesley and Rich had at times operated the machinery themselves. Anne was then unable to walk and had to be carried to her execution. There was definitely a harsh and ruthless edge to this man.

In the last days of Henry VIII, Wriothesley was identified with the conservative faction led by the Duke of Norfolk. He was particularly at loggerheads with Edward Seymour, Earl of Hertford. He was implicated in the attempt to discredit Queen Katherine Parr, along with Bishop Gardiner and, once foiled, took the full force of the king's anger. On Henry's death, Seymour became Lord Protector Somerset and Wriothesley was made Earl of Southampton. Carelessly, however, he allowed Somerset to deprive him of the Lord Chancellorship and so Wriothesley switched to supporting John Dudley, who deposed Somerset in 1549.

The Abbey

Located 1 mile north of the village beyond A27, west of a minor road to Wickham. (EH)

This is the abbey where the hapless Henry VI married Margaret of Anjou in 1445. Thomas Wriothesley, Earl of Southampton (*c.* 1505–50), was granted the monastery at the Dissolution, and he transformed it into a mansion known as Place House. Most of this was demolished in the eighteenth century, but the large **gatehouse** remains.

WARBLINGTON, 'Castle' ★★

The village is 1½ miles east of Havant. The church and castle remains lie ½ mile south of A27 Portsmouth–Brighton road. Exit A27 at the roundabout for Emsworth, but turn immediately south on a minor road.

The castle remains are scanty – some earthworks, an octagonal **turret** from the gatehouse and masonry, all on private land. However, the turret is of such dimension that it is clear this is the remnant of the huge Tudor mansion built here between 1514 and 1526 by Margaret Pole, Countess of Salisbury (1473–ex. 1541).

Margaret was a very important person – she was a Plantagenet, the daughter of George, Duke of Clarence, Edward IV's younger brother who was executed for treason in 1478. In theory, she had a much better claim to the English throne than the Tudors. Her younger brother Edward, Earl of Warwick had been executed by Henry VII in 1499, ahead of Catherine of Aragon's marriage to Prince Arthur.

In 1494 Henry VII married Margaret off to a trusted lieutenant of gentry status, Sir Richard Pole, who was a kinsman of Henry's mother, Lady Margaret Beaufort. They had four sons and a daughter. Sir Richard was Chamberlain to Prince Arthur and based in Ludlow/Bewdley in Shropshire.

Margaret Pole became firm friends with Catherine of Aragon. Sir Richard died in 1504 but, in 1513, Henry VIII reversed her father's attainder and restored Margaret's lands, at the same time creating her Countess of Salisbury (inherited through her mother, Isabel Neville, daughter of Warwick the Kingmaker) in her own right. She was godmother at Princess Mary's confirmation in 1516, and then became her governess in 1520, proving a great success. However, her daughter, Ursula, was married to Lord Henry Stafford, the son of the Duke of Buckingham, so when the duke was executed for treason in 1521 the Poles came under suspicion by the king and were expelled from court. Her eldest son, Henry, was briefly imprisoned.

As the King's Great Matter unfolded in the 1520s and 1530s Margaret supported Catherine, and was religiously conservative. In 1536 her second son, Reginald, who was based in Rome, published a scathing attack on Henry VIII's policies and actions related to the Great Matter. The king had, in fact, previously sponsored Reginald during his education and was so furious about the publication that he held the entire family responsible for Reginald's actions. Worse still, Pole had been asked by the Pope to co-ordinate a Europe-wide offensive against Henry. Cromwell had already warned the king that the Poles might join forces with the Exeters in a conservative conspiracy.

At the end of August 1538 the third Pole son, Sir Geoffrey, was sent to the Tower. There, possibly on the rack, Geoffrey divulged family secrets which implicated his mother, Margaret; his elder brother Henry, Lord Montagu; Henry Courtenay, Marquess of Exeter; and, of course, his brother, Reginald, in a treasonous conspiracy. All except the absent Reginald were sent to the Tower – Montagu and Exeter were executed in December. The Countess was held in straightened circumstances until 1541 when, without warning, the 68-year-old was butchered on Tower Green by an inexperienced axe man who took three blows to finish the job. One of the worst of many blots on Henry VIII's reputation?

Reginald was still abroad and there were now no sensible pretenders to the English throne left. Sir Geoffrey survived, but may have suffered a nervous breakdown. He lived at Lordington, in West Sussex, but spent much time travelling in Europe. He was buried in nearby Stoughton Church but, perhaps appropriately, there is no memorial. The king had been very generous to his Pole kinsmen at the beginning of his reign, but somewhere along the line, the family withheld their support to him. As usual, Henry's response was brutal. The splendid **turret** here, therefore, provides the focus for one of the biggest family tragedies in an age full of them.

WINCHESTER, Cathedral ★★★

Located in the city centre.

In the **chancel**, **north side**, a fine **chantry chapel** commemorates <u>Stephen Gardiner (*c.* 1495–1555), Bishop of Winchester</u>.

Gardiner attended Cambridge and then taught there (two of his pupils were Wriothesley and Paget). In 1523, Wolsey became his patron. Soon afterwards, he was sent on embassies to France and he became involved in the Great Matter. In 1528, he travelled with Wolsey to Rome to obtain permission for Henry's case to be decided in England. In 1529, Gardiner was appointed principal secretary to Henry VIII. He was recognised as one of the finest intellects of his day but could be overbearing and irascible. In 1531, he was made bishop. However, as the English Reformation progressed, Gardiner felt steadily less comfortable with a conflict between Crown and Church. He resisted the king in spring 1532 over supplication, and was never really fully trusted again by him. He was used only on diplomatic missions. During the 1530s he became associated with the conservative faction at court.

At a council meeting in 1546, John Dudley, Viscount Lisle, struck him during an argument and Dudley was temporarily banned from court. That same year Gardiner persuaded an exasperated Henry to launch a coup against Queen Katherine Parr. (Henry had become irritated with her hectoring debate on religious matters. He saw her heading in the same direction as Anne Boleyn.) Assisted by Wriothesley, the queen's leading women were to be arrested, their illegal books seized and Katherine sent to the Tower. Katherine, however, managed to appeal direct to the king, apologised and was forgiven. The coup attempt simply resulted in Wriothesley being humiliated by Henry when he arrived with guards to arrest the queen. Katherine Willoughby, the queen's friend and fellow religious

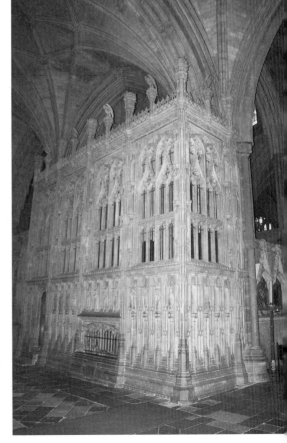

The chantry tomb of Bishop Gardiner at Winchester.

reformer, regularly crossed swords with Gardiner; she even named her dog after him – no doubt so that she could shout at him!

During the reign of Edward VI, Gardiner was imprisoned twice and, in 1551, he was deprived of his see. When Mary I came to the throne he was restored to favour, and was able to undertake his great triumph in marrying Mary and Philip of Spain in this cathedral in July 1554. Gardiner was also a noted writer on theological matters.

On the **south side** of the **chancel**, another **chantry chapel** commemorates Richard Foxe, Bishop (1448–1528). Appointed bishop in 1501, this wily character was much liked by Henry VII. He had been present with Tudor at Bosworth, and rose to be the most powerful member of his council. He was chosen to christen Prince Henry at Greenwich in 1491 while he was Bishop of Exeter. He was Lord Privy Seal from 1487–1516, and was a skilful diplomat, lawyer and churchman. He was the true inventor of 'Morton's Fork', which Henry VII used to raise extra taxes from the aristocracy. He was much involved in the negotiations for the marriages of Catherine of Aragon to Prince Arthur and then Henry VIII. He was mentor to Thomas Wolsey. He retired from government in 1516 and settled in Winchester, attending at last to his church duties. He went blind, but was still considered important enough to be interviewed on the King's Great Matter just before his death in 1528. He founded Corpus Christi College, Oxford.

WINDSOR, St George's Chapel ★★★★★ ££
Situated in the town centre, in the castle grounds. Park north of the castle near the river. Closes at 4 p.m.

This building is one of the glories of English architecture. Founded by Edward IV in 1475, the building was continued by Henry VII, at a time when he was considering being buried here rather than in his eventual resting place in Westminster Abbey. The chapel was finished by 1511. It houses an eclectic collection of church monuments from late medieval kings to modern kings and queens, plus some minor sixteenth-century aristocrats. But we are here primarily for one reason – to view the resting place of **Henry VIII**. Most people would expect him to have the most elaborate and splendid of medieval tombs, but in the **Quire** he lies beneath a plain **black marble slab**, alongside **Queen Jane Seymour** and King Charles I, who was executed during the Civil War in 1649.

Henry much admired his maternal grandfather, Edward IV, and so chose to be buried here. Jane Seymour was buried in the vault first. Henry's will decreed that he should be buried beneath an elaborate monument which he had purloined from Cardinal Wolsey, but one thing even the most powerful of kings cannot do is control events after their deaths. Henry loved to control events, and indeed, he made great efforts to control the succession after his death. However, his grave tells us something important – succeeded by his three children in turn, none of them was prepared to spend on his funeral monument. After all, Edward was only a boy, Mary's mother had been divorced and hounded to death by him, and Elizabeth's mother had been executed by him – just desserts in death?

In the **quire** there are also the **Tresilian Gates**, guarding the tomb of Edward IV (1443–83), and the **oriel window**, built by Henry VIII so that **Catherine of Aragon** could view the chapel services. It is said that Dowager Queen Katherine Parr watched the funeral service for Henry VIII from this same window. Edward IV and Queen Elizabeth Woodville's **tombs** lie in the **north quire aisle**, along with the **Hastings Chantry** commemorating William, Lord Hastings (1435–ex. 1483), Edward's friend, military support and fellow party-goer.

The **Rutland Chantry** was established for Edward IV's older and favourite sister, Anne Plantagenet (1439–76). Her first husband, the unpleasant Henry Holland, Duke of Exeter was thrown off his ship and drowned while returning from Edward IV's French campaign in 1475. She remarried Sir Thomas St Ledger, and a **brass** in the chantry commemorates them. The **tomb chest** and **effigies** there celebrate Anne's daughter, another Anne (1476–1526) and George Manners, Lord de Ros (1470–1513). He was killed fighting for Henry VIII in France (see **Bottesford**).

In the **south quire aisle** can be seen the **floor slab** marking the grave of Henry VI (1421–71), brought here in 1484 from Chertsey. Above this is the **funeral helm** of **Charles Brandon, Duke of Suffolk** who is buried in the chapel close to his monarch, in similar fashion to Lord Hastings and Edward IV. The aisle also contains modern **stained glass** of Henry VIII and his wives. Delightful painted **panels** celebrate three kings – Edward IV; his son Edward V (one of the princes in the Tower); Henry VII; and, unusually, Prince Edward (1453–71), the son of Henry VI cut down during or after the Battle of Tewksbury by the Yorkists.

The **Urswick** and **Bray chantries** commemorate household members associated with Lady Margaret Beaufort and Henry VII.

The **Beaufort Chantry** contains the **monument** to Charles Somerset, Earl of Worcester (1460–1526) and his first wife, Elizabeth Herbert (d. 1513), who was Baroness Herbert in her own right. Somerset was the illegitimate son of Henry Beaufort, 3rd Duke of Somerset. He was Knight of the Body to Henry VII, and appointed Lord Chamberlain to Henry VIII on the second day of his reign. His main achievement was to organise the Field of the Cloth of Gold. He is the direct ancestor of today's Dukes of Beaufort who, therefore, are the only surviving male line of the Plantagenets.

The **Lincoln Chapel** contains the **tomb chest** and **effigies** of Edward Clinton, Earl of Lincoln (1512–85) and his third wife, Elizabeth Fitzgerald (1527–90). Both spouses are of interest. Edward was a military man, and became Lord High Admiral during the reign of Edward VI. His first wife was none other than Bessie Blount, King Henry's former mistress, who was twelve years older than her husband – the connection being Lincolnshire, the home of Bessie's first husband, and Edward's birthplace. Elizabeth Fitzgerald, who had been married before to Sir Antony Browne, was a noted beauty who, at the age of 10 years, had caught the attention of the poet Henry Howard, Earl of Surrey. She is immortalised in verse as the 'Fair Geraldine'. She was brought up with Queen Elizabeth in the 1530s, and became her lady-in-waiting and friend.

WEST COUNTRY

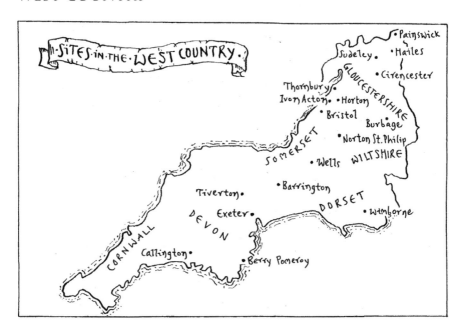

BARRINGTON COURT ★★ £

Situated at the eastern edge of the village, which is 2 miles north-east of Ilminster. Signposted off nearby A303. (NT)

Here we have two houses for the price of one!

It is the older manor house in which we are interested. A charming property which has Renaissance elements. It was built by <u>Henry Daubeny, Earl of Bridgewater (1493–1548)</u>, who came of gentry stock from Brant Boughton, Lincolnshire. His father, Sir Giles Daubeny, had been in exile with Henry Tudor and had fought at Bosworth. He became one of Henry's most trusted lieutenants and one of the few to be granted a peerage. He died in 1508 and is buried in Westminster Abbey. His son, Henry, inherited the peerage as a minor, and the estate lands in 1514. He had fought in the 1513

Barrington Court, home to the Earl and Countess of Bridgewater.

French campaign with Henry VIII, had been made Knight Banneret, and life was going well when he married Elizabeth Neville, one of the Bergavenny clan, before 1517. It was probably just after this that the house was built. No children were forthcoming, however, and Elizabeth died in 1531.

The next year a new wife was obtained, Katherine *née* Howard (d. 1554), daughter of Thomas Howard, 2nd Duke of Norfolk by his second wife Agnes Tilney – not *the* Katherine Howard, but her half-aunt. Katherine had been married before, to Sir Rhys ap Griffith who was executed on Tower Hill in 1531. Nevertheless, this was a significant step up socially for Henry. This was recognised in 1538 when he was, surprisingly, made Earl of Bridgewater. However, it all started to unravel very soon. Daubeny's new countess had previously been a senior member of her mother's (by now Dowager Duchess of Norfolk) households in Horsham and Lambeth, in which her niece – *the* Katherine Howard – was growing up. Discipline seems to have been very lax and young Katherine was left free to get unsuitably involved with her teacher, Manox, and her cousin, Francis Dereham. By the time of her marriage to King Henry, Katherine already had a track record.

Once the case against Queen Katherine had been assembled by the king's ministers, in December 1541, the countess, along with other members of the Howard family, were sent to the Tower and tried for 'misprision of treason', i.e. abetting and concealing Katherine's offences. However, they were soon pardoned after Katherine was executed.

Earl Henry died in 1548 at Brant Boughton, by which time he had managed to make himself penniless. Arthur Mee describes Henry as 'the most extravagant noble-man of an extravagant age', so perhaps this tendency, plus his wife's fall from the king's favour, are to blame for his financial ruin (Mee, *Somerset*, p. 41). Katherine also died at Brant Boughton, in 1554. (See **Queen Katherine Howard**.)

BERRY POMEROY, Castle ★★★ £

Set in beautiful countryside, 2 miles north-east of Totnes, yet only 4 miles from Torbay. Signposted off A385 Totnes–Torbay road through Berry Pomeroy village. (EH)

At first sight, not an obvious connection with Henry VIII – a medieval castle, built by a Norman family who came over with the Conqueror, within which stands the ruins of an Elizabethan house. However, our interest comes from the fact that, in December 1547, **Edward Seymour, Lord Protector and Duke of Somerset** bought the property from the Pomeroys, an impoverished local family. Somerset himself was executed in 1552 so he may never even have visited this site.

The style of the Elizabethan house is fascinating. It has clear echoes of Longleat, Lacock and Dudley Castle – all properties built by a group of enlightened men inter-ested in Renaissance architecture. Somerset was the leader of this fashion, and Sir John Thynne, his chief steward who built Longleat, the driving force. It looks as if Somerset drew up the plans for the house but work was still ongoing at his death. His son, another Edward Seymour, completed the work with the help of Thynne in the late sixteenth century.

Berry Pomeroy Castle, owned by Lord Protector Somerset.

Interestingly, the second Edward was Somerset's son by his first marriage to Katherine Filliol, who had died in 1535. Sometime in the early 1530s Somerset suddenly repudiated his marriage to Katherine, claiming that she had had an affair with his own father, Sir John Seymour, who may therefore have been the father of Somerset's two sons – including Edward above! Katherine was despatched to a nunnery (note she was not executed), where she conveniently died, leaving Somerset free to marry a second time to Anne Stanhope, who produced a second family, including two more Edwards.

In 1540 Somerset, by now a powerful player on the English political stage, was able to get an Act of Parliament passed which disinherited Katherine's sons in favour of his second family. On Somerset's death, therefore, the first Edward Seymour inherited only Berry Pomeroy and a peerage. However, the senior branch has had the last laugh – the junior line failed in the male line during the eighteenth century, enabling the seniors finally to acquire the dukedom which they hold to this day, along with this castle.

What is particularly interesting is to compare the detailed styling of the Seymour house here with that of John Dudley's at Dudley Castle. They are very similar, with Renaissance features suggesting that they were both part of the same movement. In politics, during Henry VIII's reign, they were both singled out for success by Henry as religious reformists and were in the ascendancy when Henry died. Yet by 1549, Dudley, as Duke of Northumberland, had supplanted Somerset and executed him in 1552. Does this hint at betrayal not just on a political level but also on a personal scale?

So, enjoy the ruins of the castle and house within, plus the lovely countryside. The guidebook is exceptional and there is a nice cafe. Do also call in at **St Mary's Church** in the village, where there is a splendid **monument** to Edward, Lord Seymour (d. 1593), with his own son and family.

BRISTOL, St Mark's Church ★

Located in the city centre, on the opposite side of College Green from the cathedral. It has a tower.

This church has a large collection of monuments, but we are looking for the lovely fan-vaulted **chantry chapel** founded by Sir Robert Poyntz (d. 1520) of Iron Acton. He was an Esquire of the Body of Edward IV but, like so many in the south, supported Buckingham's Revolt in 1483. He fought for Henry Tudor at Bosworth, and was knighted afterwards. Poyntz became Queen Catherine of Aragon's Vice Chamberlain and, later, Chancellor. When Catherine became pregnant in 1510, Poyntz's daughter or daughter-in-law, Elizabeth, was appointed Lady Mistress for the birthing of the new child and its subsequent care. She is seen as Catherine's choice. The baby was born on New Year's Day to much ceremony and celebration. He was christened Henry, but died after only fifty-two days at Richmond Palace under Elizabeth's care.

No blame seems to have been attached to her, and she received an annuity of £20 for her troubles. (See **Iron Acton**.)

BURBAGE (Wilts) ★★★

Wulfhall
Located 1½ miles north-east of Burbage on a very minor road to Great Bedwyn.

A puzzling site; the ancient home of the hereditary foresters of Savernake and, in particular, of the **Seymour family**, who played such an important, if not always effective, role in the events of the first half of the sixteenth century. Set deep in the Wiltshire countryside, it is definitely 'far from the madding crowd'. The location underlines that the Seymours were from modest gentry stock, even though the family had a long and illustrious pedigree going back to the Norman Conquest under the name 'St Maur'.

Today, Wulfhall is little more than a large farm. The medieval buildings have disappeared and have been replaced by an early seventeenth-century farmhouse which was much modified in the Victorian period. There is nothing in-period here. However, a few hundred metres north down the public track, in a natural hollow, lies a **redbrick house** possessing a Tudor **wing**. This is private property and is well screened from the track. It can, however, be nicely viewed from the minor road 100m back to Burbage. Go in winter for good viewing!

Could this Tudor building have been involved in the visit of Henry and Anne Boleyn in the summer of 1535?

Surely the high point for Wulfhall came in the summer of 1535, when Henry VIII and Queen Anne Boleyn visited for a few days during their summer progress. Jane Seymour was already one of her ladies-in-waiting and was already in her party. But what a signal honour for her father, Sir John, of modest background, to be visited by the king and queen. Sir John had married well, to Margery Wentworth from a powerful East Anglian family. She was a noted beauty! No doubt the Seymour brothers, Edward and Thomas, would have been on hand, with others of the family. A tradition existed that the family decamped from Wulfhall itself, leaving it for use by the king and queen alone. Perhaps they squeezed up together in the redbrick house pictured? Whatever, within a few months the king had taken up with Jane and, less than a year later, Anne had been executed.

While you are here, enjoy a walk in the lovely countryside and marvel at how isolated it must have felt in the 1530s.

Great Bedwyn, St Mary's Church
Located 3 miles north-east of Wulfhall, on the south side of the village.

In the **chancel** is a **tomb chest** and **effigy** of <u>Sir John Seymour (1474–1536)</u>, the father of Jane Seymour. Sir John was a soldier who fought for Henry VII against the Cornish rebels in 1497; for Henry VIII in France in 1513; and was present at the Field of the Cloth of Gold in 1521.

The effigy of Sir John Seymour, Jane's father.

In around 1500, he married Margery Wentworth, from a powerful East Anglian family. She was a noted beauty, who had attracted the attention of the poet John Skelton. Despite the odd marital crisis, they produced nine children, including Jane, Edward Seymour, who became Lord Protector to Edward VI, and Thomas, who married Katherine Parr after Henry VIII's death. However, Margery does not lie with Sir John, who was originally buried as per family tradition in nearby Easton Royal Priory. Margery died in 1550.

On the **north side** of the chancel, one of the lancet windows contains **stained glass** commemorating **Queen Jane Seymour**. Nearby is a **brass** of <u>John Seymour (d. 1510)</u>, Sir John's eldest son, who died young.

At Bedwyn Brail, 1 mile south, Edward Seymour began building a much larger new house in 1547. It was never finished and fell into decay after his execution in 1552. Recent excavation has revealed foundations, but nothing is visible above ground.

Sir John Seymour's mother was a Darrell, and lived at nearby Littlecote Manor, now a hotel. Also very interestingly, William Carey, who married Mary Boleyn, came from Chilton Foliat, 5 miles north. He would surely have known the Seymours.

Easton Royal, Holy Trinity Church
Located 1½ miles west of Burbage, just south of B3087 to Pewsey.

This was the resting place of the Seymours. There was a priory here until it was dissolved in 1538, and the old priory church was demolished and the present church built by a Seymour descendant in 1591. The nave includes a modern, but very pleasant, **plaque** about the Seymours.

CALLINGTON, St Mary's Church ★
On the town centre crossroads.

In the **chancel** there is a fine **tomb chest** and life-size **effigy** of <u>Robert, Lord Willoughby de Broke (1452–1502/03)</u>. Lord Robert was a Lancastrian and Tudor stalwart who had been involved in the Duke of Buckingham's revolt in 1483, had joined Henry Tudor in exile in France and had fought at Bosworth. After Henry's victory, he was given the delicate task of removing Edward, Earl of Warwick, and Princess Elizabeth of York from Sheriff Hutton Castle in Yorkshire, where Richard III had held them under house arrest. Sir Robert was immediately made Comptroller of the Household. In 1488 he was ennobled, one of only three members of Henry's close associates to be so honoured.

When Catherine of Aragon finally set sail for England in August 1501, Lord Robert was asked to arrange the formal meeting of welcome for her at Southampton, and also to organise her journey to London. Unfortunately, Catherine's fleet encountered bad storms in the Bay of Biscay and had to turn back. At the end of September she set sail again, only to be engulfed by huge seas. Her ships, therefore, ran for cover to Plymouth where she arrived on 2 October – Lord Robert was waiting at Southampton, 150 miles away! He had to undertake a hasty reschedule. He moved the formal reception to Exeter. Catherine kicked her heels for a week in Plymouth, where the locals gave her a fine, spontaneous welcome. They probably even spoke a little Spanish. Lord Robert escorted Catherine to Exeter for the reception. Everything from now on went with military precision, a testimony to de Broke's skills and experience. Catherine eventually met up with Henry VII and Arthur, Prince of Wales, at Dogmersfield near Reading in early November 1501.

CIRENCESTER, St John the Baptist Church ★★
Situated in the town centre.

You enter this wonderful church through the huge south porch, built in the 1490s by this wealthy wool town. The normally reserved Pevsner describes it as 'the most splendid of all English church porches' (Pevsner, *Gloucestershire*, p. 110). In a secure **recess in the east wall of the south aisle**, you will find the magnificent **Boleyn Cup**, which was given to the church by Dr Richard Master, physician to Queen Elizabeth. The hallmark indicates 1535, a year before **Queen Anne Boleyn's** execution. The small cup is surmounted by a crowned and sceptered falcon – Queen Anne's badge. A real treasure.

From the unusually late date of 1515, the **nave** was rebuilt and now contains a number of coloured shields on the **piers**. One of the blue shields commemorates Bishop Thomas Ruthall (d. 1522), who was councillor to both Henry VII and Henry VIII, and who was much involved in Henry VIII's surprising decision, as soon as he succeeded to the throne, to marry Catherine of Aragon after all. Ruthall was born in Cirencester. His initials, together with the badges of Catherine and the Prince of Wales (Prince Arthur or Henry?), and the arms of Henry VII occur in the **Chapel of St Nicholas and St Catherine**. Finally, the royal arms of Henry VIII are carved over the **chancel arch window**.

EXETER, Cathedral ★
Located in the city centre.

In the **retrochoir**, the Speke **chantry** commemorates Sir John Speke (d. 1518), who lived at Whitelackington in southern Somerset. Sir John and near neighbour, Sir Amyas Paulet, were detailed to escort Catherine of Aragon through Somerset on her journey from Plymouth to London, in the autumn of 1501. This was her first appearance in England, causing great excitement ahead of her marriage to Prince Arthur, eldest son of Henry VII.

They took over from Lord Willoughby de Broke, who had escorted her from Plymouth, at the county boundary between Chard and Crewkerne. All must have gone smoothly, despite the hastily revised itinerary, because Catherine was able to proceed by way of Sherborne and Amesbury to Dogmersfield, near Fleet, where she first met Henry VII, and then the Prince. Sir John may have been present at the first formal reception for Catherine at Exeter hosted by Lord Willoughby, who was Lord Steward of the king's household. A church monument also commemorates Sir Amyas Paulet (d. 1537) in Hinton St George.

The superb **west window** of the cathedral contains **glass** which celebrates the life of Miles Coverdale, Bishop of Exeter from 1551–53. Coverdale was a noted reformist and translator of the Bible into English (he is depicted writing his Bible). He officiated at the funeral of Katherine Parr at Sudeley Castle in 1548, the first Protestant royal funeral to be held.

HAILES, Abbey ★ £

Situated 2 miles north-east of Winchcombe, signposted off B4632 Winchcombe–Broadway road. (EH)

This Cistercian abbey was founded in 1246 by Richard, Earl of Cornwall and King of the Romans, brother of King Henry III. In 1270, his son Edmund presented to the abbey a phial of holy blood which had a guarantee from the Patriarch of Jerusalem, later to become Pope Urban IV, that it was the blood of Christ. The phial was placed in a shrine and, over the centuries, the abbey became one of the most popular destinations for pilgrims in England. In the early sixteenth century the abbey was, thus, very prosperous, but gained notoriety in the 1530s.

In 1527 Stephen Sagar from Lancashire was appointed abbot. He turned out to be a friend/protégé of Thomas Cromwell! In 1535, during their celebrated summer progress, Henry VIII and Queen Anne stayed at nearby **Sudeley Castle** for a week. During that time, tradition has it that Anne sent some of her chaplains to this abbey to examine the phial. They reported that it was a fake – ducks' blood or wax – but nothing further seems to have transpired.

In the summer of 1538, by which time other shrines such as Boxley and Walsingham were being denounced, Abbot Sagar wrote to Cromwell urging him to investigate the blood of Hailes. In October, the phial was removed and tested. In late November, Bishop Hilsey of Rochester preached at St Paul's Cross, London, and displayed the phial, declaring it to be a fraud, 'honey clarified and coloured with saffron'. In December 1539, the 'Trojan Horse' abbot and twenty-one monks handed over the abbey to the authorities. Sagar was given a pension of £100 p.a.

Stone from the abbey buildings was used to build a house for the Tracy family in the seventeenth century, but this was demolished. The ruins provide the usual haunting picture of the ruthless dissolution of all our monasteries, conducted with rare efficiency and speed by the king's ministers. In all, over 560 were destroyed.

HORTON, Court ★ £

Set in rural surroundings, 3 miles north-east of Chipping Sodbury. From M4, Junction 18, take A46 north towards Stroud. After 3 miles, turn left signposted to Horton Court, on minor roads. (NT)

This charming building is situated in beautiful countryside at the southern end of the Cotswolds. The north wing is Norman, from around 1140, and constitutes the remains of a prebendal school. The rest of the house was rebuilt in 1521 by Dr William Knight, chaplain to Henry VIII from 1515 and Secretary of State from 1526. Henry used him in ambassadorial roles, including a secret mission to Rome in 1527 to obtain a papal bull for his divorce from Queen Catherine. Knight became Bishop of Bath and Wells in 1541.

The interior of the house contains early Renaissance elements, together with Knight's coat of arms and an inscription. Outside, Knight built an ambulatory which survives. He is buried in **Wells Cathedral** (where a fuller biography is provided).

Horton Court, the charming home of Dr William Knight.

IRON ACTON, Court ★★ £

Located ½ mile north of the village, on B4059 to Latteridge and Rudgeway. Open only for a month each summer. Tel. 01454 228 224

The Poyntz family lived here from 1364–1680. Their memorials survive at St James's Church. Sir Robert Poyntz (d. 1520) was Catherine of Aragon's Vice Chamberlain (see **Bristol**).

Sir Robert's grandson, <u>Sir Nicholas Poyntz (1510–56)</u>, was a somewhat unruly character who was sent to the Fleet prison in 1541, and who numbered the odious Richard Rich amongst his friends. Sir Nicholas was of reformist religious persuasion, and attended the christening of Edward VI and the reception for Anne of Cleves. He was also friendly with the Seymours. He was a soldier and had naval experience against the Scots.

When, in early 1535, it was announced that Henry VIII and Queen Anne would visit Iron Acton during their summer progress, Sir Nicholas began construction of a splendid **east wing** at his property. This was completed in double-quick time ready for his royal visitors in late August. Unfortunately, an outbreak of plaque struck Bristol that summer so the royal couple remained at nearby Thornbury, and may not have even visited Iron Acton. The dangers of the medieval aristocratic lifestyle! Still, Nicholas got his reward – he was knighted that year – was left with regular financial problems over the next twenty years.

Gloriously the east wing survives. Check out the height of the panelled doors to the garderobes – too low for the tall king? A charming place to visit.

NORTON ST PHILIP, The George Inn ★
Located in the village centre, 5 miles west of Trowbridge.

This site is sure to get you very much in period! Originally a staple for the produce of nearby Hinton Priory, the upper floors were added in the fifteenth century. We can, therefore, imagine that the building overall looks very much as it did in the first half of the following century. Pevsner describes it as 'one of the most remarkable medieval inns in England' – as usual, I shall not disagree (Pevsner, *North Somerset*, p. 237).

The inn lay on the stagecoach route to the West Country, and was used as the headquarters for the Duke of Monmouth's army in 1685. Judge Jefferies held court here in the aftermath of that failed rebellion. Enjoy a drink, dinner or even stay here. The area is steeped in medieval history – Farleigh Hungerford Castle, Nunney Castle, Hinton Priory and, more particularly, over the border in Wiltshire the stunning Longleat House and Lacock Abbey, built later in the sixteenth century by acolytes of Lord Protector Somerset, Sir John Thynne and Sir William Sharrington (see **Berry Pomeroy**).

The George Inn, Norton St Philip. Treat yourself?

PAINSWICK, St Mary's Church ★★
Situated in the village centre, south of main A46 road.

St Peter's Chapel in this charming church contains a most unusual **monument**, providing three for the price of one! The original late fifteenth-century **tomb chest** belonged to a member of the powerful Talbot family, perhaps even to Thomas Talbot, who was killed at the nearby Battle of Nibley Green in 1470 (the last private battle in England, fought between Talbot and the Berkeleys). In 1540, the Tudor **canopy** was added when <u>Sir William Kingston</u> (and his second wife, <u>Mary Scrope</u>) were interred here. In the eighteenth century, the later **effigies** of Dr John Seaman and his wife were also moved here.

Born around 1476, Sir William was from a modest Painswick family, and started out as a yeoman of the guard. He was a big man, and achieved recognition as a jouster and as a soldier. In 1512, he was part of the Marquess of Dorset's ill-fated expedition to San Sebastian and, in 1513, he fought at Flodden, after which he was knighted. In 1516, he was unhorsed by King Henry at a tournament to honour Henry's sister, Queen Margaret of Scotland. He also participated in the tournament at the Field of the Cloth of Gold. In 1519, Kingston was brought into the Privy Chamber by Wolsey as part of one of the latter's purges. He was made Constable of the Tower in 1524. In late 1530, he travelled to Sheffield Park to take charge of Cardinal Wolsey, arrested on charges of treason. Kingston was with Wolsey when he died at Leicester and, afterwards, rode down to London to inform the king (see **Sheffield** and **Leicester**).

A three-in-one tomb at Painswick. The Tudor canopy belongs to Sir William Kingston and his second wife, Mary.

Kingston took an official part in the coronation of Anne Boleyn in May 1533 – Anne, of course, had lodged in her own apartments in the Tower beforehand. They were to meet again, in less favourable circumstances, in May 1536, when Queen Anne was escorted by her uncle, the Duke of Norfolk, to the Tower accused of adultery. Kingston met her at the Court Gate, by which time she was in a state of near collapse. He had orders from Cromwell to record everything she said. Four of her ladies-in-waiting, none of whom were liked by Anne, were also required to note everything down – Kingston's wife, Mary, was one of them. Kingston's reports are preserved in the British Library and have contributed to the view of many modern historians that Anne was not guilty of her charges.

Unfortunately, but not surprisingly, Anne suffered mood swings during her stay in the Tower and talked a lot – probably providing extra 'evidence' for her trial. At times, however, there seems to have been a good line in banter with Kingston during her stay. Professionally, Sir William had a stern countenance but he may have been softer underneath. He took charge of Anne's execution and escorted her to the scaffold – not a job for the faint hearted. He was made Comptroller of the Household in 1539 and a Knight of the Garter in the same year. He died in September 1540 after having, it is said, a fit in the street in Painswick.

Sir William lived at nearby **Painswick Lodge**, which Henry and Anne had used as a hunting lodge during their famous summer progress of 1535. Kingston was clearly well-briefed on his prisoner-to-be! It was also visited by Princess Elizabeth as a child. The **north** and **east wings** survive from late Tudor times. It lies 1 mile north-east of the village, on a minor road just before Sheepscombe. Head north from Painswick on the A46, Cheltenham road. After 1 mile, turn sharp right downhill on a minor road to Sheepscombe. After 1 mile, the house can be seen on the right – it is a private residence. Do not confuse this with Painswick Court, situated further on.

SUDELEY CASTLE ★★★★ ££

Situated south-east of Winchcombe village, signposted.

We are primarily interested in the restored **chapel** at the rear of the house. This contains a **tomb chest** and **effigy** commemorating **Queen Katherine Parr**, plus much **stained glass**.

Within only four months of Henry VIII's death, in 1547, his widowed queen had accepted an offer of marriage from her old flame Thomas Seymour, Lord Sudeley. The couple moved in here together with a vast array of staff, plus Princess Elizabeth and Lady Jane Grey, for whom Katherine was responsible. Given the experiences of her first three marriages, these should have been the happiest days of Katherine's life. However, there were concerns about Thomas' attentions to the young princess. Nevertheless, Katherine became pregnant in late 1547. A daughter, Mary, was born at Sudeley in September, but Katherine died soon afterwards of puerperal fever. Her funeral was held here, with Lady Jane Grey as chief mourner. It was the first Protestant royal funeral.

Evensong is held in the **chapel** on certain Sundays. On the outside of the chapel are statues to the unfortunate Henry VI and his queen, Margaret of Anjou. The house itself retains much of the original fifteenth-century structure built by the Lancastrian Ralph Boteler, Lord Sudeley and added to by Richard III when he was Duke of Gloucester. There is also an excellent Katherine Parr **museum**.

Katherine Parr's tomb at Sudeley Castle.

THORNBURY, Castle ★★

Set on the north-west edge of the village. Turn off the A38 Bristol–Gloucester road onto the B4061. After 1½ miles, bear left to St Mary's Church and the castle. The castle is now a hotel, so treat yourself in period style! A drink will be sufficient to gain access to the building.

This magnificent building, started in around 1511, represents a very personal monument to one of the losers in our story. The Stafford Dukes of Buckingham were descended directly from Edward III through his youngest son, Thomas of Woodstock. The **3rd Duke, Edward Stafford (1478–ex. 1521)**, therefore, held a better claim to the throne of England than King Henry, and had the arrogance to go with it. The Staffords had lived at Thornbury since the twelfth century, but had many other houses and estates around the country. Duke Edward chose to build a new principal residence here.

Very quickly after his accession the king was 'in Stafford's face'. The duke was known to be close to his sisters and by 1510, Henry was pursuing Edward's sister, Anne (who was wife to George, Lord Hastings), using Sir William Compton, Groom of the Stool, as an intermediary. Angry words passed between Stafford and Compton. Stafford was summoned before the king, and further angry words were exchanged. The affair soon petered out, but the duke remained a threat in Henry's eyes.

While being friendly with Catherine of Aragon, he openly disliked Wolsey. Eventually, loose words by the duke came to light (as they so often did in this reign!). He was tried by his peers and found guilty of treason. With tears streaming down his face, Thomas Howard, 2nd Duke of Norfolk pronounced the death sentence

Thornbury Castle, built by the Duke of Buckingham.

(they were brothers-in-law). Stafford was beheaded on Tower Hill in May 1521. At the duke's death, the castle had not been completed. Henry and Queen Anne stayed here for a week during the summer of 1535. The house remained uninhabited for 200 years, until being restored in the nineteenth century, appropriately by a member of the Howard family.

TIVERTON, Castle ★★ £

Located in the town centre, on the west side near the river.

This ancient castle serves as a memorial to the Courtenay family from the fourteenth century. Staunch Lancastrians during the Wars of the Roses, the Courtenays had briefly lost their titles, but regained them after Bosworth.

In 1495, William Courtenay, heir to the earldom, married Katherine Plantagenet, a younger sister of Elizabeth of York. Henry Courtenay was born around 1496 and educated alongside Prince Henry. However, the family was found to be in correspondence with the Yorkist de la Poles, and William was put in the Tower by Henry VII, and not released until Henry VIII's accession.

William carried the sword of state at Henry's coronation in 1509. He died in 1511, so his son Henry Courtenay (c. 1496–ex. 1539) succeeded to the title. Initially, the new king was kind and supportive to his maternal cousin. In 1520, he was made Knight of the Garter and Privy Councillor. He was at the Field of the Cloth of Gold and, in 1525, he was raised to Marquess (one of only two in England) and sent as envoy to secure the release of the French king, Francis I, after the Battle of Pavia. He supported Henry over the divorce and the suppression of the monasteries, from which he did extremely well financially.

In 1519, Courtenay's first wife, Elizabeth Grey, died and he married Gertrude Blount, daughter of William Blount, Lord Mountjoy, and Ines de Benegas who had come to England with Catherine of Aragon. Gertrude was a devout Catholic, who remained in close contact with Catherine even after the divorce. Presumably, with Gertrude in the van, the Exeters boycotted Anne Boleyn's coronation in 1533 (see **Wimborne Minster**). In a typical Henrician response, Gertrude was promptly chosen to carry Princess Elizabeth at her christening and, in 1537, she carried Prince Edward at his.

Exeter became head of the Privy Chamber, and sat as commissioner at Anne Boleyn's trial but, unfortunately, he had formed a dislike for Cromwell. After Anne's execution he was suspended from the council under suspicion of being involved in Sir Nicholas Carew's bid to reinstate Princess Mary, but he survived. The Exeters supported Jane Seymour, and became identified with the conservative faction. Courtenay was in regular correspondence with Reginald Pole in Rome, and in November 1538 he was arrested for plotting to usurp the throne, along with members of the Pole family. The episode became known as the 'Exeter Conspiracy'. Courtenay

The delightful south porch of Tiverton church in which Katherine Courtenay née Plantagenet is buried.

was convicted on the evidence of his correspondence with Reginald Pole, and executed by sword in December. Gertrude was accused of treasonable correspondence with Chapuys, the Imperial ambassador, but pardoned. (See **Wimborne Minster**.)

The castle is particularly associated with Countess Katherine (1479–1527), above, who lived here as a widow after her husband's death. She took a vow of perpetual chastity, and was thus able to lead an independent, if somewhat extravagant, lifestyle. A room in the castle is identified with her death. She was the last surviving child of Edward IV and Elizabeth Woodville. Her son, Henry, and his two wives, Elizabeth Grey who died in 1519 and Gertrude Blount (*c.* 1500–58), spent much time at their property in West Horsley, Surrey, because they were much absorbed at court. The castle contains some useful displays on the Yorkist family connections.

Immediately to the south of the castle stands the parish **Church of St Peter**. Countess Katherine was buried here, and her **coat of arms** are displayed on the outside of the marvellous **south porch**.

WELLS, Cathedral ★

Located in the city centre.

In the **nave** of this lovely cathedral, unusually, a **stone pulpit** commemorates Dr William Knight, Bishop of Bath and Wells 1541–47. The pulpit displays early Renaissance elements.

Born around 1475, in London, of relatively humble origins, Knight obtained scholarships to Winchester and New College, Oxford. He became one of Henry VII's secretaries and a protégé of Wolsey. Henry VIII employed him as an ambassador in Spain, Switzerland, Germany and the Low Countries, presumably because he was a good linguist (he had studied in Italy). He was at the Field of the Cloth of Gold. In 1526, he became secretary to the king.

In 1527, Henry despatched Knight on a secret mission to Rome to obtain a papal bull for his divorce from Catherine – secret, that is, from Wolsey who, by this time, was suspected by Henry of 'getting in the way' of the divorce. On his journey to visit the imprisoned Pope Clement VII, Knight was nearly murdered, but the Pope was then freed from Spanish captivity. Knight thought he could bring home to Henry a workable solution but, somehow, Wolsey was able to recover his position with the king, and Knight was eventually recalled to England. Anne Boleyn was able to ensure that Knight made financial gain out of the episode and ambassadorial roles in Paris and to the Holy Roman Emperor continued. Knight attended the christening of Prince Edward in October 1537 and, in 1541, he was consecrated Bishop of Bath and Wells. (See also **Horton Court.**)

WIMBORNE MINSTER ★★

Located in the town centre.

In the **chancel**, **north side**, is a plain **tomb chest** for Gertrude _née_ Blount, Marchioness of Exeter (_c._ 1500–58). She outlived her husband, Henry, by almost twenty years (he was executed in 1539) and lived to see her great friend, Princess Mary, become queen. She was the daughter of William Blount, Lord Mountjoy, and Ines de Benegas, one of Catherine of Aragon's ladies-in-waiting who came to England with her. Mountjoy served as Catherine's chamberlain from 1512 (he was a kinsman of Bessie Blount, Henry's mistress).

In 1519, Gertrude married Henry Courtenay, who was the king's nearest male relative (they were maternal cousins). In 1525, Courtenay was promoted to Marquess. Gertrude remained a devout Catholic so, by the 1530s, the couple were associated with the conservative faction at court. In 1532 they were banned from visiting Princess Mary, but Gertrude continued to correspond with Catherine of Aragon even after the latter's banishment from court. The couple boycotted Anne Boleyn's coronation in 1532, but the king responded by obtusely choosing Gertrude as godmother to Princess Elizabeth the following autumn. She also had to deputise at the last minute for the Marchioness of Dorset as godmother at Prince Edward's christening.

Amazingly, Gertrude also kept up a correspondence with Eustace Chapuys, the Imperial Ambassador, acting as one of his chief sources of information and visiting him in disguise. In 1536 she was the first to inform Chapuys that the king had tired of Anne Boleyn. Clearly she was dedicated to the conservative cause! In late 1538, she was arrested with her husband and son, Edward, and sent to the Tower. The Marquess was beheaded, but Gertrude and her son languished in prison, accused of treasonable correspondence with Chapuys. She briefly shared accommodation with Margaret Pole in the Tower, before being pardoned and released in 1540 (Margaret was not so lucky – see **Warblington**).

When her old friend, Mary, acceded to the throne in 1553, Gertrude was made lady-in-waiting and her son freed. At one stage Edward was considered as a possible husband for Mary, but Philip of Spain prevailed.

On the **south side of the chancel** is a fine **tomb chest** for <u>John Beaufort, 1st Duke of Somerset (1404–44)</u> and his wife <u>Margaret Beauchamp</u> of Bletsoe, Bedfordshire. They were the parents of Lady Margaret Beaufort, and thus grandparents of Henry Tudor.

The duke, in turn, was the grandson of John of Gaunt and Katherine Swynford. He returned from the French Wars in Normandy in 1443 with his reputation under a cloud, and may have taken his own life. His duchess remarried, but arranged for her daughter to be brought up in the household of her first husband's family, the St Johns of Bletsoe (see **Bletsoe**).

EAST OF ENGLAND

BLACKMORE, Jericho Priory ★★

Located 4 miles north-west of Ingatestone. The church is at the end of a cul-de-sac at the southern tip of the village.

This charming church was originally the basis of a priory established in Norman times. Its **timber tower** is very unusual, and much praised by Pevsner as perhaps the most impressive timber church tower in England.

Sometime in the 1510s, Henry VIII took out a lease from the priory on a house right by the church. The house was called 'Jericho', perhaps because the village stream was known locally as the River Jordan. It soon became common knowledge to courtiers that Jericho was Henry's 'love nest'. Surprisingly, the king only rented this property, despite having so many of his own royal palaces. Perhaps he wanted to keep the project well and truly under wraps? It is known that, when he visited the house, he took with him a very small household who were under strict rules of non-engagement with him during the stay. When asked where Henry was, courtiers left behind in London would answer that he had 'Gone to Jericho!'

Coming to Jericho, in early 1519, was Elizabeth (or Bessie) Blount, who had become Henry's mistress in 1514. She stayed several months, and in the spring gave birth here to a boy named **Henry Fitzroy, (later Duke of Richmond and Somerset)**. The matter was arranged by Cardinal Wolsey, who became the boy's godfather. The king visited a number of times and, later, formally acknowledged the boy as his illegitimate offspring. The affair with Bessie seems to have ended after this

The site of Jericho Priory, where Henry Fitzroy was born.

time, although Henry was instrumental in arranging a good marriage for Bessie to Gilbert Tailboys. (See **South Kyme**, **Kinlet** and **Framlingham**.)

Enjoy the lovely church, take in the **Jericho name plate** on the much later rebuilt house and walk round the remains of the medieval **moat** fed by the 'Jordan'. It's a charming spot, but go in summer.

The priory was dissolved early in 1527, by which time Henry had established New Hall just the other side of Chelmsford in a similar role (see **Boreham**). Enjoy a pint at the nearby 'Leather Bottle' or even browse at 'Jericho Antiques'.

BLETSOE, St Mary's Church ★
Set in the village centre, east of A6 Bedford–Kettering road.

Lady Margaret Beaufort, Henry Tudor's mother, was born at Bletsoe Castle just north of this church (nothing in-period remains). Bletsoe was the home of the St John family, into which Lady Margaret's mother, Margaret Beauchamp, had first married. When her second husband, John Beaufort, Duke of Somerset died in 1444 (probably by his own hand), Lady Margaret was brought up with her St John half-siblings.

By the **north nave door** is a fine alabaster **monument** to Sir John St John (c. 1495–1558) and his family – probably his first wife, Margaret Waldegrave (d. c. 1525), plus five sons and four daughters carved on the tomb. Sir John was the son of Sir John

senior, who was one of the half-siblings above brought up with Lady Margaret Beaufort. Sir John junior led a conventional life as a rural squire, being MP for Bedfordshire from time to time, serving ably as a soldier in France and attending at court on the big occasions – he attended the coronation of Anne Boleyn, the christening of Prince Edward and the funeral of Jane Seymour. He also helped to receive Anne of Cleves at Blackheath. He is also described as '*custos* to Princess Mary', although no detailed source confirms or explains that title. In fact, he was closer to Princess Elizabeth but died too soon after her accession to take advantage.

The charming tomb of Sir John St John at Bletsoe.

BOREHAM ★★

St Andrew's Church
Boreham is 5 miles north-east of Chelmsford, south of the A12 Colchester road. The church is at the southern edge of the village on a minor road.

In the **Sussex Chapel** lies a large **tomb chest** which commemorates three genera-tions of Ratcliffe Earls of Sussex, and which dates back to the late sixteenth century. The **effigy** of <u>Sir Robert Ratcliffe, Lord Fitzwalter and later, Earl of Sussex (c. 1483–1542)</u> lies in the centre of the tomb.

The Ratcliffes were diehard Yorkists. Robert's grandfather was killed at Ferrybridge just before the Battle of Towton, whilst his father was executed in 1496 for his part in the Perkin Warbeck fiasco. Robert served Henry VII and Prince Arthur, being present at the latter's wedding to Catherine of Aragon in 1501. He regained his father's lands and title, and then married extremely well to Elizabeth Stafford, sister to the Duke of Buckingham. He was Lord Sewer at the coronation of Henry VIII. His wife was lady-in-waiting to Catherine of Aragon, and became embroiled in the affair of her sister, Anne, Lady Hastings, with the king. She witnessed the row between the king and the Duke of Buckingham, her brother. Elizabeth was banned from court for a while as a result.

Lord Robert was a soldier who fought in France. He was very close to the king at this time, and an ally of the Boleyns, and supported the divorce. He again served as Lord Sewer at the coronation of Anne Boleyn. In 1536, he even proposed to the Privy Council that King Henry should nominate the illegitimate Henry Fitzroy as heir, ahead of Princess Mary.

His wife had died in 1532, so Robert married Margaret Stanley, daughter of the Earl of Derby, by whom he had two daughters. He had had three sons by his first wife, and was to have two more by his third wife, Mary Arundell. Oddly, the monu-ment does not focus on the wives, although they continued in the traditional roles of ladies-in-waiting to Jane Seymour, Anne of Cleves and Katherine Parr.

In 1540, Lord Robert was made Lord Great Chamberlain, head of the royal house-hold, in which role he had to brief Katherine Howard on the etiquette required when meeting her predecessor, Anne of Cleves. The other two **effigies** on this tomb relate to Robert's son, Henry, and grandson, Thomas.

New Hall
New Hall is a school, which can be viewed externally from the entrance drive. It is 3 miles north-east of Chelmsford and 1½ miles north-west of Boreham village. Access is via a drive which turns off the A130 northern ring road for Chelmsford, just before it crosses the A138 feeder road from Chelmsford to the A12 (access from the carriageway going south-east only).

Beaulieu or New Hall Palace at Boreham.

Henry VIII bought this property in 1516–17 from Thomas Boleyn, Anne's father, and proceeded to lavish £7.5 million (in today's money) on converting it into a full-scale royal palace in the Tudor brick style, with eight courtyards. Intriguingly, he renamed it 'Beaulieu', the same name as the palace in Bewdley, Shropshire, used by Prince Arthur until his death in 1502.

In 1522, he appointed William Carey, husband of Mary Boleyn, as keeper of Beaulieu. It had something of a reputation as a 'love nest', because Henry stayed here in July 1527 for a month with his new passion, Anne Boleyn. Presumably, Carey's role was to ensure discreet but total security. During this stay, the king was joined by a select group of nobles (Norfolk, Suffolk, Exeter, Fitzwalter, Rutland, Rochford, Oxford and Essex but *not* Wolsey) for a planning session on the Great Matter – for the first time, Wolsey was excluded from the centre of power.

By 1530, the palace was considered dated, and downgraded. It became the residence of Princesses Elizabeth and Mary, under the control of Sir John Shelton. Sir John's wife, Lady Anne (*née* Boleyn), was instructed to ensure a strict regime for Mary. (See **Shelton**.) From 1533, the house was leased to George Boleyn, Anne's brother; Elizabeth I sold New Hall to the Earl of Sussex in the 1560s, who rebuilt it in contemporary style. The **south facade** remains from this period.

BUCKDEN, Palace ★★

Found in the village centre, just north of the parish church and east of A1 bypass.

A fine survival of the medieval palace of the Bishops of Lincoln. Originally built in the thirteenth century, much remains of the late fifteenth-century brick additions of the outer and inner **gatehouses** and the **Great Tower**. Now run as a Catholic College, visitors are welcome to walk around the grounds.

In July 1533, **Catherine of Aragon** had still not accepted that she was no longer Queen of England, despite visits by members of Henry VIII's council (she had been banished to Ampthill, Bedfordshire). As Anne Boleyn had been crowned on 1 June, Henry became increasingly frustrated. At the end of July he ordered Catherine to be moved from Ampthill to Buckden. Buckden was further from London, and was situated close to the Great Ouse and the edge of the Fens, with a harsh climate.

Her entourage was lodged in a corner turret of the **Great Tower**. The site had a substantial moat, and lay in a remote area – to all intents and purposes Catherine was imprisoned, and visitors were forbidden by the king. By December, Catherine's health began to suffer in the damp conditions, so Princess Mary requested that she be moved to a better site. Henry proposed the old Yorkist stronghold of Fotheringhay but Catherine refused, knowing it to be in rundown condition. At this, Henry despatched Charles Brandon, Duke of Suffolk with a force to escort her to Fotheringhay. On their arrival at Buckden, a furious row broke out and Catherine locked herself in her room. Suffolk could not risk injury or worse to the aunt of the Holy Roman Emperor so, instead, tried to insist that Catherine was not referred to as the queen by her household.

Meanwhile, local people began to gather outside the palace in silent, but in some cases armed, protest in favour of Catherine. Suffolk was forced to stay there until 31 December 1533, when he departed empty-handed. Catherine found her rooms stripped and most of her servants gone. She stayed there for the rest of the winter until, in April 1534, Henry moved her to **Kimbolton Castle**, only 4 miles away but in a more congenial location.

BURY ST EDMUNDS, St Mary's Church ★★

In the town centre, near the cathedral and abbey ruins.

In the **chancel** of Bury St Edmunds' parish church lies a **tomb chest** of **Mary Tudor, sister to Henry VIII and Dowager Queen of France**. Initially, Mary was buried in the nearby St Edmundsbury Abbey but, at the Dissolution a few years later, her tomb was moved here. She and Henry had not seen eye-to-eye ever since Anne Boleyn had come into royal favour. On her deathbed she was reconciled to her brother, but Henry does not seem to have allocated much money for her tomb. Consequently, her funeral monument here is modest by contemporary standards –

after all, she was Dowager Queen of France (although it is still a lot more lavish than Henry's – see **Windsor**).

The **east end of the south aisle window** contains glass donated by Queen Victoria, which depicts the story of Mary Tudor's betrothal to the King of France and her second marriage to Charles Brandon. (Her biography is summarised under **Westhorpe**.) Brandon was buried at Windsor.

Note also the **tomb chest** and **effigies** to Sir Robert Drury, a counsellor and Knight of the Body to Henry VII and Henry VIII.

CAMBRIDGE ★★★
A city centre walk. King's Parade, St John's Street and Sidney Street.

Find your way to King's Parade at the heart of the university. Head north to find **King's College Chapel**, one of the glories of medieval England. Founded in 1441 by the pious Henry VI, with links to Eton College, the chapel was not completed until 1515 because of funding problems. After his victory at the Battle of Towton in 1461, Edward IV stopped all work until 1477. Richard III provided funds, but then Henry VII stopped work again until 1508. It was left to **Henry VIII** to complete the job.

Not surprisingly, the chapel is really as much a celebration of the Tudor triumph as of Henry VI its founder. It is festooned inside and out with **Tudor emblems** – Tudor roses, red dragons, portcullises (the emblem of **Lady Margaret Beaufort**, Henry VII's mother) and the crown in the thorn bush from Bosworth battlefield. There is original **stained glass**, said to be of **Henry VIII** and **Queen Katherine Howard**, thus dating the work rather precisely.

Return to King's Parade and head further north, up Trinity Street and St John's Street to **St John's College**. Note the splendidly elaborate heraldic carving on the sixteenth-century **gatehouse**. The carving came from Queens' College. St John's College was founded posthumously by **Lady Margaret Beaufort** in 1511.

Turn right down Bridge Street and Sidney Street to **Christ's College**, which was re-founded by **Lady Margaret Beaufort** in 1505. Once again, the **gatehouse** is covered in an enormous coat of arms resplendent in Lady Margaret's devices. She was indeed a friend to Cambridge.

CASTLE HEDINGHAM, St Nicholas's Church ★
Located in the village centre.

Castle Hedingham, a fabulous late Norman keep (which survives), was the principal residence of the de Vere Earls of Oxford, whose lineage went back to the Conquest. The 13th Earl, John de Vere (*c.* 1443–1513), was Henry Tudor's principal commander at Bosworth, whose skills in leading the vanguard against the Duke of Norfolk were crucial in ensuring victory. He subsequently carried out significant rebuilding in this church, providing the **hammer beam roof** and the frieze of shields above the **west window** outside the church, which include his **emblems** (a boar and a star) and his chain of state as Lord Great Chamberlain.

Inside the church, on the **north side of the sanctuary**, is a black marble **tomb** which commemorates another John de Vere (*c.* 1482–1540), 15th Earl of Oxford and his second wife, Elizabeth Trussell. This earl was also a soldier fighting for Henry VIII at the Battle of the Spurs in 1513. As hereditary Lord Great Chamberlain from 1526, a largely ceremonial, but important, post managing the Palace of Westminster, de Vere got to attend most of the great events of the reign – he bore the crown at Anne Boleyn's coronation; later, he served on the commission which tried the queen; he attended the christening of Prince Edward in 1537 (he was said to be the first Protestant Earl of Oxford); followed by the funeral of Jane Seymour. He was in the King's retinue at the reception for Anne of Cleves on Blackheath in early 1540. But, the holder of this most prestigious of earldoms was unable to contribute much to the government of the country during the reign, just like so many of his fellow peers.

You may wish to visit the splendid Norman **castle** where the earls of Oxford lived, just up the hill from the church.

COGGESHALL, Paycocke's ★ £
In the village centre. (NT)

This lovely **Tudor house** was built in 1509, as a home and showroom for Thomas Paycocke, a wealthy clothier. Pevsner describes it as 'one of the most attractive half-timbered houses of England'. It provides a fine example of mid-Tudor middle-class architecture. There are **brasses** of Paycocke's descendants in the nearby parish church.

DUNSTABLE, St Peter's Church ★★
In the town centre, on A505 road to Luton, just east of the major crossroads with A5, London–Milton Keynes road.

One of the joys of visiting historic sites occurs when a site far exceeds expectation. I came to Dunstable parish church thinking only of the prosaic Bedford vans which used to be made in this town, and was therefore totally unprepared for this ex-priory church, built in the late twelfth century in the glorious late Norman style. Despite the loss of two towers over the centuries much of the structure remains, particularly the **west front**. The other priory buildings do not survive, with the exception of a **gatehouse** south-west of the church.

Paycocke's house in Coggeshall.

The stunning Dunstable Priory, where Archbishop Cranmer held court.

The church is worth visiting in its own right, but the particular reason for coming here is because, on 10 May 1533, Archbishop Cranmer convened a special ecclesiastical court to consider the annulment of Henry VIII's marriage to **Catherine of Aragon**. One of the most important steps in the English Reformation was held in the **Lady Chapel** of this church. The bishops of London, Winchester (Gardiner), Lincoln (Longland) and Bath sat with him in judgement.

At the time, Catherine was residing at Ampthill, just 6 miles away. Cranmer summoned Catherine to the court, but she would not recognise his authority to take judgement on the case and refused to attend. Cranmer declared her contumacious (disobedient to authority) and proceeded anyway. After considerable discussion, Cranmer announced the verdict of the court on 23 May: the marriage was declared null and absolutely void, and contrary to divine law, thus making it inappropriate for the Pope to dispense in the case. Five days later, Cranmer reviewed the marriage of Henry and Anne Boleyn and, at Lambeth Palace, in contrast, pronounced it to be good and valid. After six long years Henry had got what he wanted, but only by having taken some big steps along the way! Anne was crowned on 1 June, and by July the Pope had annulled all proceedings at Dunstable and would have excommunicated Henry had not Catherine stopped him.

FELSTED, Holy Cross Church ★★
In the village centre.

A large standing **wall monument** commemorates Richard, Lord Rich (c. 1496–1567), universally recognised as one of the most unscrupulous men of the Tudor era. Unfortunately he rose to be Lord Chancellor!

A protégé of Audley and Cromwell, he became Solicitor General in 1533 and his evidence against Fisher and More, obtained through trickery and betrayal, was crucial to their conviction and execution. He also played a major part in the downfall of Cromwell, his erstwhile mentor. From 1536, he played a large role in the Dissolution of the Monasteries, enriching himself at the same time. On the death of Catherine of Aragon, he advised Henry VIII on how he might legitimately lay his hands on her possessions, even though they were divorced. In 1539, he was appointed as Groom to the Privy Chamber, and went to Calais to greet Anne of Cleves.

Rich's *pièce de résistance* was, however, in 1546 when, as Solicitor General, he personally took part in the only recorded racking of a gentlewoman in the Tower – the evangelical Anne Askew. Along with Wriothesley, Secretary of State, he apparently took his turn at the wheel!

In his private life, Rich was conventionally Catholic and had fifteen children with his wife, Elizabeth Jenks. Perhaps to atone for his 'mistakes' in his career, Rich endowed a school in the village. From the church door, go under the arch in the

Leez Priory, near Felsted – a delightful wedding location built on the ill-gotten gains of Richard Rich.

house opposite onto the road. Turn around, and you will see a **plaque** on the **Old School House** recording Rich's benefaction.

But this extremely wealthy man wasn't finished yet! Take the B1417 Chelmsford road and, after 2 miles, turn left to **Leez Priory** (signposted). In the remains of the priory Richard, Lord Rich built a full-scale Tudor house around 1540. Much of the house survives as a fabulous memorial to a dreadful man. There are two gatehouses, ranges and barns. The property is in use as a wedding venue, but access can be obtained from reception. A fantastic wedding location for any couple interested in history.

FRAMLINGHAM ★★★★

St Michael's Church
In the village centre, up the hill.

On the **north** wall of the **chancel** is the **tomb chest**, with **effigies** of Henry Howard, Earl of Surrey (c. 1516–ex. 1547) and his wife Frances de Vere (1516–77). This magnificent tomb reflects Surrey's character – there is no more colourful character in this book.

The eldest son of the 3rd Duke of Norfolk and Elizabeth Stafford, Henry Howard should have had a long career as England's premier duke. However, he was different – for a start, he was one of England's foremost poets, but he was also unstable, hot-tempered and wild. He began well enough – as a youth, Henry VIII chose him as companion for his illegitimate son, Henry Fitzroy. They remained firm friends, both attending the execution of Anne Boleyn.

The king held young Howard in high regard and, after Fitzroy's early death, seemed to transfer some of his paternal affection to him. However, Surrey's intemperate behaviour got the better of him and he was imprisoned at least twice – once for

The tomb of Henry Fitzroy and his wife Mary Howard at Framlingham.

The funeral helm of the 2nd Duke of Norfolk at Framlingham. He was the victor of Flodden.

punching Edward Seymour, Lord Hertford, in the face during an argument, and once for being drunk and disorderly in London with friends, behaviour unbecoming of a leading nobleman. Surrey had, however, developed a reputation as a brave and effective, if somewhat reckless, soldier. He led the army in France until 1546, when he was recalled because he had lost fourteen captains in the siege of St Etienne. He was replaced by Edward Seymour, by now very much his rival at court.

Through his Stafford mother, daughter of the Duke of Buckingham, Surrey possessed royal blood from Edward III's youngest son, Thomas of Woodstock. This seems to have made him arrogant and, in the final years of Henry's reign, drove him to covet the regency of Edward VI. He even went as far as applying to the College of Arms to quarter his arms with those of Edward the Confessor. Obviously a gesture towards his royal ancestry, but a strange one, since the saintly Edward very famously had no children or other descendants. Was it a cryptic reference to Henry VIII's reproductive problems? Mock-ups of the proposed arms were found in Surrey's house near Norwich.

Betrayed by his own supporter, Sir Richard Southwell, and by his own sister, Mary, who had been married to Henry Fitzroy but with whom he had fallen out, Surrey was finally dumped by his father, the 3rd Duke, in order to save his own skin. He was executed on Tower Hill in January 1547, just days before the king died. His father survived. Surrey was married in 1532 to Frances de Vere, daughter of the 15th Earl of Oxford, a prestigious but impecunious earldom. She was a lady-in-waiting to Anne Boleyn. They had five surviving children, of whom Thomas became the 4th Duke.

High up on the **south wall** of the **chancel** is the funerary **helm** of the 2nd Duke of Norfolk, who was the victor over the Scots at the Battle of Flodden in 1513 (see **Thetford**). Below the helm is the fine early Renaissance **tomb chest** and **effigies** of **Thomas Howard, 3rd Duke of Norfolk** and his wife, Anne Plantagenet (1446–1510). Thomas played a major part in Henry VIII's reign and Anne was a daughter of Edward IV, and had four children, though none survived.

To the **left** of the **altar** is a **tomb chest** with **effigies** of **Henry Fitzroy, Duke of Richmond and Somerset** and his wife Lady Mary Howard (1519–56). Fitzroy was Henry VIII's only acknowledged illegitimate son, whose mother was Elizabeth Blount, a member of Catherine of Aragon's household (see **Kinlet** and **South Kyme**). In a match brokered by Anne Boleyn, he was married in 1533 to Mary Howard, daughter of the 3rd Duke of Norfolk, yet further indication of the close ties between Henry VIII and the Howards. Mary was a lady-in-waiting to her cousin, Anne Boleyn, and may have had a similarly lively character. At any rate, she fell out with her brother, Henry Howard, and dropped him in it when arrested in 1546. Intriguingly, Fitzroy and Mary were forbidden to consummate their marriage (by the king?).

Fitzroy was originally buried secretly by the Duke of Norfolk, in Thetford, on the king's orders. Henry then changed his mind and castigated Norfolk for not giving Fitzroy a funeral in keeping with his status! His remains were moved here after the Dissolution.

1 *Henry VIII as a young man. (Getty Images)*

2 Henry VIII in his prime. (Getty Images)

3 Queen Catherine of Aragon. (Royal Collection Trust)

Anna Bollein Queen.

4 Queen Anne Boleyn. (British Library)

5 *Queen Jane Seymour by Holbein.*

6 *Queen Anne of Cleves by Holbein.*
(Getty Images)

7 *Queen Katherine Howard. (Royal*
Collection Trust)

8 Queen Katherine Parr.
(National Portrait Gallery)

9 Katherine Parr in stained glass in the chapel at
Sudeley Castle.

10 The Tudor Royal Family – an allegory of the succession. (Getty Images)

11 The haunting ruins of Cowdray House.

12 The splendid Deal Castle, built by Henry VIII.

13 The west frontage of Hampton Court.

14 *The royal arms outside the Chapel Royal, Hampton Court.*

15 *Henry VIII in procession. (British Library)*

16 Just the right sentiment from London Transport.

in confpectu fanctorum tuorum
patri S icut erat.

17 Henry VIII and his fool, the mysterious Will Somers. (Getty Images)

18 *Sir Philip Hoby at Bisham church.*

19 *Lady Elizabeth Hoby, wife of Sir Thomas.*

20 The east wing of Iron Acton Court, built especially for a visit from Henry and Anne Boleyn.

21 Lord Rich's tomb at Felsted: magnificent in death but certainly not so in life.

22 *Exquisite tomb of Henry Howard, Earl of Surrey, and his wife, Frances de Vere, at Framlingham.*

23 *Probably a copy of Tudor stained glass at Stanford-on-Avon.*

24　Original stained glass of the Shelton family, including Lady Anne (née Boleyn).

25 *The wonderful Golden Chapel at Tong.*

Castle £

Just east of the church. Signposted. (EH)

This fine medieval castle was home to the earls and dukes of Norfolk from the twelfth century, and has much stonework remaining.

The Howard dukes tended to move their power base northwards into Norfolk, perhaps so that they could be more securely surrounded by their tenants and supporters. The 3rd Duke based himself at Kenninghall in Norfolk, which is a long way from anywhere! After the attainder of the 3rd Duke in 1546, Henry VIII's will gave Framlingham to Princess Mary. It was at this castle that she raised her standard on Edward VI's death in July 1553, having left Hunsdon in a hurry. On 15 July, she rode out from here to make her successful bid for the throne against John Dudley, Duke of Northumberland.

There are a number of features within the castle which are of interest – the **gatehouse**, rebuilt at the beginning of the sixteenth century by <u>Thomas Howard, 2nd Duke (1446–1524)</u>; in the Inner Court, the **Tudor Room**; the **Chamber Block** where **Princess Mary** is reputed to have resided during her stay in July 1553; and the **Chapel**. The 2nd Duke died here in 1524, and his coffin lay in this chapel prior to his burial at Thetford Priory (see **Thetford**). He was immensely popular, and over 900 mourners are said to have accompanied the hearse on its two-day journey to Thetford.

GREAT HALLINGBURY, St Giles Church ★★★

Located 2 miles south-east of Bishop's Stortford across M11. Access is from Birchanger Services junction. From the roundabout, take B1256 east to Takeley. Take the first right on a minor road to Great Hallingbury. The church is on the right towards the end of the straggling village.

This charming church has eleventh-century origins, and unusually incorporates Roman bricks in the chancel arch. It is thought that the present church is built on a Roman religious site. In medieval times, it was the mausoleum of the Parker family, Lords Morley, and there was a Morley monument on the north wall of the nave. When the church was enlarged in the nineteenth century this monument was removed, but some of the **tablets** and **inscriptions** were relocated to the **choir vestry**. Two of these tablets relate to <u>Sir William Parker (d. 1510)</u> and his wife, <u>Alice Lovell (d. 1518)</u>.

Sir William was a privy councillor to Richard III, and his standard bearer at Bosworth. Although not attainted by Henry VII after that battle, he was never really trusted by the king – he appears to have suffered from periods of insanity which cannot have helped. In fact, there is a decidedly Yorkist flavour to the Parker family. In addition to Sir William, his father-in-law, William Lovell, was called to the House of Lords from 1469–71, during the reign of Edward IV. His son, Henry, married Elizabeth de la Pole, whose family were staunch supporters of Edward. Elizabeth's

tablet survives. Slightly surprisingly, therefore, Sir William's son, Henry, was brought up and educated by Lady Margaret Beaufort, mother of Henry VII. As a result, Henry Parker, Lord Morley (1476–1556) was later married to Alice St John (1486–1552), the daughter of John St John (see **Bletsoe**). The St Johns were descended from Lady Margaret's half siblings.

Alice's **tablet** survives in the church. It is known that Henry was also buried in the church and the **figure** of death displayed here may have been part of their monument. Young Henry showed academic promise, and went up to Oxford – paid for by Lady Margaret. He became a member of her household and of her inner circle for the last ten years of her life. She was instrumental in obtaining Henry a place in the household of the new king in 1509. In fact, as her cupbearer he accompanied Lady Margaret to Henry VIII's coronation feast in Westminster Hall in late June 1509, along with a carver (one of whose roles was usually to check the food before the aristocrat ate it). According to Parker, very soon after eating cygnet at the feast Lady Margaret was taken ill and retired to the precincts of nearby Westminster Abbey. Amidst much pain and weeping, here she died five days later. Poisoned? Or was it just bad luck? In his letters, Parker was quite up front about it being down to the cygnet. At any rate there is no suggestion that Parker, or the carver, were held to account for the death.

Whatever the cause of her death, Henry VIII was now monarch and head of his small family, all alone at the tender age of 18 years – he didn't seem too overawed! Subsequently, Parker spent much time on translation and literary work. In 1516, he was made gentleman usher to the king, but his involvement in court matters was sporadic – perhaps he suffered from bouts of mental illness as well? In 1523, he was ennobled by Henry VIII as Lord Morley, the title descending through his mother from her father, William Lovell.

In 1530, Lord Henry signed the letter from peers to the Pope requesting assent to the king's divorce; he also helped to carry Princess Elizabeth at the christening of Prince Edward in 1537 and attended the funeral of Henry VIII in 1547. He was a staunch Catholic, even keeping up very friendly relations with Princess Mary. Alice predeceased her husband, as did their son, Henry, largely because Lord Morley lived to the ripe old age of 80 years.

Unfortunately, there is one more Parker associated with this church, and this brings us to one of the most melancholic stories in this book. Henry Parker had two daughters, the elder of whom was Jane. Jane Parker (c. 1505–ex. 1542) is better known to history as Lady Rochford or Jane Boleyn. Before 1520, Jane joined the household of Catherine of Aragon and accompanied her to France at the Field of the Cloth of Gold. She took part in the celebrated Chateau Vert pageant, for Lent in 1522, as Constancy.

During 1524, her father undertook negotiations with Sir Thomas Boleyn for the marriage of Jane to George Boleyn, Viscount Rochford, Anne's brother. Sir Thomas (a grasping man) demanded an astronomic dowry of £90,000 in today's money, well outside Lord Morley's capability. Amazingly, the king made up the difference

– apparently not an unusual event! Agreement was reached and the wedding took place in late 1524, or during 1525. No record exists of the event, but the most obvious location is at this church (or at the chapel of nearby Hallingbury Place, the Parkers' principal seat). This proved to be one of the most infamous marriages in English history – George went to the block in 1536, found guilty of incest with his sister, Queen Anne, largely based on information supplied by his wife Jane. Jane herself followed in 1542, for her part in the downfall of Queen Katherine Howard.

George was extrovert, intelligent and fun-loving, and probably promiscuous, perhaps quite different from Jane's character. Whatever, the marriage does not seem to have worked – after eleven years there were no children. George was also a leading evangelical, along with his sister, Anne. Jane's motives could have been religious – her own beliefs are not known, but it is quite likely she followed her father's staunch Catholic views. The normal view is that she was driven by jealousy, because of the very close, and perhaps incestuous, relationship of George with his sister, the queen.

Jane had been a lady-in-waiting to her sister-in-law, Anne, and in 1534 Anne enlisted her support in heading off a new mistress of the king's. The gambit back-fired, and Jane was banned from court for a while. On her return in 1535 relations with Queen Anne were never as close. Jane's involvement in the downfall of Queen Katherine Howard was even murkier. She seems to have acted as some sort of go-between for the queen and her lover, Thomas Culpepper (see Katherine Howard).

HATFIELD, Bishop's Palace ★★

Situated south-east of Old Hatfield and the railway station. Signposted off A1000. It is possible to view the Old Palace before reaching the entrance booth for the main house.

In the 1480s, John Morton, Bishop of Ely, (1450–1500) built an early Tudor house here in Henry VII's reign, when he was Archbishop of Canterbury and a cardinal. A clever and determined man, he worked well with Lady Margaret Beaufort and had been a major figure in ensuring the Tudor triumph in 1485.

What survives is only about a quarter of the original building, but includes a splendid **gatehouse** and **hall**. Henry VIII liked the house and, sometime in the 1520s, took over the property. Catherine of Aragon was sent here for a short time in 1532. Henry undertook renovations so that, like nearby Hunsdon, it could be used for his children. From 1532 onwards, all three stayed here from time to time but the palace is most associated with **Princess Elizabeth**. Her household came here when she was 3 months old, under the management of Sir John Shelton. Elizabeth was here in 1557 when the news came through that her sister, Queen Mary, had died and therefore she was queen in her turn.

HUNSDON ★★

House

Located 1½ miles south of the village centre on the east side of a minor road to Harlow (via A414) which forks off B180 Stanstead Abbots road. The church is next to the road, with the house behind. (This is a private residence – it can only be glimpsed through the hedge.)

A house was built here in the mid-fifteenth century by Sir William Oldhall. Around 1525, **Henry VIII** purchased it from the Duke of Norfolk and rebuilt it as a royal palace. Much remains, including the **Tudor gatehouse**. Henry apparently bought the property as a retreat from the plague, because of its 'wholesome airs'. Certainly all three of his children lived here at one time or another. The house is most associated, however, with **Princess Mary** who was based here from 1527. It was from here that she launched her successful bid for the throne in 1553, as Edward VI lay dying in Greenwich. Deceiving John Dudley, Duke of Northumberland she headed northeast to her supporters in Norfolk.

St Dunstan's Church

In front of the house.

This church was rebuilt in the fifteenth and sixteenth centuries – sometimes in brick. In the **chancel**, **north side** is a **wall-mounted tomb** of Francis Poyntz (*c.* 1486–1528). He was a member of the royal household, which evacuated here to escape the plague in 1528. Unfortunately, he already had the disease and died at Hunsdon. He was Esquire of the Body, and carver, and was the younger son of Sir Robert Poyntz (see **Iron Acton**).

In the **south chapel** is a **wall monument** to Sir John Carey, 3rd Lord Hunsdon (d. 1617). He was the younger son of Henry Carey, who was ennobled by Elizabeth I. Henry was the son of Mary *née* Boleyn, and therefore Elizabeth's maternal cousin (see **Westminster Abbey**).

Note also the **east window**, which was installed by Sir William Oldhall in the mid-fifteenth century. Sir William was a prominent Yorkist at the beginning of the Wars of the Roses. He was Richard, Duke of York's military advisor and 'Mr Fix-it'. He was captured by the Lancastrians in 1459 and imprisoned. Without him, the Yorkist army was surrounded at the Battle of Wakefield the next year and Duke Richard killed. Oldhall disappeared from history's view around the same time.

INGATESTONE ★★★

St Edmund and St Mary's Church
In the town centre, on the High Street.

A splendid church with an imposing west tower in brick. Between the **chancel** and **south chapel** lies a fine alabaster **tomb chest** commemorating Sir William Petre (c. 1505–72) and his second wife, Anne Browne (d. 1582).

Sir William was a major figure in the government of England for more than thirty years, being Secretary of State under four monarchs from the mid-1530s until his retirement in 1566. He came from relatively humble origins – his father was a farmer and tanner in Devon – but attended Oxford University as a lawyer. There he became tutor to George Boleyn, Anne's brother, and through the Boleyns he met Thomas Cromwell. After a spell in France, by 1536 Petre had, in effect, become Cromwell's deputy and was much involved in the Dissolution of the Monasteries. This is how he acquired Ingatestone Hall.

In 1544 he was appointed one of two advisors to Queen Katherine Parr, when she acted as regent during Henry VIII's expedition to Boulogne. After Henry's death, Petre had the ability to twist and turn through all the crises of the reigns Edward VI, Mary I and Elizabeth I, managing to keep his head on his shoulders. He had something of a reputation as a negotiator – the Duke of Chatillon, a French diplomat, complained that their cause had been frustrated by 'the man who said nothing'. He has been described as the first civil servant.

Sir William's first wife, Gertrude Tyrell (d. 1541), lies next to his tomb, but is remembered only by a plain **floor slab**.

The tomb of Sir William Petre and his second wife, Anne Browne, at Ingatestone.

Ingatestone Hall, built in the 1540s.

Hall £

Situated 1½ miles south of the church. Head south for ½ mile towards A12 south. Take a left turn across the level crossing near the station. The Hall is ½ mile further, on a bend.

The manor of the nunnery of Barking Abbey came into the hands of <u>Sir William Petre</u> in 1539. By 1548, he had largely constructed this fabulous Tudor **house**, much of which is unchanged. It has interesting **portraits** and is altogether delightful.

IPSWICH ★★

The great **<u>Cardinal Thomas Wolsey</u>** rose from the ranks to be the second most powerful man in England in the 1520s. He was, of course, the son of an Ipswich butcher (actually, he was more probably a wealthy cloth merchant).

Cardinal College Gateway

In College Street, south of the town centre, at the bottom end of St Peter Street.

Unfortunately, the sparse remains of Wolsey's proposed college are in poor condition, and surrounded by dereliction and vehicular traffic. At the time of his death the college building was not finished, but the school was in full swing. Wolsey proposed an

Public house in Ipswich.

*The gate to Cardinal College,
built by Wolsey in Ipswich.*

institution linked to his Cardinal College at Oxford (now Christchurch) in the same way that Eton was linked to King's Cambridge – all came to nought with his abrupt fall. The **gatehouse** catches the eye. **St Peter's Church**, round the corner, was part of the college. See the arms of **Henry VIII** on the outside of the chancel.

Queen Street / St Peter's Street
In the town centre, south of Buttermarket shopping centre.

In this busy shopping street, there is a modern **statue** of Cardinal Wolsey in his pomp, and nearby, a **public house**, 'The Thomas Wolsey', in which to celebrate his unexpected rise to power and puzzle over his rapid demise.

KIMBOLTON, Castle ★★★ £
In the village centre. The castle is now a private school, but the premises are open to the public twice a year, in March and November (01480 861763).

This was a medieval manor house owned by the Duke of Buckingham. After his execution in 1521, it passed to the Crown. **Catherine of Aragon** was moved here, in May 1534, after she complained so bitterly about her previous accommodation at **Buckden**. Although only 4 miles away, Kimbolton lies on higher ground, further away from the dreaded Fens. Confined to one room, Catherine was, in effect, imprisoned with only a small staff and her gaolers, Sir Edmund Bedingfield and Sir Edward Chamberlain. Her food was prepared and then tasted for fear of poison. She established some kind of routine, revolving around prayers and needlework. In late 1535 she was taken seriously ill. She was visited by Chapuys, the Imperial ambassador, and by Maria de Salinas, Lady Willoughby, her old lady in waiting, but died on 7 January 1536. It is thought cancer of the heart was the cause.

The remains of the manor are encased in the current school building.

LAVENHAM ★

Guildhall of Corpus Christi £
In the village centre, on the market place. (NT)

Lavenham is a fabulous survival of a medieval building, most of which was built between 1460 and 1530, and provides the perfect example of Henrician middle-class housing. This guildhall was built right at the end of the woollen boom – within a generation, the village/small town was in depression.

St Peter and St Paul's Church
Located ½ mile south-west of the village centre, on B1115 to Sudbury.

This church celebrates the Tudor triumph at the Battle of Bosworth in 1485. It was much rebuilt in the late fifteenth century by <u>John de Vere, 13th Earl of Oxford (*c.* 1443–1513)</u>, in partnership with wealthy clothiers – particularly the extremely wealthy Spring family. The church and the spectacular **south porch** are festooned with the Oxford arms and emblems, and there is an Oxford **Chantry** with parclose screen.

LEIGHTON BROMSWOLD, St Mary's Church ★★
At the eastern end of the village street, 1 mile north of A14 Huntingdon–Kettering road and 3 miles west of Huntingdon. Best to turn off A14 on B660 north at Brington, and access Leighton from Old Weston on a minor road. (KAL)

Fortunately tucked away from the A14, this is a lovely spot with a nice pub.

In the **north transept** of the church are two much-battered **tomb effigies**. One commemorates <u>Sir Robert Tyrwhitt (*c.* 1504–72)</u> and his second wife, <u>Elizabeth *née* Oxenbridge (*c.* 1519–78)</u>. For once, we are more interested in the wife! Elizabeth, from Brede in East Sussex, married Sir Robert before 1539. She became a gentlewoman of Katherine Parr's privy chamber, and took up similar duties when Katherine became queen. She was known to Katherine through the latter's first

The battered effigy of Sir Robert Tyrwhitt at Leighton Bromswold.

marriage to Lord Borough. She had evangelical religious tendencies which matched easily with Katherine and she later published a book of prayers. She became a firm favourite of Katherine's along with Katherine's sister, Anne Herbert.

When the conservative faction at court tried to move against Katherine in 1546, Elizabeth and Anne were arrested and questioned, but Katherine talked her way out of trouble with the king. After Henry's death in 1547, Elizabeth and her husband stayed on with Katherine. Elizabeth was present at Katherine's deathbed a year later, after giving birth to her child with her new husband, Thomas Seymour. Elizabeth testified to the Privy Council on how, in her delirium, Katherine ranted against Seymour for long periods. The tone of delivery adopted by Elizabeth in her testimony indicated a strong dislike for Seymour.

Sir Robert was also employed by Katherine as Comptroller of her household, and later, Master of the Horse. He served in France on the military expedition of 1544. However, Sir Robert's first wife, Lady Bridget Wingfield (who is not buried here), is also of great interest. Sir Robert was her third husband, and she died in 1534. As Lady Wingfield, during her first marriage, she was lady-in-waiting to Anne Boleyn and had witnessed various 'goings-on'. In her deathbed ramblings in 1534, she referred to these and they were allowed as evidence two years later, at the trial of Anne Boleyn.

The other, much mutilated, effigy celebrates Lady Katherine Darcy (d. 1567), the daughter of Sir Robert and Lady Elizabeth, who predeceased her parents. After death, time has not been kind to this family.

LITTLE WALSINGHAM, Priory ★★★ £
In the village centre.

In the Middle Ages, the Priory of Our Lady of Walsingham was one of the most popular pilgrimage destinations in England. Kings like Edward IV had come here. It was also a favourite of Catherine of Aragon, who visited both before and after the birth of Princess Mary in 1516.

Its special significance in our story is that, immediately after the birth of Prince Henry on New Year's Day 1511, **Henry VIII** came here on pilgrimage to give thanks for the safe arrival of a son and heir. At the time, this would have been at least a two-week round trip, so Henry must have thought it sufficiently important to invest so much time at the height of winter. On Henry's return to London, the celebrations began in earnest with tournaments and pageants. It all came to nought, however, for on 22 February the baby prince died at Richmond Palace. How different might English history have been if this prince had survived? From this moment, Henry's Great Matter began to take shape.

In order to enjoy this important site the following itinerary is recommended:

Tudor architectural delights at East Barsham.

Take the B1105 north from Fakenham to **East Barsham**. Enjoy a pint in the White Horse Inn (or even stay there). Over the wall is a truly phantasmagorical **Tudor mansion**, built in the 1520s by Sir Henry Fermor, but unfortunately not open to the public – go in winter for the best view. Henry VIII stayed here when he came on pilgrimage and walked the two miles into Walsingham.

Visit **All Saints Church** next door, which is used by pilgrims. Next to the church take the minor road west, signposted to West Barsham. After 1 mile, turn right to North Barsham. Keep right in North Barsham, on Little Walsingham Road which becomes the old pilgrim route. Pass the Roman Catholic **Slipper Chapel**, where King Henry would have changed into slippers and walked the final mile into Little Walsingham. Cardinal Wolsey also came here on pilgrimage in 1517, after recovering from a bout of the sweat which had hit the country particularly hard that year.

Proceed to the centre of the village and enjoy the **ruins** of the medieval priory, which are sparse but very well kept. A peaceful spot.

NETTLESTEAD, St Mary's Church ★

Set in the depths of the Suffolk countryside, 4 miles south of Stowmarket. Turn off the A14 West at Stowmarket onto A1120 and then B1113 to Needham Market. Turn right here onto B1078 to Barking and Ringshall. At Barking Tye, take the minor road left to Offton and Somersham. At the beginning of Somersham, take the very minor road left for 1 mile to the hamlet of Nettlestead.

A charming spot, set in lovely countryside. **The Chace** next to the church was built on the site of the medieval hall of the Wentworths, lords of the manor since the fifteenth century. An **arch** from the hall is all that remains of the current building.

In the **nave** of the church is a **small floor brass** showing a medieval knight in armour. It is dated to around 1500, which fits well with <u>Sir Henry Wentworth</u>, who was lord of the manor until his death in 1499/1500. Sir Henry was the father of Margery Wentworth, wife to Sir John Seymour and mother to Jane Seymour, Henry VIII's third queen.

The Wentworths came from a Yorkshire family with strong Lancastrian sympathies (as had so many in Yorkshire). With Clifford and Ros blood from the female lines, plus a descent from Edward III's youngest son, Margery was quite a catch for the Seymours. Their powerful affinity was linked to the Duke of Suffolk. Sir Henry's Lancastrian father, Philip, had been executed after the Battle of Hexham in 1464, but Henry was married to Anne Saye who had a Yorkist background. Anne predeceased Henry, who then married Elizabeth Neville, niece of Warwick the Kingmaker, but there were no children of this union.

Henry and Anne's eldest son, Thomas, was made a peer in 1529 and was buried in Westminster Abbey on his death in 1550. Thomas Wentworth, Earl of Strafford, the ill-fated minister of Charles I, was also a direct descendant.

OXBOROUGH, Hall and St John's Church ★★★ £

Signposted off A134 Thetford–King's Lynn road, 2 miles north-east of Stoke Ferry. (NT) 01366 328258

This early Tudor moated house is a wonderful survival. Built from 1482 by Sir Edmund Bedingfield, Pevsner describes the gatehouse as 'tremendous'.

Originally a Yorkist, Sir Edmund managed to avoid Bosworth, and then joined Henry VII for the Battle of Stoke Field. After his death in 1496, his estates were held by his three sons successively. His third son, another <u>Sir Edmund Bedingfield (d. 1558)</u>, acted as Catherine of Aragon's 'gaoler' when Henry VIII moved her to Kimbolton Castle in 1535. She adopted a policy of non-cooperation with Sir Edmund and they didn't see one another for weeks. He was present when she died in early 1536.

He was married to <u>Grace Marney</u>, who was Chief Mourner at Catherine's funeral in Peterborough Abbey. There are similarities between this hall and Layer Marney Tower, in Essex, built by Grace's father and brother.

St John's Church stands outside the hall grounds, managed by the National Trust. It houses the splendid **terracotta monuments** to the first Sir Edmund and his wife, Margaret Scott, plus the **tomb** of <u>Sir Henry Bedingfield (d. 1583)</u>, who was the son of the second Sir Edmund above, and who followed into his father's line of work – he was Governor of the Tower of London in Mary I's reign and looked after Princess Elizabeth while she 'resided' there.

PETERBOROUGH, Cathedral ★★★★

In the city centre.

In the **north aisle** of the **nave** lies the reconstituted **tomb of <u>Catherine of Aragon</u>**, who died at nearby Kimbolton.

Following the divorce from Henry VIII, Catherine actually died not as a queen, but as Dowager Princess of Wales in recognition of her status as Prince Arthur's wife. In Henry's eyes, this did not warrant a London funeral and he ordered she be buried in the nearest great abbey – in fact, she probably deserved a more prestigious burial location within this church.

Perhaps as a late attempt at honouring Catherine, Henry granted cathedral status to Peterborough in 1541. So, when we admire the magnificent architecture and massive size of this late Norman/Gothic building, bear in mind that, for 400 years, it was not a regional centre of religion – it was just one of a fair number of great abbeys in England, alongside Gloucester, Tewkesbury, St Albans, nearby Thorney and Bury St Edmunds. In an agrarian society often struggling to keep starvation at bay, these institutions demanded the diversion of massive amounts of resources, both to construct and to maintain, and used income from monastic lands and the 'farming' of tithes from surrounding parishes and elsewhere. In 1536, this building would have appeared absolutely massive to the local population. The Dissolution of the Monasteries sprang out of this misallocation of resources and the perceptions surrounding it.

Catherine of Aragon's original tomb was despoiled during the Civil War.

The restored grave of Catherine of Aragon in Peterborough Cathedral.

SAFFRON WALDEN, St Mary's Church ★

Located at the north end of town, between the Cambridge and Linton roads, near the town museum.

This splendid church is a large and lavish testimony to the prosperity of this wool town in the late fifteenth and early sixteenth centuries. All the more reason to be disappointed that the **monument** commemorating a major English historical figure, Thomas, Lord Audley of Walden (c. 1488–1544), now resides tucked away in the vestry!

Audley was born at Earls Colne near Colchester. He became a barrister at Middle Temple and town clerk for **Colchester**, where he is commemorated with a **statue** on the **town hall** on the north side of the High Street. He was Speaker of the Commons 1529–33 and Lord Chancellor 1533–44, thus presiding over some of the most important legislation passed by Parliament in its history. What's more, he succeeded in dying in harness in his own bed – a real achievement during those turbulent decades.

His success was achieved at a cost though; the urbane Audley was seen as a king's man through and through. He supported the king's divorce, and marriage to Anne Boleyn, presiding at the trials of Fisher and More. He was also very much part of the downfall of Anne Boleyn, establishing the commission through which his lawyer friend/acquaintance, Cromwell, sought out 'evidence' and by passing the death sentence on Anne's 'lovers' in Westminster Hall. He was a witness at Anne's execution.

On the other hand, he presided over the trials of the conservative faction – the Marquess of Exeter and the Poles – in 1538. In 1540, he managed the passage of the parliamentary attainder against his old 'friend' Cromwell, and the dissolution of the king's marriage to Anne of Cleves. In 1542, he led the interrogation of the Duchess of Norfolk, while assembling evidence against Katherine Howard. So, a man very much at the heart of the events of our story, but who was a facilitator not policy instigator.

SALLE, Norfolk, St Peter and St Paul's Church ★

Located 1 mile north of Reepham. Access from B1145, Aylsham road. Turn left ½ mile north of Reepham, onto a minor road and turn left again.

This splendidly large and self-confident church stands today in a small hamlet. Unusually, it was built all of a piece in the Perpendicular style, 1400–30 (the magnificent tower came later in the century). At that time there was plenty of money in the parish from wool.

The Boleyns came from Salle, and it is most likely that Anne Boleyn's ancestors helped to fund the building work, along with the other three landowners in the parish. Two are recognised in the church – Thomas Boleyn (d. 1411), through an inscription in a **window**, and Geoffrey Boleyn (d. 1440) and wife Alice, whose **brass** lies in the **nave**. Geoffrey's son, another Geoffrey, was a mercer, and was so

Boleyn ancestor in Blickling church.

The church at Salle, home of the Boleyns.

successful that he became Lord Mayor of London in 1457. In 1459, he purchased two new properties – Hever Castle in Kent and nearby Blickling Hall. These two properties were both inherited by Thomas Boleyn, Anne's father, in 1505, and he chose to allow his brother, Sir James, to live at Blickling, preferring to use Hever because of its closeness to London.

Blickling is only 5 miles from here. It lies on the B1354 Aylsham–Saxthorpe road, and the hall is well signposted. Park for **St Andrew's** church, which affords a fine view of the Jacobean hall (no medieval survivals). St Andrews is another church of the Boleyns, containing three **brasses** of Anne's ancestors.

SHELTON, St Mary's Church ★★
Situated 2 miles south-east of Long Stratton, on a minor road, next to Shelton School.

This delightful and unusual brick church was the mausoleum of the Shelton family, who lived at the nearby Shelton Hall. It was built in the Perpendicular style by Sir Ralph Shelton and his heirs, from the late fifteenth century.

There are **tomb chests** and family **emblems** in the chancel, but our main interest is in the **stained glass** in the **east window**, some of which is original early sixteenth century. There are portraits of Sir Ralph and his wife Margaret Clere, and portraits of their son <u>Sir John Shelton (d. 1539)</u> and his wife, <u>Lady Anne Boleyn (1475–1555)</u>, Queen Anne's paternal aunt. Sir John certainly is buried in this church.

The delightful brick church at Shelton.

By July 1536, Sir John was Steward of the Household to Princess Elizabeth and Princess Mary at Hatfield. His wife had been governess to Princess Mary since 1533, with orders from Queen Anne to preserve a strict and harsh regime. In June 1536, Lady Anne had been one of four women appointed to attend Queen Anne in the Tower with instructions to record everything Anne said. None of the four were liked by Anne. It is not clear why relations between the two women were so bad (see **Boreham New Hall** and **Hatfield**).

Sir John and Lady Anne's son, another John (d. 1558), married Margaret Parker, sister of Jane Parker who married George Boleyn. One of John's sisters, Madge or Mary Shelton, was said to be Henry VIII's mistress in 1534/35, perhaps encouraged in the role by their cousin Queen Anne? These close connections between the three families were to have disastrous consequences the following year (see **Great Hallingbury**).

STANDON, St Mary's Church ★★★
Located at the village centre, south of A120, Bishop's Stortford road. On a minor road to Much Hadham.

The church is built on rising ground, so the inside is dominated by two **wall-monuments** in the **chancel**. These commemorate <u>Sir Ralph Sadler (1507–87)</u> and his son, Thomas (d. 1606).

Ralph was from a modest background and was a protégé of Thomas Cromwell. He became an ambassador and civil servant who spent much time on Scottish affairs, before becoming joint principal Secretary of State to Henry VIII with Thomas Wriothesley. He survived the fall of Cromwell, but was thrown into the Tower by the conservative faction in 1541, although he was released. He was replaced as Secretary in 1543, becoming Master of the Great Wardrobe.

In the will of Henry VIII, he was made a member of the Regency Council to Edward VI, and continued to contribute to national affairs right through to the reign of Elizabeth. He was also a fighting man, and had been present with Edward Seymour, Lord

The tomb of Sir Ralph Sadler at Standon.

Hertford, in 1547 at the Battle of Pinkie when the Scots were defeated. Sadler's **helmets**, **sword**, **spurs** and the **pole** from the Scottish standard make a fine addition to his monument.

As far as one can tell, Sadler seems to have been a nicer than normal Tudor gentleman. However, his private life was flawed. In 1533, he married Ellen Barre, a widow (*née* Mitchell). By the mid-1540s, they had seven surviving children when, suddenly, Ellen's first husband turned up – he had abandoned Ellen, gone abroad and had been thought dead. With some nimble footwork, Sir Ralph managed to get a private Act through Parliament, without publicity, which legitimised both his marriage to Ellen and the children.

It is not known when Ellen died, and she is not buried with Sir Ralph. However, their eldest son, Thomas, is commemorated by the other monument in the chancel. He was named after Thomas Cromwell. There were compensations for Sir Ralph who, at his death, was reputedly the wealthiest commoner in England.

Below the **chancel steps** can be found another memorial – there is an **indent** in the floor slab from where a brass, of <u>Sir William Coffin (or Cosyn c. 1495–1538)</u>, at some time was stolen. He was a prominent jouster and member of the Privy Chamber. He became Master of the Horse to Anne Boleyn and then Jane Seymour. In the 1520s he married a widow, Margaret Vernon *née* Dymocke, who was one of the four ladies who attended on Anne Boleyn while she was in the Tower (see **Haddon Hall**).

Return to the A120 and turn left across the River Rib. After ½ mile take the first left on the minor road to Barwick. After ¾ mile, you will arrive at the drive for **'The Lordship'**. This is a private house, but the drive is a public footpath down to the fine **Tudor property**. It was built in 1546 by <u>Sir Ralph Sadler</u> out of his burgeoning wealth.

THETFORD, Priory of our Lady ★★★

Situated ½ mile west of the town centre, north of the Little Ouse River. Turn sharp left off 'Old A11', going north just after the bridge. Signposted.

This book is full of hard-nosed, self-seeking and ruthless men on the make, but in the **ruins** of this priory church is buried someone who rose above that unattractive norm. Until the Dissolution, the priory was the burial site of the Mowbray and Howard Dukes of Norfolk. Here are buried John Howard, 1st Duke, killed at the Battle of Bosworth, and his son, <u>Thomas Howard, 2nd Duke (1443–1524)</u>. Thomas was given precedence in front of the altar because he was the victor at the Battle of Flodden in 1513. A **plaque** marks the spot. Thomas literally bounced into history in 1483, leading the small force that carried out Richard III's coup by rushing into the council chamber, arresting William, Lord Hastings, and nearly killing Thomas, Lord Stanley. The Howards, an ebullient lot led by father John, were granted the dukedom by Richard III, but suffered a reverse at Bosworth. After his father's death, Thomas saved the lives of himself and his men by ordering them to lay down their arms on the battlefield.

Henry VII reluctantly allowed Thomas to keep the family estates, but withheld the dukedom – he was known by the junior title of Earl of Surrey. Thomas, an experienced fighting man, made himself useful to both Henry VII and VIII. When Henry VIII departed for France in 1513, Howard was left behind to defend the northern border with Scotland under the regency of Catherine of Aragon. His stunning victory at Flodden fully restored the family fortunes including the dukedom, but more particularly destroyed the Scottish threat for a generation (see **Flodden**).

Thomas was hereditary Earl Marshal, and so occupied a key role in government. His sister, Elizabeth, became the wife of Thomas Boleyn and mother to Mary, Anne and George. By the early 1520s, the Howards had become the backbone of the regime of Henry VIII. Thomas was required to preside over the court that tried the Duke of Buckingham, his brother-in-law, for treason in 1521. He is said to have pronounced the death sentence with tears rolling down his face.

WESTHORPE, St Margaret's Church ★★
We are well away from it here – 8 miles north of Stowmarket and A14. Access the church via B1113 Stowmarket–Rickinghall (Diss) road. Heading north, turn left in Finningham on a minor road to Westhorpe. The church is at the western end of the village.

This village is proud of its links to **<u>Mary Tudor, Dowager Queen of France and Duchess of Suffolk</u>**, who was Henry VIII's younger sister. In the lovely old church is a modern **memorial** to her. She lived at nearby Westhorpe Hall from her marriage to Charles Brandon, Duke of Suffolk in 1515, until her death. They were frequently at court, at least in the early years, but could hardly have chosen a more remote location for their country property.

Mary was said to be Henry VIII's favourite sister – Henry was brought up with his sisters rather than with Prince Arthur, so they must have been close as children. After Arthur's death, Mary developed a friendship with Catherine of Aragon as well. As she got older, Mary was lined up to marry Charles of Castile, the eventual Holy Roman Emperor. All was planned for the spring 1515, when Henry fell out with Ferdinand of Spain. A treaty with the French was hastily put in place by Wolsey, and Mary was betrothed instead to King Louis XII of France, by now in his fifties. This brought the Boleyn girls to France in Mary's entourage.

Charles and Mary had three children. Frances, the elder daughter, became the mother of Lady Jane Grey, the 'Nine Day Queen' whose claim to the throne came from Mary. Fairly quickly, Mary developed an intense dislike of Anne Boleyn, and the Brandons began boycotting court from 1529 onwards. Unfortunately, Mary became terminally ill, but she was reconciled to Henry in a final letter to him. He was not

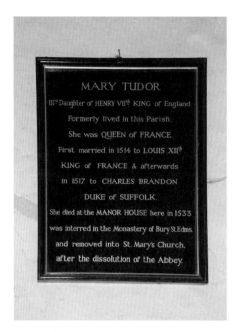

A modern commemoration of Mary Tudor, Henry VIII's sister, at Westhorpe.

so kind to her after death (see **Bury St Edmunds**). In his will, of late 1546, he did recognise Frances and her sister as potential heirs to the throne after his own children.

At the eastern end of the village is a small **green**. On the **northern** edge of this lies a care home which occupies the site of **Westhorpe Hall.** The access **bridge** is Tudor and the remains of **moats** can also be seen.

WINGFIELD, St Andrew's Church ★★

Wingfield is a small and dispersed village 2 miles west of Fressingfield. Take the turning out of Fressingfield to Hoxne. After 2½ miles, turn right across the stream to Wingfield. The church is up the hill on the right.

This is about as good as a rural site gets. Before the Reformation this was a collegiate church of the de la Pole Dukes of Suffolk, whose country seat was at nearby Wingfield Castle. The family rose to prominence in the fourteenth and fifteenth centuries as businessmen and financiers from Hull.

The 1st Duke, celebrated here in **stained glass**, dominated the government of the enfeebled Henry VI in the 1440s. He was murdered in a small boat in Deal Roads with a rusty sword as he tried to flee the country in 1450. His son, John de la Pole (1429–89) married Elizabeth Plantagenet (1444–1503), sister to Edward IV and Richard III, but he never really pulled his weight during the Wars of the Roses. Their lovely **tomb chest** survives.

Their son, another John, Earl of Lincoln, was made of sterner stuff and, after the death of Richard III's son in 1484, became Richard's heir presumptive. John junior became President of the Council of the North, based at Sheriff Hutton where a number of Yorkist notables were held under house arrest, including Elizabeth of York. John was killed at the Battle of Stoke in 1487 rebelling against Henry VII. After the battle, Henry seemed particularly keen to secure Lincoln alive but even his body could not be recovered. However, the de la Pole claim to the throne through Elizabeth was kept alive by Lincoln's younger brothers, right up until 1524.

EAST MIDLANDS

ASLOCKTON, Cranmer's Mound ★★
In the village centre, ¾ mile north of A52, 2 miles east of Bingham. The footpath is signed east for 300 yards from the church.

Aslockton is the birthplace of **Archbishop Thomas Cranmer** and the village is, rightly, proud of this connection. Virtually every amenity has a Cranmer prefix – the Cranmer Trail, Cranmer House (where his family lived), the Cranmer Centre at the church and the Cranmer Arms (worth a look). However, it is the much older Cranmer's Mound which interests us here. Situated in fields behind the church, this is in fact the surviving earthworks of a small **motte and bailey castle**, perhaps early post Norman Conquest. The motte and remains of a moat survive. Very good information boards are provided, and everything is done tastefully – well done Aslockton! A fine memorial to a man who made a real difference to England.

Cranmer's family were members of the gentry and his father's **effigy** survives in St John of Beverley's Church in the adjoining village of **Whatton**.

BOTTESFORD (Leicestershire), St Mary's Church ★★
Situated in the village centre, north of A52 Grantham–Nottingham road, and 400m west of the station.

The **chancel** of this immaculately kept church contains a treasure trove of monuments to the Manners family, Dukes of Rutland. We are interested in <u>Thomas Manners, 1st Earl of Rutland (c. 1488–1543)</u> and his second wife, <u>Eleanor *née* Paston (d. 1551)</u>, daughter of Sir William Paston and Bridget Heydon, both from well-known Norfolk families.

The Manners originated in Northumberland but, through highly advantageous marriages, in two successive generations had first become Lords of Ros (see **Windsor**) and then, in 1526, Thomas was made Earl of Rutland, the title held by Edward IV's younger brother, Edmund, who was cut down by the Lancastrians on Wakefield Bridge at the end of 1460. By contrast the Ros were diehard Lancastrians, so a nice balance was achieved. Thomas' maternal grandmother was Anne Plantagenet, Edward IV's elder sister, so Plantagenet blood flowed in these veins.

After the dissolution of the local monasteries in 1538, monuments were brought here from Croxton Abbey and Belvoir Priory. The Manners still live at nearby Belvoir Castle. Thomas, like his father, was a soldier and was much involved in the suppression of the Pilgrimage of Grace in both Lincolnshire and Yorkshire in 1536. In 1542, he accompanied the Duke of Norfolk on the invasion of Scotland. He also attended the Field of the Cloth of Gold. He was at the coronation of Anne Boleyn, but also sat in judgement at her trial in 1536. He was appointed Lord Chamberlain to Jane Seymour and, in 1539, he was similarly appointed Lord Chamberlain to Anne of

Cleves and met her at Shooters Hill outside London on her way from Dover. Later, he was appointed to the same position for Katherine Howard – he must have known much that would be of interest to us today!

Unlike other members of the upper aristocracy, he managed to keep out of trouble with the king – probably by being a reliable servant. He acquired lands from many monasteries in the Midlands and north, and became very wealthy. He died in his own bed.

BRADGATE, House ★★

Situated in Bradgate Country Park, 6 miles north-west of Leicester. From A46 northern bypass for Leicester, take the exit for Anstey north. Continue on a minor road to Newtown Linford and on to the car park (signposted).

This one is a little different. The ruins of the medieval house remain in their original park setting in beautiful countryside. Park your car and walk a mile or so through Little Matlock to the **ruins**. This gives you some idea of the scale on which the medieval aristocracy lived. The house was built at the end of the fifteenth and early sixteenth centuries by the father and son, Thomas Grey, Marquess of Dorset. Thomas Grey senior contrived the idea of moving his principal residence from nearby Groby, devised detailed plans and commenced building. His son completed the work.

Actually, the Dorsets were more important at this time for who they were, rather than for what they achieved. The senior Thomas was the elder son of Edward IV's queen, Elizabeth Woodville, from her first marriage to Sir John Grey who was killed at the Battle of Towton in 1461, fighting for the Lancastrians against Edward. Edward's choice of queen in 1464 thus baffled most of the nation!

Thomas got on well with his new stepfather, but gained a reputation as something of a womaniser in the company of the king and Lord Hastings. He was made Marquess in 1475 but, after Edward's death in 1483, he vacillated between Henry Tudor and Richard III. He tried to desert Henry's cause in France, but was prevented from so doing. Henry never really trusted him thereafter.

Thomas junior had a good start in life – he was tutored by Wolsey. However, he was imprisoned by Henry VII for supporting the de la Pole threat to the throne. Henry VIII released him, and he became something of a favourite at court because of his skills at the joust. Thomas took part, for example, in the joust in February 1501 to celebrate the wedding of Prince Arthur and Catherine of Aragon, and that of 1511 to celebrate the birth of the ill-fated Prince Henry.

He was also a soldier – he led the expedition to San Sebastian/Biarritz in 1512, which ended in fiasco when Ferdinand of Spain, Catherine's father, duped Henry VIII and didn't show up! Thomas escaped censure and joined Henry in France in 1513 and 1520. He became a gentleman of the Privy Chamber in 1523, and was made Lord of

Princess Mary's Council of Wales, but held no other household position. During the investigations into Catherine's and Prince Arthur's marriage he testified that, in his opinion, Arthur had been fit and healthy and the couple had indeed 'done the deed'. But really not a major contribution for a marquess.

When Thomas' son, Henry, inherited the powerful affinity in 1530 at an early age, a family tragedy began slowly to unfold. In 1533, Henry married Frances Brandon, the daughter of Charles Brandon, Duke of Suffolk and Henry VIII's sister, Mary Tudor. On religious matters, Henry turned out to be a reformer. He was chief mourner at Henry VIII's funeral and Lord High Constable at the coronation of Edward VI. Mary Tudor died in 1533, whilst Frances' brother, Henry Brandon, died the following year, aged 18 years. At a stroke Frances herself moved up in the succession stakes in the event that Henry VIII died.

In 1537 Frances gave birth to Lady Jane Grey (1537–ex. 1554), here at Bradgate. Jane was an intelligent and studious girl who, in the summer of 1553, was pushed forward by John Dudley, Duke of Northumberland as a Protestant successor to the dying Edward VI. She was married, much against her will, to his son, Guildford Dudley, in order to block the Catholic Mary Tudor. The attempt was doomed from the start, as the power of the Tudor brand name proved too strong. Lady Jane and Guildford were executed in July 1553 – she had ruled for just nine days. Jane's father, Henry Grey, went to the scaffold a year later for his part in Wyatt's rebellion against Mary – a true family disaster.

GAINSBOROUGH, Old Hall ★★★ £
Located in Parnell Street, on the north side of the town centre, near All Saints' Church.

If this building was located in, say, Buckinghamshire or Surrey it would be nationally famous. As it is, it represents something of a hidden gem – a remarkable survival of medieval architecture. Originally it was built around 1460 by Sir Thomas Burgh, one of Edward IV's favourites. In 1470, it was attacked and burnt down by the Lancastrians, but subsequently rebuilt. Adroitly, Burgh sided with Henry Tudor and was ennobled. His son, Edward was declared a lunatic, but his grandson, another Thomas Burgh (or Borough) (c. 1488–1550) escaped that fate and rebuilt the family's fortunes. He regained the peerage in 1529, and in 1533 was appointed Lord Chamberlain to Anne Boleyn. He rode in her coronation procession. However, in 1536 he was also one of twenty-six peers chosen to sit on the jury at Anne's trial.

In 1529, Thomas' son, another Edward Burgh (c. 1508–33), was married to **Katherine Parr**, as her first husband. Interestingly, recent research has revealed that Edward was not an old man at the time of the wedding as previously thought but, in fact, much of an age with Katherine. The couple lived here in the hall, but life proved to be somewhat tempestuous because of the rages of his father, Thomas. The couple

The spectacular Gainsborough Old Hall, where Katherine Parr lived during her first marriage.

moved out to Kirton-in-Lindsey to their own property. Edward himself may have suffered from mental illness, and there were rumours of homosexuality. He died in the spring of 1533.

GREEN'S NORTON, St Bartholomew's Church ★
On the northern edge of the village, 1 mile west of A5, Watling Street.

Green's Norton church provides a lovely celebration of the eponymous family which held sway here from the fourteenth to the sixteenth centuries. Maud Green married Sir Thomas Parr in 1508, perhaps in this church. They were the parents of Katherine Parr.

Maud's ancestors are buried here, including her parents <u>Sir Thomas Green (d. 1506)</u> and <u>Joan Fogge, daughter of Sir John Fogge of Ashford</u>. The **marble slab** from their tomb stands at the **east end** of the **south aisle** and Joan's **brass** is still in situ.

The Greens descended from Sir Henry Green of Boughton, who was Lord Chief Justice from 1361–65 (there were two branches of the family in Northamptonshire). Along with her sister Ann, Maud was co-heiress to Sir Thomas who, in an unusual manoeuvre, had joined forces with his stepfather, Nicholas Lord Vaux, and together they wooed and married the sisters. Clearly the Greens were wealthy indeed.

Although the Parrs hailed from Kendal in Cumbria, it is now thought that Sir Thomas and Maud more likely lived in the manor house here (nothing remains), as well as their town house in the Strand (See **Kendal**).

The church is proud of its Green connections, and provides a number of useful family trees.

GRIMSTHORPE, Castle ★★ £
Situated just west of the village centre and A151 Bourne–Colsterworth road. Signposted.

More of a pile than a castle!

In 1516, the manor was granted to Lord William Willoughby d'Eresby on his marriage to Maria de Salinas, compatriot and lady-in-waiting to Catherine of Aragon. On his death in 1526, their only daughter, <u>Katherine Willoughby (1519–80)</u>, inherited both the estate and title. **Charles Brandon, Duke of Suffolk** bought her wardship, and then caused a stir in 1533 by marrying her, then aged 14 years – he was 48 years old, and it was his fourth marriage!

Grimsthorpe became the principal residence of Brandon, who switched his focus to Lincolnshire, being very active in the suppression of the Pilgrimage of Grace. He quickly set about rebuilding the medieval house. The **south front** is still largely his Tudor rebuild, and can be viewed from the gardens. When Henry VIII announced that he would visit with his new queen, Katherine Howard, in the summer of 1541, Brandon had to hastily finish off the works. A meeting of the Privy Council was held here, in August 1541, during that ill-fated summer progress. It was said that Grimsthorpe was the only overnight stay when the queen did *not* sleep with one of her lovers!

When Brandon died in 1545, his wife, as Baroness in her own right, continued to live here with her second husband, Richard Bertie. She was an active religious reformer and Hugh Latimer preached here (see **Spilsby**). After the death of Katherine Parr in childbirth in 1548, her good friend, Baroness Willoughby, looked after her child, Mary Seymour, here at Grimsthorpe. Initial problems with funds were overcome, but Mary is lost to history – she is presumed to have died as a child (see **Sudeley**).

HADDON, HALL ★★★★ £
Located 2 miles south-east of Bakewell, on the A6 Matlock–Bakewell road. Signposted.

Set in delightful surroundings above the River Wye, this is a fourteenth-century castle with later modifications.

From around 1170 the property was owned by the Vernon family. <u>Sir Henry Vernon (d. 1515)</u> made many alterations, including the **Gate Tower**, the Tudor **dining room** and the **Great Chamber**. He was appointed chamberlain and treasurer to Prince Arthur in 1492. Although Arthur spent much time at Ludlow and Bewdley as he grew up, he also spent time at Haddon, certainly in 1501, presumably

Haddon Hall, home of the Vernons, which Prince Arthur regularly visited.

Henry VIII's fool, Will Somers. What is he doing at Haddon Hall?

before his wedding to Catherine of Aragon. **Prince Arthur** is reputed to have given a **tapestry** to the Vernons which hangs behind the dais in the **banqueting hall**. Tradition holds that a room was reserved here for the visits of the young prince.

The ceiling of the **dining room** depicts the Tudor Rose, the Talbot Dog and the coats of arms of the Vernon and Dymoke families. The dog celebrates Sir Henry's wife, Anne Talbot (d. 1494), daughter of the Earl of Shrewsbury. Margaret Dymoke (date of death not known) had married Sir Henry's son, Richard, who died in 1517. In 1536, Margaret was one of the ladies-in-waiting detailed to accompany Anne Boleyn to the Tower and report Anne's utterances to Sir William Kingston.

Above the **fireplace** are **carvings** of the Tudor Rose, the three feathers of the Prince of Wales and the letters 'EP' for Prince Edward, later Edward VI. In the **window recess** are carved portraits of **Henry VII** and his queen, **Elizabeth of York**, together with Will Somers (d. 1560). Somers was Henry VIII's last and much-loved court jester – it is most surprising to find him here!

HAINTON, St Mary's Church ★★★
Located 3 miles south-east of Market Rasen. Turn off A157 Lincoln–Louth road at Hainton on a sharp bend onto a minor road to Sixhills. Take the first left to the church.

This is a delightful site which needs more visitors. The Heneages have lived here since the Conquest, and still do in rural tranquillity. The church contains **Heneage Chapel**, where many of their ancestors are buried. In the **chancel** is a **tomb chest** with wall-mounted brasses to Sir Thomas Heneage (c. 1480–1553), his wife Katherine Skipwith (c. 1484–1575) and his daughter, Elizabeth (d. 1555).

Relatively late in life, Thomas became a member of Wolsey's household, based at Hampton Court. Alongside Russell, he became one of Wolsey's main court followers and, in 1528, Wolsey managed to get him a position in the king's Privy Chamber. Heneage developed a good relationship with Anne Boleyn, while becoming a Cromwell man. He was one of only three witnesses at the secret wedding of Henry and Anne in January 1533. He somehow managed to escape any implication in the downfall of Anne three years later, and indeed succeeded the ill-fated Henry Norris as Groom of the Stool (head of the Privy Chamber). He managed to hold on to this dangerous position for ten years, despite Cromwell's fall. In this role, he organised many key events such as the reception for Anne of Cleves at Blackheath and Katherine Parr's wedding to Henry.

Thomas' brother-in-law always maintained that the Pilgrimage of Grace started in this vicinity in 1536, when a mob attacked Heneage. But Sir Thomas is best known for his testimony at the enquiry into the annulment of Henry's marriage to Anne of Cleves, 'In so often that his Grace went to bed with her, he ever grudged and said plainly he mistrusted her to be no maid, by reason of the looseness of her breast and

The charming tomb of Sir Thomas Heneage, his wife Katherine and daughter Elizabeth at Hainton.

other tokens. Furthermore, he could have no appetite with her to do as a man should do with his wife, for such displeasant airs as he felt with her.' As so often is the case with Henry, we know too much detail, but really we know nothing!

HORTON, St Mary's Church ★

This hamlet is 6 miles south-east of Northampton on B526 to Newport Pagnell. The church is east of a sharp bend on B526, in the centre of the hamlet. The church is currently closed.

A **tomb chest** and **effigies** commemorate <u>William, Lord Parr of Horton (1483/84– 1546)</u> and his wife, <u>Mary Salisbury</u>. Mary brought Horton manor to the marriage as her dower, and her relations are also commemorated in **brass** nearby in the church. The couple had four daughters.

William was Katherine Parr's uncle and was the younger son of Sir William Parr of Kendal (a great favourite of Edward IV) and his second wife, Elizabeth Fitzhugh. Young William was a soldier who fought for Henry VIII in France but was also Esquire to the Body for both Henry VII and VIII. His elder brother, Sir Thomas (and Katherine's father), was a great favourite of Henry VIII but died of the sweat in 1517. William provided great support to his sister-in-law, Maud, who chose not to remarry. She lived at nearby Green's Norton.

During the 1520s he became chamberlain to Henry Fitzroy, Duke of Richmond and Somerset, Henry VIII's illegitimate son. Once his niece Katherine had married Henry in 1543, he was appointed chamberlain of her household, and was a member of her council when she acted as regent while Henry returned to France in 1544. Parr was ennobled in 1546, but the title died with him.

KNESSALL, Old Hall Farm ★
Located on the west side of the village, on a bend on A616 Newark–Ollerton road, across from the church.

It's not a lot, but a pleasant visit can be constructed by repairing to the farm shop next door which has a good cafe. Underneath a modern roof and windows survives a hunting lodge thought to have been built by <u>John, Lord Hussey (c. 1465–ex. 1536)</u>. It is now a private house.

John's father had been Lord Chief Justice, and the family came from Sleaford. He had opposed the rebels on Blackheath in 1497, was knighted and became Knight of the Body to Henry VII. Later, he became Chief Butler of England. He (together with his second wife, Anne Grey, daughter of the Earl of Kent) was appointed chamberlain of Princess Mary's household.

After Anne Boleyn's execution in 1536, Henry, perhaps surprisingly, moved against the conservative faction. Lady Hussey was arrested and imprisoned in the Tower, but soon released. Lord Hussey joined the rebels in the Pilgrimage of Grace in Lincolnshire, against his will he later claimed. He certainly did not oppose them as the king would have expected. He was tried by the court of the Lord High Steward under the Marquess of Exeter and found guilty, along with Lord Darcy. He was beheaded in 1537, but exactly where is unclear – Tower Hill, Lincoln or Sleaford. Exeter himself was to follow within eighteen months. Was Hussey's execution about the Pilgrimage of Grace, or suppression of the religious conservatives?

LAUNDE, Abbey ★★★
Set in the surprising rural charm of eastern Leicestershire, close to the Rutland border, 6 miles north-east of Uppingham. Approach on minor roads from Loddington from the south or Tilton-on-the-Hill from the west. Set in Launde Park, now a retreat for the diocese of Leicester.

During the Dissolution of the Monasteries, **Thomas Cromwell** earmarked Launde Priory for himself (his notebook survives). Work quickly started on building a house amongst the ruins of the priory. This **house**, although much modified, still stands and thus represents the only memorial to this important but controversial figure. Although he acquired twelve other dissolved properties, there is good reason to assume that Cromwell intended Launde as his principal country residence. Lewes Priory was a big one, but the Cromwells disliked the accommodation there.

On Cromwell's execution, his only son, <u>Gregory, Lord Cromwell (*c.* 1516–51)</u>, inherited and completed the house. Gregory went to Cambridge, but seemed to lack both his father's intelligence and his drive. In the late 1530s he had become a member of the parliament which attainted his father in 1540. Gregory appears to have escaped any serious consequences of his father's fall from power. In fact, he was ennobled by Henry only five months later.

Gregory had married Jane Seymour's widowed sister, Elizabeth (she had previously been married to Sir Antony Oughtred). They produced three sons and two daughters. He was knighted at the coronation of Edward VI, who had become his nephew.

The Cromwells appear to have lived very quietly at Launde, Gregory regularly attending the Lords and taking his place in shire government, but doing nothing of consequence. He died of the sweat in 1551, just as his mother had done, and his **tomb chest** survives in the **chapel** within the house. The tomb is much liked by Pevsner. His wife Elizabeth had obviously found life at Launde too quiet – just days after Gregory's death she married Sir John Paulet, who was to become Marquess of Winchester. He will have proved a deal livelier than Gregory! (See **Old Basing**.)

LEICESTER, Abbey ★★★

Located 1 mile north of the city centre in Abbey Park, next to the River Soar and between the A6 Loughborough road and the A607 Melton Mowbray road. Access is from Abbey Park Road, where street parking is possible. The scant abbey ruins are 200m inside the park.

Excavations have revealed the foundations and footings of the large and prosperous Augustinian abbey which was virtually obliterated at the Dissolution.

In nicely kept surroundings, a modern **stone** marks the place where **Cardinal Wolsey** was buried, following his death in the abbey en route to London in November 1530. Wolsey's fall from power was swift, but in two phases. In October 1529, Wolsey was deprived of the office of Lord Chancellor after having locked horns with the rising star of Anne Boleyn. Pushed by the Duke of Norfolk, he retired to his see of York, where he planned to be consecrated Archbishop only sixteen years after taking up the position!

However, on 4 November, Wolsey was arrested for treason by Henry Percy, Earl of Northumberland at Cawood, the archbishop's palace outside York. Wolsey was taken to Sheffield Park (belonging to the Earl of Shrewsbury) where he stayed for two weeks under house arrest. While there, he contracted dysentery. Sir William Kingston, the Lieutenant of the Tower, arrived to escort Wolsey back to London and the party struggled down to Leicester Abbey, where he died on 29 November.

The low-key grave of Cardinal Wolsey at Leicester.

Note also, the ruins of Cavendish House nearby in the park. It was built with stone from the abbey, but destroyed in the Civil War by Royalist soldiers. The park **wall** in Abbey Park Road was built in around 1500 (see also **Sheffield Manor Park**).

LINCOLN, Cathedral ★★
Located on the north side of the city centre, on a hill.

In the **south aisle** of the **retrochoir** there are two chantry chapels. On the left is the smarter of the two, which celebrates Bishop John Russell, Lord Chancellor to Richard III. The **chantry** on the right celebrates <u>Bishop John Longland (1473–1547)</u>, who had, perhaps, the most difficult (or the easiest depending on how you view it!) job in medieval England – Henry VIII's almoner and confessor! Fairly soon after his appointment in 1521, Longland became the first person to whom Henry confided his doubts about the validity of his marriage to Catherine of Aragon. Longland later indicated that much spiritual discussion followed, but Henry didn't give up until the bishop was won over.

Although naturally a religious conservative, Longland became a big supporter of the King's Great Matter, the Act of Succession and the Dissolution of the Monasteries. In other words, he perhaps bent to the King's will to a certain extent, as so many others had to do. His reward, despite his tricky position, was to die in his bed in his mid-70s. Longland also acted as confessor to Katherine Howard in the Tower just before her execution. She swore to him that she was innocent of the crimes she had been condemned for, and that she had never 'so abused my sovereign's bed'. However, she did not hide the follies of her youth.

Just across the south aisle lie two **tomb chests** to a mother and daughter. The mother is none other than <u>Katherine Swynford (*c.* 1350–1403)</u>, mother of the Beauforts and thus Henry VIII's great-great-great-grandmother. Her daughter was <u>Joan Beaufort (d. 1440)</u>, grandmother of Richard Neville, Warwick the Kingmaker. Since the later Beauforts provided much of the military leadership for Henry VI in the Wars of the Roses, we have here the maternal ancestors of opposing sides from this conflict, in which the English aristocracy tore itself apart! Katherine lived close by at Kettlethorpe during her first marriage to Sir John Swynford, a retainer of John of Gaunt. Her first child with John of Gaunt was conceived in double adultery in 1372. They produced three more before the children were legitimated by the Pope and the couple married in this cathedral in 1396. A very romantic story, but was it a sound basis for the Tudor royal house?

MELTON MOWBRAY, 'The Anne of Cleves' ★★
Located in the town centre, immediately south of the parish church.

On the annulment of their marriage after only five months, in July 1540, **Anne of Cleves** received a very generous settlement from Henry VIII. In return for going so quietly, she was given the status of the King's Sister, with a female rank below only the queen, and a handsome financial settlement of £4,000 p.a. Her main residences

This house in Melton Mowbray was one of Anne of Cleves' many properties granted to her by Henry in the divorce settlement.

were the superb Richmond Palace and Bletchingley Place in Surrey, but in addition she acquired several manors to generate income. This splendid Tudor survival, now a **public house** with period interiors, was one of them. In fact it had been owned briefly by **Thomas Cromwell**, who had also acquired nearby Launde Abbey. Cromwell was attainted and executed in 1540 so, as usual, his lands had passed to the Crown at just the right time for Anne!

Enjoy a pint or a meal here, perhaps after visiting nearby Launde (see also **Bletchingley** and **Lewes**).

SOUTH KYME, St Mary and All Saints' Church ★★

The village is 4 miles north-east of Heckington. From A14, 2½ miles east of Heckington, take B1395 north. The church is at the west end of the village. Turn left after the sharp right-hand bend.

Welcome to the Fens – a very different environment!

In the **nave/vestry** of this former priory church is found an incomplete **brass** and **inscription** commemorating Sir Gilbert Tailboys (d. 1530) and his wife **Elizabeth (Bessie) Blount (1501–40)**.

It is a modest memorial, which belies the importance of Bessie to our story. She was the mother of Henry Fitzroy, the only illegitimate child acknowledged by Henry VIII (see **Kinlet**). She had been the mistress of the king since 1514, when her attractive looks and dancing skills first brought her to his attention. Fitzroy was born in 1519. By 1522, Bessie was married to Gilbert, the eldest son of Sir George Tailboys, a wealthy member of the gentry, with lands in six counties from Northumberland to Somerset. Sir George (d. 1538) had his principal seat at Goltho, near Lincoln, but he suffered from bouts of insanity and so he was, at times, in the custody of the Duke of Norfolk.

Gilbert was a member of the household of Cardinal Wolsey, who was godfather to Fitzroy and had overseen his birthing arrangements at 'Jericho' (see **Blackmore**). From 1522, Gilbert received grants of extra land and Bessie was given a dowry from Tailboys' lands by Act of Parliament. In 1525, Fitzroy was unveiled to the political nation, Gilbert was knighted and went on to be MP and sheriff for Lincolnshire. Gilbert and Bessie had three more children before Gilbert predeceased his father in 1530. Bessie continued her unexceptional, normal gentry existence by marrying her much younger neighbour Edward, Lord Clinton in 1534, with whom she had three more daughters.

In front of the church, you will see a fourteenth-century **tower house** built by Sir Gilbert de Umfraville, which was part of the medieval manor pulled down in the 1720s.

SPILSBY, St James's Church ★★
In the town centre, on the crossroads.

There were Willoughbys in Spilsby from 1302, and in the **Willoughby Chapel** lie the monuments to a good number of them and their Bertie successors. One in particular catches the attention – described by Pevsner as 'a most remarkable monument' (Pevsner, *Lincolnshire*, p. 68), it covers the whole of the chapel west wall and commemorates <u>Baroness Katherine Willoughby d'Eresby (1519–80)</u> and her second husband <u>Richard Bertie (1516–82)</u>.

Katherine was a most remarkable woman. She was the only child of Lord Willoughby d'Eresby and his second wife, Maria de Salinas, a lady-in-waiting to Catherine of Aragon. Maria was very close to Queen Catherine, and nursed her through her final illness in 1535. Lord Willoughby had died in 1526, leaving young Katherine as sole heiress to his considerable estate, based in Lincolnshire. The king sold her guardianship to his old friend Charles Brandon, Duke of Suffolk, and Katherine was betrothed to Brandon's son, Henry.

However, Charles' first wife, Mary Tudor the king's sister, died in 1533. In an extreme version of Tudor aristocratic marriage, Brandon overrode his son's betrothal and, only three months into his widowhood, the 48-year-old duke married Katherine himself. She was all of 14 years old at the time, and it was his fourth marriage! Clearly her inheritance had some influence here. The couple lived primarily at Katherine's residence at Grimsthorpe in Lincolnshire (see **Grimsthorpe**), which enabled Brandon to wield influence in a new part of the country. He was on hand to suppress the Pilgrimage of Grace which actually started in the county. The new duchess attended Catherine of Aragon's funeral in Peterborough Abbey, and she carried Prince Edward at his christening in 1537. At Deal, in Kent, the duke and duchess formally welcomed Anne of Cleves to England at the end of 1539.

Katherine quickly produced two sons, who tragically were to die of sweating sickness within an hour of one another in Cambridge in 1551. Brandon died in 1545. Katherine, by now, had become an independent-minded and outspoken religious reformer – very surprising, given her mother's strong Catholic links. She developed a close friendship with Katherine Parr, with whom she debated religious issues along with other like-minded ladies at court. She also possessed a sharp tongue. She is said to have named her dog 'Gardiner' after her adversary the conservative bishop of Winchester!

Late in Henry's reign, there were rumours that Katherine might become his seventh wife, as Katherine Parr came under pressure from the conservatives! However, Parr survived and the two women's friendship continued. In 1548, when the Dowager Queen Katherine died in childbirth at Sudeley, Katherine took custody of the newborn baby, Mary Seymour, at Grimsthorpe but the child is thought to have died young.

In 1551, Katherine married again, this time for love to Richard Bertie (pronounced Bartie), a member of her household. When Mary I claimed the throne, the couple went into exile on the continent, returning when the queen died. Their son, Peregrine, became a noted courtier and soldier under Elizabeth I. Katherine and Richard continued to live at Grimsthorpe and she ended her days still sharp-witted but rather eccentric.

STANFORD-ON-AVON, St Nicholas's Church ★

Located 2 miles east of junction 19 of M1, and just north of A14. Access is from the roundabout on A14, via Swinford. Approach on M1 from the north only. The church is next to the hall.

Set in charming rural surroundings and despite the proximity of major trunk roads, this church is a treasure trove for the historian. In the sixteenth century the manor was owned by the Cave family, some of whose members are commemorated here.

We are interested in the very striking **stained glass** in the **east window**. This is a commemoration of Tudor triumph, in the form of portraits of **Henry VII and Elizabeth of York** together with Tudor emblems, plus members of the Cave family from the sixteenth century. The colours, however, seem rather too vivid and Pevsner tells us they are likely to be Victorian. Glass was found hidden away in Stanford Hall in 1932 and fitted this window perfectly. Perhaps the originals had been damaged in earlier centuries (the Civil War?) and a replacement made but never fitted? Whatever, it seems likely that a sixteenth-century Cave was really pleased about the Tudor triumph. If the glass is a faithful representation of an original, it is a unique survival of such commemoration in a parish church.

WEST MIDLANDS AND WALES

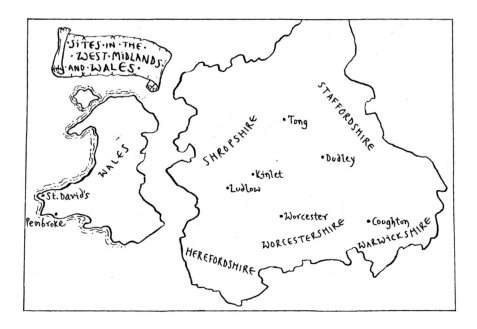

COUGHTON, Court ★★ £

Situated on A435 Studley–Alcester road, 2 miles south of Studley. Signposted. (NT)

The star of the show is the Tudor **gatehouse**, built from 1510 by Sir Robert Throckmorton (d. 1519) and his son Sir George Throckmorton (c. 1489–1552). Inside, the house, tower and dining rooms are especially good. Next door is **St Peter's Church**, where Sir George is buried on the north side of the **chancel**. There are fine **brasses** on the tomb.

Sir George was a fervent Catholic who openly opposed the Reformation. He was a leading member of the 'Queen's Head' group, who met in London to resist reform and the King's Great Matter. In 1532, he made a very strong speech in the Commons and was hauled up in front of Henry VIII to explain why he opposed the king's marriage to Anne Boleyn. Almost unbelievably, he is said to have replied, 'It is thought that ye have meddled with both the mother and the sister [of Anne]' – i.e. Elizabeth Boleyn *née* Howard and Mary Boleyn. Rather weakly, Henry responded, 'Never with the mother'. Cromwell stepped in to deny that the king had ever slept with Anne's sister either. Courage, or foolhardiness – but Sir George got away with it. This exchange remains the only objective proof we have for Henry's affair with Mary. Elizabeth Howard was over ten years older than Henry, and the daughter of his biggest supporter, the Duke of Norfolk, so what was that astonishing claim about? During the Pilgrimage of Grace, Sir George was arrested, but again survived by making a full apology to the king.

Coughton Court, home of the Throckmortons.

In 1512, George had married Katherine Vaux, who was Katherine Parr's aunt by marriage. He and Katherine had nineteen children and 112 grandchildren.

His father, Sir Robert, also had constructed a big **tomb chest** in the **nave**, but he died on pilgrimage in 1519 (a later Sir Robert is now buried there). Sir Robert had fought for Henry VII at the Battle of Stoke Field. He rebuilt the church.

DUDLEY, Castle ★★★ £

The castle grounds contain a zoo! Access is from junction 2 of M5 on A4123 to Dudley. Follow the signs to the zoo from A4123. Park in the zoo car park and use the zoo entrance. Climb up to the castle keep and make sure you take the children for this one!

A Norman castle was established soon after the Conquest on this natural outcrop. It became the home of the Sutton family, who had been ennobled in the middle of the fifteenth century.

In the late 1530s **John Dudley, Earl of Warwick, later Duke of Northumberland, (1501–ex. 1554)** acquired the castle from his cousin John Sutton, Lord Dudley. Warwick had climbed steadily during the reign of Henry VIII and had become a prominent member of the Protectorate for Edward VI. He was a member of a small group of courtiers around Lord Protector Somerset who were denizens of Renaissance architecture, and who expressed this interest through building in the new style.

This range was built by John Dudley, Duke of Northumberland.

Warwick rebuilt the **Great Hall** and other domestic buildings here to form, what the guidebook calls, 'a Renaissance Palace'. The styling is uncannily similar to Protector Somerset's rebuild at **Berry Pomeroy**, and has much in common with the more familiar houses at Longleat (Sir John Thynne) and Lacock Abbey (William Sharrington). All were members of Somerset's circle (see **Berry Pomeroy**). Warwick displaced Somerset and became Duke of Northumberland and, in effect, Lord Protector in 1551.

After his execution by Queen Mary, the castle reverted to the Sutton line. This exciting architecture makes a fine legacy for a man who had a much more dubious political legacy.

Good displays and exhibits.

KINLET, St John the Baptist Church ★★

The village lies at the junction of the B4194 Bewdley–Bridgnorth road with the B4363 Cleobury Mortimer–Bridgnorth road. The church is reached 1 mile north-west on a minor road, from the above junction, leading to a school.

The park of Kinlet Hall was extended in the eighteenth century, the village moved and the road diverted. The church remains in the grounds of the hall, which is now a school. The church is very peaceful, and in a charming setting. It contains a number of monuments to the Blount family, kinsmen of the barons Mountjoy, but actually much more important to our story.

Sir John Blount and his wife Catherine at Kinlet. They were the parents of Bessie.

A **tomb chest** and **effigies** in the **Blount Chapel** celebrate <u>Sir John Blount</u> <u>(d. 1531)</u> and his wife <u>Catherine Peshall, of Knightley, Staffs</u>. They were the parents of Elizabeth (Bessie) Blount, Henry VIII's mistress from 1514 (see **South Kyme** and **Framlingham**). Sir John attended the funeral of Henry VII and the coronation of Henry VIII. He was a soldier who accompanied Henry to France in 1513.

Another monument commemorates Bessie's brother, <u>Sir George Blount (1503–81)</u>. Finally, there is a second **tomb chest** and **effigies** in the chapel of <u>Sir Humphrey</u> <u>Blount (d. 1471)</u>, grandfather to Sir John above. He wears a sun-and-roses Yorkist collar. He fought for Edward IV at Tewksbury, was knighted after the battle and died the same year. His grandson, Sir John, by contrast wears a Lancastrian 'SS' collar – a good example of how many supporters of Edward IV turned to Henry Tudor after Edward's death in 1483, rather than to Richard III. Henry's promise to marry Edward's daughter, Elizabeth of York, was a key factor in this switch.

LUDLOW ★★★★★

Castle £
In the town centre, at the western end near the market place.

The unusual circular Norman chapel in Ludlow Castle.

This formidable fortress holds a position centre stage in the drama of the King's Great Matter. **Prince Arthur, Prince of Wales** had spent much of his childhood here. After his wedding to **Catherine of Aragon** in November 1501, it seemed quite natural for him to bring his new bride here, so that he could resume his duties in the principality. Catherine was somewhat reluctant, perhaps having been told that the castle was cold and damp in winter, but was persuaded by Henry VII to make the journey. The couple struggled up here in foul weather just after Christmas.

By April 1502, Arthur was dead from sweating sickness – Catherine was also ill, but recovered. Some said Arthur had been weakened from too much sex! However, the question arising twenty-five years later, after Catherine's marriage to Arthur's brother Henry VIII, was, had her first marriage to Arthur in fact been consummated? There were of course opposing views. During their brief stay, Arthur and Catherine occupied the top floor of the **Solar Wing** (also known as **Prince Arthur's** chamber). Presumably Arthur died here. Don't miss the delightful circular Norman **chapel** once known as Prince Arthur's chapel.

The castle occupies a magnificent position above the River Teme. Walk west out of the castle, down the minor road to Bromfield and cross the river bridge to find the best view.

St Laurence's Church
Located in the town centre, north of the High Street.

A **plaque** in the **chancel** denotes that the heart of **Prince Arthur** was buried in this church – the rest of his body was taken to Worcester. Victorian stained glass in the nave includes Arthur.

From 1492, perhaps oddly, Prince Arthur spent most of his time away from London. In addition to Ludlow, he spent quite a lot of time at Bewdley, 18 miles away next to the River Severn. He lived there at Tickenhill Manor or Beaulieu Palace, an established royal palace (unfortunately, although the location is known, nothing survives of relevance – but see **Boreham**). He also spent a fair amount of time at **Haddon Hall** in Derbyshire, the home of his childhood guardian, Sir Henry Vernon, where a room was reserved for him. A much travelled young man.

ST DAVID'S, Cathedral ★★
In the city centre, signposted.

In the **sanctuary** is the splendid **tomb chest** and **brass** of Edmund Tudor (1430–57), father of Henry VII. Edmund died in Carmarthen Castle while in the custody of Yorkists and before the birth of his son by Lady Margaret Beaufort. He was initially buried in Carmarthen Priory, but at the Dissolution his remains were moved here. The brass is a nineteenth-century replacement. (See **Henry VII** biography.)

If you are journeying to St David's, why not call in to **Pembroke Castle** (Cadw), where **Henry VII** was born just a few weeks after his father's death. He was born in a **tower** in the outer ward which now bears his name. His mother, Lady Margaret, was only 13 years old and had a very difficult childbirth. The castle belonged to Edmund's brother, Jasper Tudor (1431–95), who was a Lancastrian and Tudor stalwart. The castle is signposted and easy to find.

TONG, St Bartholomew's Church ★★★
Tong is immediately north of junction 3 of M54, on A41 to Newport. Turn right off A41 to the village.

A real gem, and a treasure trove for the medieval historian. A college was established here in 1409 which became the family mausoleum of the Vernons, who lived at Tong castle and at **Haddon Hall** in Derbyshire. They were powerful members of the gentry in the Peak District.

Amongst the many church monuments we are interested in the **Golden Chapel**, which commemorates Sir Henry Vernon (d. 1515), his wife Lady Anne *née* Talbot (d. 1494) and their youngest son Sir Arthur Vernon (*c.* 1482–1517). Sir Henry was Prince Arthur's guardian and treasurer (see **Haddon**). The furnishings in the chapel are sumptuous, especially for a rural church – the Vernons obviously had plenty of money at this time. The delightful **tomb chest** and **effigies** represent Sir Henry and Lady Anne.

Their son, Sir Arthur, is commemorated by a lovely **floor brass** and a very unusual **wall-mounted bust**. He was rector of nearby Whitchurch and was a Cambridge graduate. Arthur was not a common name at the time, so was he named after Prince Arthur?

Monument to the mysterious Sir Arthur Vernon at Tong.

The Golden Chapel at Tong, with effigies of Sir Henry Vernon and his wife Anne Talbot.

Elsewhere in the church are monuments to two more of Sir Henry and Lady Anne's children – Sir Humphrey Vernon (d. 1542), who succeeded his father, and Richard Vernon (d. 1517) and his wife Margaret Dymocke (date of death not known). So, what with two sons dying in the same year and maybe an Arthur connection and the lavish monuments, is there a story here? (See **Standon**, for Margaret.)

WORCESTER, Cathedral ★★★★
Located in the west side of the city centre, by the River Severn.

This delightfully situated cathedral is home to a very important monument in our story.

On the **south** side of the **chancel** lies the lovely **Prince Arthur's Chantry**, which commemorates **Prince Arthur**, eldest son of Henry VII, who died so tragically young at Ludlow. Because he had been married for five months to Catherine of Aragon, he took centre stage in the debates around Henry VIII's 'Great Matter' in the 1520s and 1530s (see **Ludlow**). The chantry is covered in Tudor emblems – roses, the Beaufort portcullis and pomegranates, the emblem of Catherine.

Nearby, in the **south-east transept** is a **tomb chest** for Sir Gryffyth Ryce (d. 1523), who was Prince Arthur's boyhood friend from his days in Ludlow. Ryce requested to be buried near his friend.

The spectacular inside of Prince Arthur's chantry in Worcester Cathedral.

THE NORTH

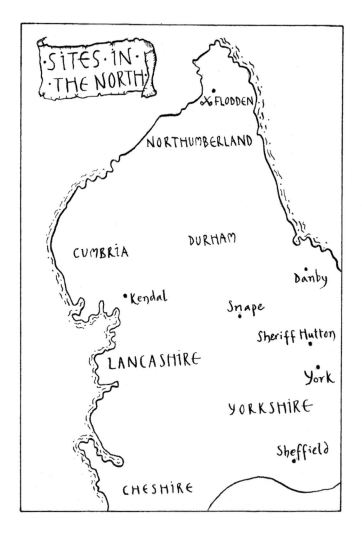

DANBY (near Guisborough), Castle ★★

Situated in the North York Moors between Guisborough and Whitby. Approximately 7 miles east of Guisborough, take the minor road south, off A171 Whitby road. Head south through Danby village over a railway bridge, and turn left through the hamlet of Ainthorpe on a narrow road for 1 mile.

Dramatically situated in beautiful Eskdale, this fourteenth-century castle belonged to the Neville Lord Latimers, one of whom was the husband of **Katherine Parr**. In 1534, she married her second husband <u>John Neville, 3rd Lord Latimer (1493–43)</u>, whose main residence was Snape Castle in north-west Yorkshire.

Danby Castle, owned by the Latimer Nevilles. Katherine Parr spent time here during her second marriage.

The castle ruins adjoin a farmhouse which sports a modern **plaque** on its front. The property does B&B, and is now a wedding venue. A bit out of the way if you're living in London, but fantastic if one or both of you are history buffs! (See also **Dartford** and **Felsted**. For more on Latimer see **Snape**.)

THE BATTLE OF FLODDEN (9 September 1513) ++++

Strategic Background

At the end of June 1513, Henry VIII arrived in the English possession of Calais at the head of an army of southern English levies, which might be described as his 'First XI'. His intention was to invade France in concert with his Spanish father-in-law, King Ferdinand. By mid-August, Henry had won a minor victory in northern France called the 'Battle of the Spurs'.

Meanwhile, King James IV of Scotland, who was married to Henry's elder sister, Margaret, and had signed a number of peace treaties with Henry, could not resist the temptation to invade England in Henry's absence and renew hostilities with the 'auld enemy'. On 19 August the Scots mustered at Edinburgh, and then crossed the Tweed at Coldstream with a huge army of perhaps 40,000 men on 22 August. They proceeded to besiege and overrun the English border castles in the area – Norham, Wark, Etal and Ford. By 5 September, they had encamped on Flodden Hill, a few miles south-east of Coldstream, and awaited the arrival of an English defensive force.

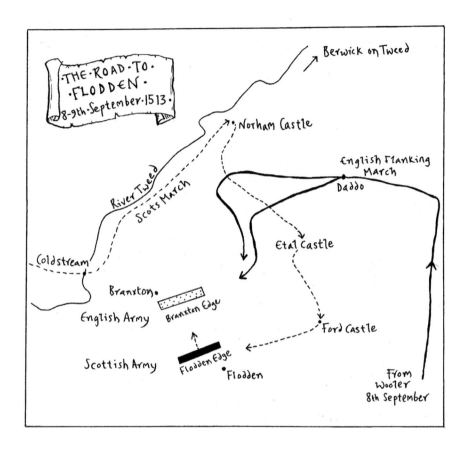

On his departure to France, Henry VIII had appointed Queen Catherine as his regent, to govern the country in his absence with the help of a council which included Archbishop Warham of Canterbury and Thomas Howard, Earl of Surrey. Thomas was an experienced soldier, and had fought against Henry Tudor at Bosworth where his father was killed. Thomas' life was spared, but the family lost their dukedom of Norfolk. Thomas may have expected to go to France with Henry, but instead was chosen to 'captain the Second XI', as Lord Lieutenant of the Northern Marches, possibly because he did not get on with Wolsey.

Queen Catherine was much involved in the raising of troops to combat the Scots, and joined a reserve army stationed in Buckinghamshire. Surrey first heard of the Scots' crossing of the Tweed on 25 August at Pontefract as he marched north with his army. They reached Newcastle on 30 August. Here, he was partially provisioned by a fleet of supply ships, led by the *Mary Rose*, which had been depleted by storms in the North Sea.

The English army mustered near Alnwick, where Surrey was joined by 1,000 crack troops detached from the king's French campaign, commanded by his eldest son, another Thomas Howard (later 3rd Duke of Norfolk).

In a sense, King James had already achieved his first military objective. The army now comprised 20–25,000 men. Heralds were exchanged by the two armies, and Surrey offered battle to commence on 9 September, probably influenced by his shortage of supplies. His offer was accepted by the Scots, so Surrey continued to march north, arriving near Wooler on 6 September. The next day, he received intelligence regarding the strength of the Scottish position on Flodden Hill where their 'big guns' were now dug in. A direct frontal assault uphill against their positions would have been suicidal.

However, nearby Etal Castle was held by the prominent Manners family and neighbouring Ford Castle by the Herons. Tradition has it that the 'Bastard Heron', the owner's illegitimate brother and Border renegade, devised a cunning plan for Surrey. On 8 September, the English army broke camp and embarked on an audacious outflanking manoeuvre to the east and north of the Scottish position. Keeping out of sight of the Scots on their march, the English camped overnight at Barmoor and, before first light on 9 September, divided into battle groupings and marched the remaining 11 miles to Branxton Edge, immediately **north** of Flodden. Unfortunately, along the way the division of archers commanded by Sir Edward Stanley became detached and fell behind – this kind of 'mishap' quite often happened to the Stanleys in battle.

The English army now stood between King James and Edinburgh, while facing a less dramatic slope up to the Scottish camp on Flodden Hill. The Scots were forced to completely turn their heavy guns around to face the English. In addition, the lower slopes of Branxton Hill contained a nasty, marshy dip which was to disrupt the Scottish battle line. The initial, huge advantage in terms of numbers and position held by the Scots had been somewhat nullified.

The choice of armaments by the two armies was also to have a significant effect on the outcome of the battle. The Scots had recently adopted the hugely successful Swiss pike, under the direction of French officers. The pike outranged other traditional thrusting weapons but, for success, needed the battle line to be very disciplined and maintain cohesion. The Scots had also acquired huge siege guns, which were difficult and slow to deploy and had slow rates of fire. The English had more conventional armaments, including the very manoeuvrable billhook.

The Battle

Battle commenced in mid-afternoon with an artillery exchange, the faster firing English field guns having much the better of it. Nevertheless, at about 4.30 p.m., it was Lord Home's 'Borderers' and the Earl of Huntly's 'Highlanders' who left their higher position on Branxton Hill and charged at the English vanguard, which was commanded by Edmund Howard, Surrey's second son.

There were approximately twice as many Scots opposing Howard, whose vanguard was almost overwhelmed before being relieved by Lord Dacre's 'Cumbrians'. This

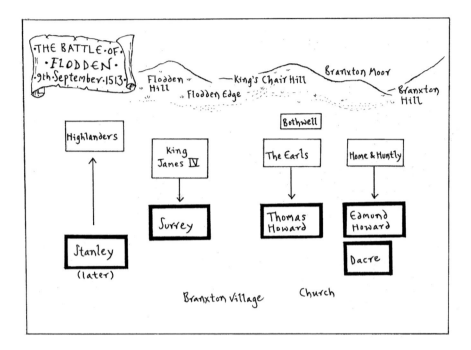

success led King James to order the advance, first of the centre division under Earls Errol, Crawford and Montrose, and then of his own vanguard, which may have comprised as many as 15,000 pikes. However, both these attacks lost cohesion as they encountered the marshy dip; the pikes were discarded for swords, which could not match the range of the agile English billhooks, and many fled the field.

The English line, commanded by the Earl of Surrey and his eldest son, Thomas, was not broken and, in the traditional melee that developed, was dominant. King James was killed leading a charge against Surrey, whilst many members of the Scottish nobility met their deaths elsewhere on the field. There followed two hours of carnage, during which the Scots were thoroughly defeated.

Aftermath

The scale of the slaughter at Flodden was dreadful – approximately 1,500 dead on the English side, but up to 8,000 Scots, including the king, twenty-three members of the nobility and 300 gentry. This resulted in relative quiet along the Borders for a generation or more.

Margaret Tudor became regent of Scotland on behalf of her infant son, King James V. The family which gained the most from Flodden was, of course, the Howards. They were rewarded by a grateful Henry VIII with the return of their Norfolk dukedom, which they had lost after the Battle of Bosworth. Thomas, the younger, was given the junior title of Earl of Surrey.

However, we are most interested in the effects of this battle on the relationship between Henry VIII and Queen Catherine of Aragon. Catherine had proved a shrewd regent, and had had a good war. Henry was still in France when the news from Flodden came through. She made the mistake of comparing 'her' victory (for Flodden was very much Catherine's victory) favourably with Henry's rather inconsequential victory at the Battle of the Spurs. In truth, Henry had achieved little of consequence in France but his ego required him to be told differently.

When Henry's Spanish alliance foundered on the third betrayal of Henry by Catherine's father, King Ferdinand, Catherine felt the full force of Henry's tongue. Politically, the honeymoon period at the beginning of Henry's reign was over and he dropped her as a close advisor. It may also give the first indication that their private life may not have been perfect.

Location and What to See

The battlefield is set in lovely countryside, just 4 miles south of Coldstream and the Scottish border.

For a long period English and Scottish historians could not even agree on the battle's name! The Scots favoured Flodden, because that was where King James had dug in on the hill before the battle. The English preferred Branxton, because their field positions were just in front of Branxton village. Technically, most people would opt for Branxton but the Scottish view prevailed. The whole area is rewarding to visit because there has been little disturbance over the centuries.

A large **monument** has been erected on Piper's Hill, ½ mile to the west of Branxton village, which is signposted off the A697 Coldstream–Wooler road. In recent years, a **battlefield trail** has been constructed from the car parks at the village. This traverses the area of intense fighting that occurred at the battle's climax in the marshy dip. The information boards are excellent and ensure an interesting walk. A good way to approach Branxton from the south is to turn off the A697 just north of Milfield village, on a minor road to Flodden and Branxton. Flodden Edge and Flodden Hill can be seen to the right. After 3 miles, turn right at the T-junction and immediately left down Branxton Hill, passing the marshy dip on the way.

Finally, make sure to visit nearby **Etal Castle** on the east side of the A697. The ground floor of the **Tower House** displays a fine exhibition on the battle and the events leading up to it.

The Scots charged down this incline but were heavily defeated at Flodden Field.

The battle cross at Flodden.

KENDAL ★★

Holy Trinity Church

Situated ¾ mile south of the town centre, on the west bank of the River Kent. The best approach is on A6, from the south.

In the **Parr Chapel** is the large tomb of Sir William Parr (d. 1484), a member of the powerful family based in Kendal and grandfather of Queen Katherine Parr. Sir William began the Wars of the Roses as a retainer of the Nevilles, and actually fought for Warwick the Kingmaker at the Battle of Edgcote, against the forces of Edward IV in 1469. At Doncaster in 1470, however, Sir William took up Edward's offer of a pardon and deserted Warwick.

He fought for Edward at both Barnet and Tewkesbury, and quickly became a favourite of the king's. He was appointed Comptroller of the Household and made a Knight of the Garter. On Edward's death, he sided with Richard III and was made a member of his council, but died before Bosworth.

Note the brasses to the Bellinghams, who lived at Burnside and were arch rivals of the Parrs.

Castle

Located on the east bank of the river, ¾ mile east of the church. From the church, walk across the footbridge over the river and head up Parr Street to find a footpath uphill through trees.

This castle was the ancestral home of the Parr Family. It was granted to them by Richard II in the late fourteenth century. However, by the end of the fifteenth century it was probably no longer in use. Since Katherine Parr's father, Sir Thomas, married a wealthy heiress from Northamptonshire, it is much more likely that Katherine was born down there (see **Green's Norton**), than in this rather draughty and outdated pile.

The castle sits on a natural mound now covered in trees. It was re-sited here in the late twelfth century. Remnants of the stone curtain wall survive. There are extensive views from the mound, so go in winter to maximise these.

SHEFFIELD ★★★

Cathedral
In the city centre, on the north side of Fargate.

In the **Shrewsbury Chapel**, a fine **tomb** and **effigies** celebrate <u>George Talbot, Earl of Shrewsbury (1468–1538)</u>, and his two wives <u>Anne Hastings (d. 1507)</u> and <u>Elizabeth Walden (d. 1567)</u>.

Although the Talbot family was strongly Lancastrian, George's first wife, Anne, was the daughter of Lord William Hastings, Edward IV's right-hand man. As a result, George fought on the wrong side at Bosworth aged 17 years, but was pardoned by Henry VII. He fought for the new king at the Battle of Stoke Field in 1487. He attended both Henry's coronation and his wedding to Elizabeth of York. At the former, he carried the Curtana (ceremonial sword), and again at Henry VIII's coronation. He carried the young Prince Henry at the ceremony when he was created Duke of York. He attended the funerals of Prince Arthur and Henry VII.

In 1502, Talbot was made Lord Steward, whose job it was to run the royal household. This was no sinecure – it involved running twenty-five departments and 500 staff, with a management team of treasurer, vice treasurer and Comptroller. He was one of the two witnesses to the wedding of Henry VIII and Catherine in 1509. Because of his role, he probably attended virtually all the major state occasions.

He married his first wife, Anne, in 1481 and they proceeded to have eleven children. His second wife, Elizabeth, had attended Catherine of Aragon at the Field of the Cloth of Gold in 1520. George seems to have been one of the nicer characters encountered in this story – gentle George? He broke cover only once in 1528, when he was interviewed regarding the King's Great Matter. He was asked his opinion on whether Prince Arthur had consummated his marriage to Catherine. He quoted from own his experience, saying words to the effect that he had consummated his own marriage at 15 years old (he was married at 13) and that Arthur looked a strong boy, so surely he had! Better to give the king what he wanted to hear on this particular matter?

Talbot died, in harness, in 1538. When he died, George was the sole remaining member of the nobility who had fought in the Wars of the Roses, and life had become very different.

Manor Park Ruins
Situated 1½ miles south-east of the city centre. Take A6135 to Killamarsh/Eckington (City Road) from the central area. After 1¼ miles, turn left onto Manor Lane just before the cemetery. The park and ruins are on the left after ¼ mile.

Wolsey stayed here on his way back to London.

Manor Park was originally a hunting lodge when the Talbot Earls of Shrewsbury were based at Sheffield Castle. In 1510, the 4th Earl built a much larger property on this site, which survives as the second structure along Manor Lane but is very ruinous.

It is known as **Wolsey's Tower** because <u>Cardinal Wolsey</u> stayed here on his final journey from York. Arrested on the king's orders at Cawood Palace near York by Henry Percy, Earl of Northumberland, Wolsey made his way to this spot via Pontefract and Doncaster. Imagine him coming up the hill from the north-east on his donkey – tiring travel? He arrived on 8 November and was met by Sir William Kingston, Constable of the Tower of London, who was to escort him to that place. This much unsettled the cardinal, as well it might. He stayed here for two weeks because he had contracted dysentery. Finally, the party proceeded south via Hardwick Hall and Nottingham. Wolsey died at Leicester Abbey on 29 November. The question is, could Kingston have brought with him a phial of poison from the king, to save everybody the embarrassment of a lengthy and revealing trial? (See also **Leicester**.)

Fine views are afforded from the park of the surrounding city. Do look round the late sixteenth-century **Turret House** built to house Mary Queen of Scots.

SHERIFF HUTTON, Castle ★★

Located on the south-eastern edge of the village along a cul-de-sac, go east to visit the church.
01347 878341

The scant but imposing remains of this important medieval fortress can be visited by appointment. Alternatively, you can walk round the outside on public footpaths. Start or finish at the nearby **Castle Inn**.

The castle was a Neville stronghold, and passed by marriage to Richard, Duke of Gloucester (later, Richard III). After Richard's coup in 1483, he assembled quite a collection of political prisoners here, under the supervision of John de la Pole, Earl of Lincoln (1460–87). His prisoners included **Princess Elizabeth of York** and one or two of her sisters, plus Edward Plantagenet, Earl of Warwick (1475–ex. 1499), and his sister Margaret Pole (1473–ex. 1541). An ideal set-up for a house party? Lincoln was the son of Richard's sister, Elizabeth (see **Wingfield**), and was most probably Richard's heir presumptive after the death of Richard's only son in 1484. Lincoln was killed at the Battle of Stoke Field, fighting against Henry VII.

It was from Sheriff Hutton that Elizabeth and the Earl of Warwick were escorted by Sir Robert Willoughby, in 1485, under orders from the victorious Henry Tudor after the Battle of Bosworth. Elizabeth was destined for marriage to Henry, honouring the pledge he made while in exile in France at Christmas 1483, whilst Warwick was secretly taken to the Tower, never to emerge alive. Probably mentally feeble, Warwick was cruelly executed in 1499 as part of Henry VII's cleaning up operation ahead of Prince Arthur's marriage to Catherine of Aragon.

Henry Fitzroy nominally ran the Council of the North.

Do visit **St Helen's church** further along the cul-de-sac. An alabaster effigy there is said to commemorate Edward, Prince of Wales, only son of Richard III.

SNAPE, Castle ★★★

Located at the west end of the village, 3 miles west of A1 (M) and 2 miles south of Bedale. Leave A1 (M) at Bedale/Leeming.

Snape was the home of the Neville, Lords Latimer, a parallel branch to that of Warwick the Kingmaker. The first Lord Latimer, George, who was unfortunately of unsound mind, was a sibling of Richard, Earl of Salisbury and Cecily Neville, mother of Edward IV and Richard III.

In spring 1534, <u>John Neville, 3rd Lord Latimer (*c.* 1493–1543)</u> married his third wife, **<u>Katherine Parr</u>** – herself already the widow of Edward, Lord Borough (see **Gainsborough**). Katherine had joined one of the most powerful families in the north, although it had been somewhat reduced after the Kingmaker's demise in 1471. Lord Latimer was implicated in the Pilgrimage of Grace in 1536, but managed to talk himself out of trouble.

The castle is somewhat ruinous, and was much modified at the end of the sixteenth century. Follow the directions to the **chapel** at the **rear** of the building where there is a nice display on Queen Katherine.

Snape Castle was the primary residence of Lord Latimer, Katherine Parr's second husband.

Just 2 miles down the road is **Well**, a lovely little village with **St Michael's Church** at the east end. Here, in the **Neville Chapel**, there is a plain **tomb chest** celebrating Lady Dorothy Neville (d. 1526), the first wife of John, Lord Latimer. She was the daughter and co-heiress of John de Vere, 14th Earl of Oxford. Unfortunately, Latimer missed out on her inheritance as she died too soon. Their son, another John, 4th Lord Latimer, has a high **tomb chest** in the chapel.

YORK, King's Manor and St Mary's Abbey ★★

In the city centre, 300m west of York Minster in Exhibition Square. The abbey is in the small park behind the manor buildings.

Henry VIII only came to the north once. He arrived here on his summer progress with Queen Katherine Howard in September 1541. He was met by the Archbishop and pardoned 200 men who had been involved in the Pilgrimage of Grace. He was also due to meet his nephew, King James V of Scotland, his sister's son. James never showed up so Henry went off to Hull.

While in York, the royal couple stayed at the **King's Manor**, which had been specially built or renovated for them. The nearby abbey had only just been dissolved so stone was available to create a palatial building, probably on the site of the former abbot's house. By this time, Queen Katherine was having nightly assignations with

Henry VIII stayed at the King's Manor, York, during his one and only visit to the north, accompanied by Katherine Howard.

her alleged lover, Thomas Culpepper. It was said that these occurred at every over-night stop, except at Grimsthorpe on the way home!

The manor later housed the Council of the North, and has been much altered over the centuries. It is a fine medieval building with the **coat of arms** of the ill-fated Thomas Wentworth, Earl of Strafford. He was President of the Council, but was executed by a desperate Charles I in 1641.

The building is now used by the University of York, but the outside can be easily viewed. Take the side footpath which leads into the park behind the Manor. This houses the **Yorkshire Museum** and the **ruins** of **St Mary's Abbey** which was used to provide hospitality for the royal couple.

BIBLIOGRAPHY

Baldwin Smith, Lacey, *Catherine Howard*, Amberley, 2010

Bernard, G.W., *The King's Reformation*, Yale, 2005

Chrimes, S.B., *Henry VII*, Yale, 1999

Elton, G.R., *Reform and Reformation*, Edward Arnold, 1977

Fox, Julia, *Jane Boleyn*, Phoenix, 2008

Harrison, Brian et al., *The Oxford Dictionary of National Biography*, Oxford University Press, 2004

Hart, Kelly, *The Mistresses of Henry VIII*, The History Press, 2009

Hutchinson, Robert, *The Last Days of Henry VIII*, Phoenix, 2008

Hutchinson, Robert, *Thomas Cromwell*, Phoenix, 2006

Hutchinson, Robert, *Young Henry*, Phoenix, 2012

Ives, Eric, *The Life and Death of Anne Boleyn*, Blackwell Publishing, 2005

Ives, Eric, *The Reformation Experience*, Lion, 2012

Jones, Michael K. and Underwood, Malcolm G., *The King's Mother*, Cambridge University Press, 1992

Jones, Philippa, *The Other Tudors – Henry VIII's Mistresses and Bastards*, New Holland, 2009

Lacey, Robert, *The Life and Times of Henry VIII*, Weidenfeld and Nicolson, 1992

License, Amy, *In Bed with the Tudors*, Amberley, 2012

License, Amy, *Elizabeth of York*, Amberley, 2013

Lindsey, Karen, *Divorced, Beheaded, Survived*, Addison-Wesley, 1996

Lipscombe, Suzannah, *A Visitor's Companion to Tudor England*, Ebury Press, 2012

Lipscombe, Suzannah, *1536 – The Year that Changed Henry VIII*, Lion, 2009

Loach, Jennifer, *Edward VI*, Yale, 2002

Loades, David, *The Boleyns*, Amberley, 2011

Loades, David, *Henry VIII*, Amberley, 2011

Mackie, J.D., *The Earlier Tudors*, Oxford University Press, 1972

Mee, Arthur, *The King's England* series, Hodder & Stoughton, 1936

Norton, Elizabeth, *Anne Boleyn*, Amberley, 2011

Norton, Elizabeth, *Catherine Parr*, Amberley, 2011

Norton, Elizabeth, *Jane Seymour*, Amberley, 2009

Norton, Elizabeth, *Margaret Beaufort*, Amberley, 2010

Okerlund, Arlene Naylor, *Elizabeth of York*, Palgrave Macmillan, 2009

Penn, Thomas, *The Winter King*, Allen Lane, 2011

Pettifer, Adrian, *English Castles*, Boydell Press, 2002

Pevsner, Sir Nicholas, *The Buildings of England* series, 1950s onwards

Porter, Linda, *Katherine the Queen*, Pan Books, 2011

Rex, Richard, *The Tudors*, Amberley, 2011

Ridley, Jasper, *Henry VIII*, Constable, 1984

Scard, Margaret, *Tudor Survivor – The Life and Times of William Paulet*, The History Press, 2011

Scarisbrick, J.J., *Henry VIII*, Yale, 1997

Seward, Desmond, *The Last White Rose*, Constable, 2010

Skidmore, Chris, *Edward VI – The Lost King of England*, Phoenix, 2008

Starkey, David, *Henry – Virtuous Prince*, Harper Press, 2008

Starkey, David, *Six Wives*, Vintage, 2004

Tremlett, Giles, *Catherine of Aragon*, Faber and Faber, 2011

Weir, Alison, *Britain's Royal Families*, Pimlico, 1996

Weir, Alison, *Children of England – The Heirs of King Henry VIII*, Vintage, 2008

Weir, Alison, *Henry VIII – King and Court*, Vintage, 2008

Weir, Alison, *The Lady in the Tower*, Vintage, 2010

Weir, Alison, *Mary Boleyn*, Jonathan Cape, 2011

Weir, Alison, *The Six Wives of Henry VIII*, Pimlico, 1991

Whitelock, Anna, *Mary Tudor*, Bloomsbury, 2009

Wilkinson, Josephine, *Anne Boleyn – The Young Queen to be*, Amberley, 2011

Williams, Penry, *The Later Tudors*, Oxford University Press, 1998

Wilson, Derek, *A Brief History of Henry VIII*, Constable and Robinson, 2009

INDEXES

INDEX OF PEOPLE

Bold indicates location of biographical detail; <u>underline</u> indicates site of a memorial or building; Henry VIII's entry focuses on his biography and historic sites only

INDEX OF HISTORIC SITES

SS indicates secondary sites